In Defense of Sanity

In Defense of Sanity

The Best Essays of G. K. Chesterton

Selected by Dale Ahlquist, Joseph Pearce,
and Aidan Mackey

IGNATIUS PRESS SAN FRANCISCO

Cover art:
Astonished at the World by Timothy Jones
© 2011 by Timothy Jones
Photograph courtesy of the artist

Cover design by John Herreid

ISBN 978-1-58617-489-7 (PB)
ISBN 978-1-68149-256-8 (eBook)
Library of Congress Control Number 2011926404
Printed in the United States of America ∞

CONTENTS

FOREWORD

Aidan Mackey

The essay is, for the moment, perhaps the most neglected literary form. I say "for the moment" because unless the moral and literary decadence of our day proves to be irreversible, the essay will eventually spring back into vigorous new life. The best essays have given us such a richness of erudition, elegance, wit, information, and sheer high bubbling fun that we must know beyond doubt that the essay will not perish.

It is with no disrespect at all to the classic masters of the form—Addison, Steele, Hazlitt, Arnold, Dr. Johnson, and Charles Lamb—that I declare my own high indebtedness to the essayists of the twentieth century, especially Robert Lynd, Belloc, E. V. Lucas (who, in addition to writing his own radiant essays, thought up the witty titles for some of G. K. Chesterton's own collections of the form: *Alarms and Discursions*, *Tremendous Trifles*, *Come to Think of It*, *A Shilling for My Thoughts*, and others), and—the essayist most recent so far as my own knowledge goes—Bernard Levin, who died in 2004 and whose memory I salute.

It is, though, with Chesterton himself that this volume is concerned. After my boyhood introduction to him through *The Man Who Was Thursday*, I next discovered his essays and was, at the age of fourteen, ushered into a new and more spacious sphere of literary experience than that offered by the yarns of boys' adventures, upon which I had previously fed.

Later, in my days as a schoolmaster, I had the pleasure and the fun of introducing many twelve- and thirteen-year-old pupils to my slightly abridged versions of a few of those illuminating pieces. "A Piece of Chalk" was always popular, as was "The Twelve Men". I have long maintained that we frequently and culpably underestimate the ability of young people to understand adult concepts, provided that we explain and discuss them lucidly.

But the most rewarding essay to my charges seemed always to be "What I Found in My Pocket", in which G. K. C. finds himself in a railway compartment without books or newspapers. The hearts of my pupils were won by the account of Chesterton being reduced to searching his pockets and unearthing tram tickets, upon which were "short . . . scientific essays about some kind of pill", and a box of matches that prompted him to meditate on fire, "which is stronger even than steel, the old, fierce female thing we all love, but dare not touch".

Then, especially enjoyed by the boys, came the passage: "The next thing that I took out was a pocket-knife. . . . I saw a vague and violent battle, in which the stone axes broke and stone knives were splintered against something shining and new in the hand of one desperate man. . . . I saw all the swords of Feudal and all the wheels of Industrial war. *For the knife is only a short sword; and the pocket-knife is a secret sword.*"

The emphasis in that last sentence is mine. As for the whole passage, many times I have seen its effect upon the young imagination and have myself been warmed and rewarded by it.

If you, reader of this volume, are fortunate enough to have contact with young readers of our own day, do, I implore you, introduce them to the essay form—and there is no better place to start than with G. K. Chesterton.

PREFACE

Joseph Pearce

"I am interested in getting to know the works of G.K. Chesterton. Could you recommend a good place to start?" When I hear this question—one of the most frequently asked during my travels on the lecture circuit—I experience a sinking feeling deep inside. I am obviously not disappointed that my interlocutor desires to get to know Chesterton. (Perish the thought!) On the contrary, I am always delighted to learn of another would-be convert to the magic of G.K.C. The truth is that the sinking feeling overcomes me in spite of such delight, souring its sweetness. I have come to realise that this seemingly inexplicable sense of apprehension is caused by the knowledge that I have just been asked a question that is much easier to ask than it is to answer.

The first difficulty in answering such a question is that I need to know more about the person asking it before I am able to offer an adequate reply. Does he prefer fiction or non-fiction? Does he like poetry? Is he the type of reader who likes to battle with the big questions of metaphysics, or does he prefer the truth served up in bite-size (or byte-size) chunks? I feel that I would have to sit down with my interlocutor and become his inquisitor, preferably over a pint or two of ale or a glass or two of wine. Since time seldom affords us the luxury of such pleasures, it becomes necessary to cut to the chase. Therefore, in the absence of all the necessary data, I offer the eminently sensible suggestion that he begin his study of Chesterton by buying my own biography of him! Such a solution has the added bonus of offering him the opportunity to instantly gratify his new-found enthusiasm for G.K.C. by purchasing a copy of the said volume even as he speaks, ample stocks of which are available at the author's book-table at which he is presently standing.

In defence of such shameless salesmanship, and in defiance of those who wish to scoff, I explain that my biography is peppered throughout with liberal and lengthy quotations from many of Chesterton's works. These serve as an appetizer or a sampler of G. K. C.'s considerable corpus, an hors d'oeuvre to his oeuvre. In fairness to Messieurs Ahlquist and Mackey, my co-conspirators in the compiling of the present volume, they have also published works that serve as good introductions to Chesterton. Needless to say, my interlocutor remains blissfully ignorant of these rival volumes as he is seduced into buying mine.

But let's return to our original question and try to answer it in general terms in spite of our knowledge that every man is not Everyman and that, therefore, he will differ in his preferences from his fellow men. Should our interlocutor prefer fiction, he should be told that *The Man Who Was Thursday* is indubitably Chesterton's finest novel but that it is less accessible and perhaps less fun than *The Ball and the Cross*. It is certainly more confusing on a first reading, whereas *The Ball and the Cross* offers the reader an unabashed battle between its Catholic and atheist protagonists in decidedly unambiguous terms. If he prefers poetry, he should be introduced to *The Ballad of the White Horse* or to "Lepanto" but should not be deprived of the delights of Chesterton's less ambitious voyages into verse, such as "The Donkey", "The Fish", "The Skeleton", and "The Rolling English Road"; nor should he be allowed to overlook relatively unknown and priceless gems, such as "The Strange Music" and "The Crystal". If he wants to do battle with the great metaphysical truths underpinning reality, he should grapple with the acrobatic brilliance of *The Everlasting Man* or *Orthodoxy*. If he wants hagiography worthy of hallowing to the heights, he should read G. K. C.'s pen portrait of Saint Thomas Aquinas or Saint Francis of Assisi. And we have not even mentioned the works of literary biography, or the detective stories, or the works of history, politics, or economics. Or the essays.

As to the last, it is a sorry fact that Chesterton's essays are sadly neglected in relation to the rest of his corpus, and this in spite of the fact that Chesterton is one of the finest essayists ever to grace the English language. In atonement for this sin of omission and this tradition of neglect, the present volume endeavours to bring together some of Chesterton's finest essays. I am pleased to have partnered Messieurs Ahlquist and Mackey in this noble project in which we have wallowed self-indulgently in *la crème de la crème* of Chestertonian *belles-lettres*. We have rectified a crime by being partners in cream!

[Having soured the cream of Chesterton with the worst of puns, the author exits stage left, rather hurriedly, to a chorus of boos and hisses . . .]

INTRODUCTION

Dale Ahlquist

If I may myself imitate the timid and tentative tone of the true essayist, I will confine myself to saying that there is something in what I say.

—G. K. Chesterton, "On Essays"

And who do we think we are calling any collection of Chesterton essays the "best"? The prospect of putting such a collection together seemed not just presumptuous, but impossible. Nonetheless, I agreed to participate in putting this volume together, especially since it was obvious that my presence on the committee would be necessary to balance those two Englishmen. So I arranged their choices along with mine and did what good editors do, which is nothing. Thus we have a pure dose of Chesterton the Master Essayist. But no matter how large the book, any such collection will leave out shining literary gems, essays that are not merely outstanding, but perfect. Perfect, I say. How could a perfect essay not be included among the "best"? But I assure you we left several perfect essays out. And yet, here we are, trying to pass this collection off as *The Best Essays of G. K. Chesterton.*

We begin with the first essay of Chesterton's first book, and we end with the last essay of his last book. (There will be pedants who point out that neither of these statements is true, but as Chesterton would say, they need not detain us.) Most of these essays are from previously compiled collections; however, a few of them are collected here for the first time. Two of the essays are not really essays but are transcripts of talks given by

Chesterton. Why are they included? Because, as Chesterton's wife and others attested, he talked just like he wrote.

In his essays, Chesterton can move from what seems to be the ridiculous to what is unmistakably the sublime in just a few paragraphs. He can start by lying in bed, contemplating painting the ceiling with a broom, and finish by reflecting on the inversion of values in modern society. He can start by losing a piece of chalk and finish with a profound meditation on the meaning of purity.

He takes on any topic—vulgarity; the police; sex; Jane Austen; mysticism; architecture; Shakespeare; voting; gargoyles; free verse; Mary, Queen of Scots; bureaucrats; demon possession; cheese; fantasy; religious tolerance—and he does not merely enlighten, he illuminates. He fills us with light and sheds light on everything else. There is, as he says, something in what he says. He combines his literary powers—a crispness of style, a lightness of touch, and a clarity of thought—to point to the truth. That is his goal. He gets there, and he gets there beautifully, often taking the scenic route.

As he neared the end of a long and prolific literary career, he promised to end with a bang. But all of his essays end with a bang. They begin with a bang too. He understands the value of both a good opening line and a good closing line. It is not just because he has a gift for aphorism. It is because he is a good mystery writer.

Yes, Chesterton the master essayist is still best remembered for his detective stories. But all of his essays are like detective stories. A good essay begins not just with an intriguing hook but a dilemma that needs to be solved—a fresh corpse, if you will. How did this victim get here? What are the clues? Who are the characters in this story, the suspects, the sleuth? We pursue the possible leads and gather information in each paragraph. Every sentence is suggestive. But then something thrilling happens. The solution when it is revealed comes as a surprise, even a shock. He has been leading us along in one direction, but then he abruptly changes course and stuns us with a conclusion that we had not been anticipating. At the same instant we realize that it is the only possible solution. Better still, it has been obvious all along. We just didn't see it till he pointed it out to us.

Read Chesterton's essay "The Twelve Men". It builds perfectly to an ending that is utterly unexpected but completely satisfying. (No wonder all three of us had that one on our list. It shows that the other two guys were at least paying attention. There is hope even for England.)

"The immortal writer", says Chesterton, is "he who does something universal in a special manner".[1] This quality that he recognized in other great writers was something that he himself exhibited. He is a teacher who paints with words. Each of his essays is both a lesson and a work of art.

[1] G. K. Chesterton, *Charles Dickens* (London: Wordsworth Editions, Ltd., 2007), p. 148.

Introduction to *The Defendant*

The Defendant, 1901

In certain endless uplands, uplands like great flats gone dizzy, slopes that seem to contradict the idea that there is even such a thing as a level, and make us all realise that we live on a planet with a sloping roof, you will come from time to time upon whole valleys filled with loose rocks and boulders, so big as to be like mountains broken loose. The whole might be an experimental creation shattered and cast away. It is often difficult to believe that such cosmic refuse can have come together except by human means. The mildest and most cockney imagination conceives the place to be the scene of some war of giants. To me it is always associated with one idea, recurrent and at last instinctive. The scene was the scene of the stoning of some prehistoric prophet, a prophet as much more gigantic than after-prophets as the boulders are more gigantic than the pebbles. He spoke some words—words that seemed shameful and tremendous—and the world, in terror, buried him under a wilderness of stones. The place is the monument of an ancient fear. If we followed the same mood of fancy, it would be more difficult to imagine what awful hint or wild picture of the universe called forth that primal persecution, what secret of sensational thought lies buried under the brutal stones. For in our time the blasphemies are threadbare. Pessimism is now patently, as it always was essentially, more commonplace than piety. Profanity is now more than an affectation—it is a convention. The curse against God is Exercise I in the primer of minor poetry. It was not, assuredly, for such babyish solemnities that our imaginary prophet was stoned in the morning of the world. If we weigh the matter in the faultless scales of imagination, if we see what is the real trend of humanity, we shall feel it most probable that he was stoned for saying that the grass was green and that the birds sang in spring; for the mission of all the prophets from the beginning has not been so much the pointing out of heavens or hells as primarily the pointing out of the earth.

Religion has had to provide that longest and strangest telescope—the telescope through which we could see the star upon which we dwelt. For the mind and eyes of the average man this world is as lost as Eden and as sunken as Atlantis. There runs a strange law through the length of human history—that men are continually tending to undervalue their environment, to undervalue their happiness, to undervalue themselves. The great sin of mankind, the sin typified by the fall of Adam, is the tendency, not towards pride, but towards this weird and horrible humility.

This is the great fall, the fall by which the fish forgets the sea, the ox forgets the meadow, the clerk forgets the city, every man forgets his environment and, in the fullest and most literal sense, forgets himself. This is the real fall of Adam, and it is a spiritual fall. It is a strange thing that many truly spiritual men, such as General Gordon, have actually spent some hours in speculating upon the precise location of the Garden of Eden. Most probably we are in Eden still. It is only our eyes that have changed.

The pessimist is commonly spoken of as the man in revolt. He is not. Firstly, because it requires some cheerfulness to continue in revolt, and secondly, because pessimism appeals to the weaker side of everybody, and the pessimist, therefore, drives as roaring a trade as the publican. The person who is really in revolt is the optimist, who generally lives and dies in a desperate and suicidal effort to persuade all the other people how good they are. It has been proved a hundred times over that if you really wish to enrage people and make them angry, even unto death, the right way to do it is to tell them that they are all the sons of God. Jesus Christ was crucified, it may be remembered, not because of anything he said about God, but on a charge of saying that a man could in three days pull down and rebuild the Temple. Every one of the great revolutionists, from Isaiah to Shelley, have been optimists. They have been indignant, not about the badness of existence, but about the slowness of men in realising its goodness. The prophet who is stoned is not a brawler or a marplot. He is simply a rejected lover. He suffers from an unrequited attachment to things in general.

It becomes increasingly apparent, therefore, that the world is in a permanent danger of being misjudged. That this is no fanciful or mystical idea may be tested by simple examples. The two absolutely basic words "good" and "bad," descriptive of two primal and inexplicable sensations, are not, and never have been, used properly. Things that are bad are not called good by any people who experience them; but things that are good are called bad by the universal verdict of humanity.

Let me explain a little: Certain things are bad so far as they go, such as pain, and no one, not even a lunatic, calls a toothache good in itself; but a knife which cuts clumsily and with difficulty is called a bad knife, which it certainly is not. It is only not so good as other knives to which men have grown accustomed. A knife is never bad except on such rare occasions as that in which it is neatly and scientifically planted in the middle of one's back. The coarsest and bluntest knife which ever broke a pencil into pieces instead of sharpening it is a good thing in so far as it is a knife. It would have appeared a miracle in the Stone Age. What we call a bad knife is a good knife not good enough for us; what we call a bad hat is a good hat not good enough for us; what we call bad cookery is good cookery not good enough for us; what we call a bad civilisation is a good civilisation not good enough for us. We choose to call the great mass of the history of mankind bad, not because it is bad, but because we are better. This is palpably an unfair principle. Ivory may not be so white as snow, but the whole Arctic continent does not make ivory black.

Now it has appeared to me unfair that humanity should be engaged perpetually in calling all those things bad which have been good enough to make other things better, in everlastingly kicking down the ladder by which it has climbed. It has appeared to me that progress should be something else besides a continual parricide; therefore I have investigated the dust-heaps of humanity, and found a treasure in all of them. I have found that humanity is not incidentally engaged, but eternally and systematically engaged, in throwing gold into the gutter and diamonds into the sea. I have found that every man is disposed to call the green leaf of the tree a little less green than it is, and the snow of Christmas a little less white than it is; therefore I have imagined that the main business of a man, however humble, is defence. I have conceived that a defendant is chiefly required when worldlings despise the world—that a counsel for the defence would not have been out of place in that terrible day when the sun was darkened over Calvary and Man was rejected of men.

A Defence of Skeletons

The Defendant, 1901

Some little time ago I stood among immemorial English trees that seemed to take hold upon the stars like a brood of Ygdrasils. As I walked among these living pillars I became gradually aware that the rustics who lived and died in their shadow adopted a very curious conversational tone. They seemed to be constantly apologizing for the trees, as if they were a very poor show. After elaborate investigation, I discovered that their gloomy and penitent tone was traceable to the fact that it was winter and all the trees were bare. I assured them that I did not resent the fact that it was winter, that I knew the thing had happened before, and that no forethought on their part could have averted this blow of destiny. But I could not in any way reconcile them to the fact that it *was* winter. There was evidently a general feeling that I had caught the trees in a kind of disgraceful deshabille, and that they ought not to be seen until, like the first human sinners, they had covered themselves with leaves. So it is quite clear that, while very few people appear to know anything of how trees look in winter, the actual foresters know less than anyone. So far from the line of the tree when it is bare appearing harsh and severe, it is luxuriantly indefinable to an unusual degree; the fringe of the forest melts away like a vignette. The tops of two or three high trees when they are leafless are so soft that they seem like the gigantic brooms of that fabulous lady who was sweeping the cobwebs off the sky. The outline of a leafy forest is in comparison hard, gross, and blotchy; the clouds of night do not more certainly obscure the moon than those green and monstrous clouds obscure the tree; the actual sight of the little wood, with its gray and silver sea of life, is entirely a winter vision. So dim and delicate is the heart of the winter woods, a kind of glittering gloaming, that a figure stepping towards us in the chequered twilight seems as if he were breaking through unfathomable depths of spiders' webs.

But surely the idea that its leaves are the chief grace of a tree is a vulgar one, on a par with the idea that his hair is the chief grace of a pianist. When winter, that healthy ascetic, carries his gigantic razor over hill and valley, and shaves all the trees like monks, we feel surely that they are all the more like trees if they are shorn, just as so many painters and musicians would be all the more like men if they were less like mops. But it does appear to be a deep and essential difficulty that men have an abiding terror of their own structure, or of the structure of things they love. This is felt dimly in the skeleton of the tree: it is felt profoundly in the skeleton of the man.

The importance of the human skeleton is very great, and the horror with which it is commonly regarded is somewhat mysterious. Without claiming for the human skeleton a wholly conventional beauty, we may assert that he is certainly not uglier than a bull-dog, whose popularity never wanes, and that he has a vastly more cheerful and ingratiating expression. But just as man is mysteriously ashamed of the skeletons of the trees in winter, so he is mysteriously ashamed of the skeleton of himself in death. It is a singular thing altogether, this horror of the architecture of things. One would think it would be most unwise in a man to be afraid of a skeleton, since Nature has set curious and quite insuperable obstacles to his running away from it.

One ground exists for this terror: a strange idea has infected humanity that the skeleton is typical of death. A man might as well say that a factory chimney was typical of bankruptcy. The factory may be left naked after ruin, the skeleton may be left naked after bodily dissolution; but both of them have had a lively and workmanlike life of their own, all the pulleys creaking, all the wheels turning, in the House of Livelihood as in the House of Life. There is no reason why this creature (new, as I fancy, to art), the living skeleton, should not become the essential symbol of life.

The truth is that man's horror of the skeleton is not horror of death at all. It is man's eccentric glory that he has not, generally speaking, any objection to being dead, but has a very serious objection to being undignified. And the fundamental matter which troubles him in the skeleton is the reminder that the ground-plan of his appearance is shamelessly grotesque. I do not know why he should object to this. He contentedly takes his place in a world that does not pretend to be genteel—a laughing, working, jeering world. He sees millions of animals carrying, with quite a dandified levity, the most monstrous shapes and appendages, the most preposterous horns, wings, and legs, when they are necessary to utility. He sees the good temper of the frog, the unaccountable happiness of the hippopotamus. He sees a whole universe which is ridiculous, from the animalcule, with a head too big for its body, up to the comet, with a tail too big for its head. But when it comes to the delightful oddity of his own inside, his sense of humour rather abruptly deserts him.

In the Middle Ages and in the Renaissance (which was, in certain times and respects, a much gloomier period) this idea of the skeleton had a vast influence in freezing the pride out of all earthly pomps and the fragrance out of all fleeting pleasures. But it was not, surely, the mere dread of death that did this, for these were ages in which men went to meet death singing; it was the idea of the degradation of man in the grinning ugliness of his structure that withered the juvenile insolence of beauty and pride. And in this it almost assuredly did more good than harm. There is nothing so cold or so pitiless as youth, and youth in aristocratic stations and ages tended to an impeccable dignity, an endless summer of success which needed to be very sharply reminded of the scorn of the stars. It was well that such flamboyant prigs should be convinced that one practical joke, at least, would bowl them over, that they would fall into one grinning man-trap, and not rise again. That the whole structure of their existence was as wholesomely ridiculous as that of a pig or a parrot they could not be expected to realise; that birth was humorous, coming of age humorous, drinking and fighting humorous, they were far too young and solemn to know. But at least they were taught that death was humorous.

There is a peculiar idea abroad that the value and fascination of what we call Nature lie in her beauty. But the fact that Nature is beautiful in the sense that a dado or a Liberty curtain is beautiful, is only one of her charms, and almost an accidental one. The highest and most valuable quality in Nature is not her beauty, but her generous and defiant ugliness. A hundred instances might be taken. The croaking noise of the rooks is, in itself, as hideous as the whole hell of sounds in a London railway tunnel. Yet it uplifts us like a trumpet with its coarse kindliness and honesty, and the lover in "Maud" could actually persuade himself that this abominable noise resembled his lady-love's name. Has the poet, for whom Nature means only roses and lilies, ever heard a pig grunting? It is a noise that does a man good—a strong, snorting, imprisoned noise, breaking its way out of unfathomable dungeons through every possible outlet and organ. It might be the voice of the earth itself, snoring in its mighty sleep. This is the deepest, the oldest, the most wholesome and religious sense of the value of Nature—the value which comes from her immense babyishness. She is as top-heavy, as grotesque, as solemn, and as happy as a child. The mood does come when we see all her shapes like shapes that a baby scrawls upon a slate—simple, rudimentary, a million years older, and stronger than the whole disease that is called Art. The objects of earth and heaven seem to combine into a nursery tale, and our relation to things seems for a moment so simple that a dancing lunatic would be needed to do justice to its lucidity and levity. The tree above my head is flapping like some gigantic bird standing on one leg; the moon is like the eye of a cyclops. And, however much my face clouds with sombre vanity, or vulgar vengeance, or contemptible contempt, the bones of my skull beneath it are laughing for ever.

On Certain Modern Writers and the Institution of the Family

Heretics, 1905

The family may fairly be considered, one would think, an ultimate human institution. Every one would admit that it has been the main cell and central unit of almost all societies hitherto, except, indeed, such societies as that of Lacedaemon, which went in for "efficiency," and has, therefore, perished, and left not a trace behind. Christianity, even enormous as was its revolution, did not alter this ancient and savage sanctity; it merely reversed it. It did not deny the trinity of father, mother, and child. It merely read it backwards, making it run child, mother, father. This it called, not the family, but the Holy Family, for many things are made holy by being turned upside down. But some sages of our own decadence have made a serious attack on the family. They have impugned it, as I think wrongly; and its defenders have defended it, and defended it wrongly. The common defence of the family is that, amid the stress and fickleness of life, it is peaceful, pleasant, and at one. But there is another defence of the family which is possible, and to me evident; this defence is that the family is not peaceful and not pleasant and not at one.

It is not fashionable to say much nowadays of the advantages of the small community. We are told that we must go in for large empires and large ideas. There is one advantage, however, in the small state, the city, or the village, which only the willfully blind can overlook. The man who lives in a small community lives in a much larger world. He knows much more of the fierce varieties and uncompromising divergences of men. The reason is obvious. In a large community we can choose our companions. In a small community our companions are chosen for us. Thus in all extensive and highly civilised societies groups come into existence founded upon what is called sympathy, and shut out the real world more sharply than the gates of a monastery. There is nothing really narrow about the clan; the thing which is really narrow is the clique. The men of the clan live together because they all wear the same tartan or are all descended from the same sacred cow; but in their souls, by the divine luck of things, there will always be more colours than in any tartan. But the men of the clique live together because they have the same kind of soul, and their narrowness is a narrowness of spiritual coherence and contentment, like that which exists in hell. A big society exists in order to form cliques. A big society is a society for the promotion of narrowness. It is a machinery for the purpose of guarding the solitary and sensitive individual from all experience of the bitter and bracing human compromises. It is, in the most literal sense of the words, a society for the prevention of Christian knowledge.

We can see this change, for instance, in the modern transformation of the thing called a club. When London was smaller, and the parts of London more self-contained and parochial, the club was what it still is in villages, the opposite of what it is now in great cities. Then the club was valued as a place where a man could be sociable. Now the club is valued as a place where a man can be unsociable. The more the enlargement and elaboration of our civilisation goes on the more the club ceases to be a place where a man can have a noisy argument, and becomes more and more a place where a man can have what is somewhat fantastically called a quiet chop. Its aim is to make a man comfortable, and to make a man comfortable is to make him the opposite of sociable. Sociability, like all good things, is full of discomforts, dangers, and renunciations. The club tends to produce the most degraded of all combinations—the luxurious anchorite, the man who combines the self-indulgence of Lucullus with the insane loneliness of St. Simeon Stylites.

If we were to-morrow morning snowed up in the street in which we live, we should step suddenly into a much larger and much wilder world than we have ever known. And it is the whole effort of the typically modern person to escape from the street in which he lives. First he invents modern hygiene and goes to Margate. Then he invents modern culture and goes to Florence. Then he invents modern imperialism and goes to Timbuctoo. He goes to the fantastic borders of the earth. He pretends to shoot tigers. He almost rides on a camel. And in all this he is still essentially fleeing from the street in which he was born; and of this flight he is always ready with his own explanation. He says he is fleeing from his street because it is dull; he is lying. He is really fleeing from his street because it is a great deal too exciting. It is exciting because it is exacting; it is exacting because it is alive. He can visit Venice because to him the Venetians are only Venetians; the people in his own street are men. He can stare at the Chinese because for him the Chinese are a passive thing to be stared at; if he stares at the old lady in the next garden, she becomes active. He is forced to flee, in short, from the too stimulating society of his equals—of free men, perverse, personal, deliberately different from himself. The street in Brixton is too glowing and overpowering. He has to soothe and quiet himself among tigers and vultures, camels and crocodiles. These creatures are indeed very different from himself. But they do not put their shape or colour or custom into a decisive intellectual competition with his own. They do not seek to destroy his principles and assert their own; the stranger monsters of the suburban street do seek to do this. The camel does not contort his features into a fine sneer because Mr. Robinson has not got a hump; the cultured gentleman at No. 5 does exhibit a sneer because Robinson has not got a dado. The vulture will not roar with laughter because a man does not fly; but the major at No. 9 will roar with laughter because a man does not smoke. The complaint we commonly have to make of our neighbours is that they will not, as we express it, mind their own business. We do not really mean that they will not mind their own business. If our neighbours did not mind their own business they would be asked abruptly for their rent, and would rapidly cease to be our neighbours. What we really mean when we say that they cannot mind their own business is something much deeper. We do not dislike them because they have so little force and fire that they cannot be interested in themselves. We dislike them because they have so much force and fire that they can be interested in us as well. What we dread about our neighbours, in short, is not the narrowness of their horizon, but their superb tendency to broaden it. And all aversions to ordinary humanity have this general character. They are not aversions to its feebleness (as is pretended), but to its energy. The misanthropes pretend that they despise humanity for its weakness. As a matter of fact, they hate it for its strength.

Of course, this shrinking from the brutal vivacity and brutal variety of common men is a perfectly reasonable and excusable thing as long as it does not pretend to any point of superiority. It is when it calls itself aristocracy or aestheticism or a superiority to the bourgeoisie that its inherent weakness has in justice to be pointed out. Fastidiousness is the most pardonable of vices; but it is the most unpardonable of virtues. Nietzsche, who represents most prominently this pretentious claim of the fastidious, has a description somewhere—a very powerful description in the purely literary sense—of the disgust and disdain which consume him at the sight of the common people with their common faces, their common voices, and their common minds. As I have said, this attitude is almost beautiful if we may regard it as pathetic. Nietzsche's aristocracy has about it all the sacredness that belongs to the weak. When he makes us feel that he cannot endure the innumerable faces, the incessant voices, the overpowering omnipresence which belongs to the mob, he will have the sympathy of anybody who has ever been sick on a steamer or tired in a crowded omnibus. Every man has hated mankind when he was less than a man. Every man has had humanity in his eyes like a blinding fog, humanity in his nostrils like a suffocating smell. But when Nietzsche has the incredible lack of humour and lack of imagination to ask us to believe that his aristocracy is an aristocracy of strong muscles or an aristocracy of strong wills, it is necessary to point out the truth. It is an aristocracy of weak nerves.

We make our friends; we make our enemies; but God makes our next-door neighbour. Hence he comes to us clad in all the careless terrors of nature; he is as strange as the stars, as reckless and indifferent as the rain. He is Man, the most terrible of the beasts. That is why the old religions and the old scriptural language showed so sharp a wisdom when they spoke, not of one's duty towards humanity, but one's duty towards one's neighbour. The duty towards humanity may often take the form of some choice which is personal or even pleasurable. That duty may be a hobby; it may even be a dissipation. We may work in the East End because we are peculiarly fitted to work in the East End, or because we think we are; we may fight for the cause of international peace because we are very fond of fighting. The most monstrous martyrdom, the most repulsive experience, may be the result of choice or a kind of taste. We may be so made as to be particularly fond of lunatics or specially interested in leprosy. We may love negroes because they are black or German Socialists because they are pedantic. But we have to love our neighbour because he is there—a much more alarming reason for a much more serious operation. He is the sample of humanity which is actually given us. Precisely because he may be anybody he is everybody. He is a symbol because he is an accident.

Doubtless men flee from small environments into lands that are very deadly. But this is natural enough; for they are not fleeing from death. They are fleeing from life. And this principle applies to ring within ring of the social system of humanity. It is perfectly reasonable that men should seek for some particular variety of the human type, so long as they are seeking for that variety of the human type, and not for mere human variety. It is quite proper that a British diplomatist should seek the society of Japanese generals, if what he wants is Japanese generals. But if what he wants is people different from himself, he had much better stop at home and discuss religion with the housemaid. It is quite reasonable that the village genius should come up to conquer London if what he wants is to conquer London. But if he wants to conquer something fundamentally and symbolically hostile and also very strong, he had much better remain where he is and have a row with the rector. The man in the suburban street is quite right if he goes to Ramsgate for the sake of Ramsgate—a difficult thing to imagine. But if, as he expresses it, he goes to Ramsgate "for a change," then he would have a much more romantic and even melodramatic change if he jumped over the wall into his neighbour's garden. The consequences would be bracing in a sense far beyond the possibilities of Ramsgate hygiene.

Now, exactly as this principle applies to the empire, to the nation within the empire, to the city within the nation, to the street within the city, so it applies to the home within the street. The institution of the family is to be commended for precisely the same reasons that the institution of the nation, or the institution of the city, are in this matter to be commended. It is a good thing for a man to live in a family for the same reason that it is a good thing for a man to be besieged in a city. It is a good thing for a man to live in a family in the same sense that it is a beautiful and delightful thing for a man to be snowed up in a street. They all force him to realise that life is not a thing from outside, but a thing from inside. Above all, they all insist upon the fact that life, if it be a truly stimulating and fascinating life, is a thing which, of its nature, exists in spite of ourselves. The modern writers who have suggested, in a more or less open manner, that the family is a bad institution, have generally confined themselves to suggesting, with much sharpness, bitterness, or, pathos, that perhaps the family is not always very congenial. Of course the family is a good institution because it is uncongenial. It is wholesome precisely because it contains so many divergencies and varieties. It is, as the sentimentalists say, like a little kingdom, and, like most other little kingdoms, is generally in a state of something resembling anarchy. It is exactly because our brother George is not interested in our religious difficulties, but is interested in the Trocadero Restaurant, that the family has some of the bracing qualities of the commonwealth. It is precisely because our uncle Henry does not approve of the theatrical ambitions of our sister Sarah that the family is like humanity. The men and women who, for good reasons and bad, revolt against the family, are, for good reasons and bad, simply revolting against mankind. Aunt Elizabeth is unreasonable, like mankind. Papa is excitable, like mankind. Our youngest brother is mischievous, like mankind. Grandpapa is stupid, like the world; he is old, like the world.

Those who wish, rightly or wrongly, to step out of all this, do definitely wish to step into a narrower world. They are dismayed and terrified by the largeness and variety of the family. Sarah wishes to find a world wholly consisting of private theatricals; George wishes to think the Trocadero a cosmos. I do not say, for a moment, that the flight to this narrower life may not be the right thing for the individual, any more than I say the same thing about flight into a monastery. But I do say that anything is bad and artificial which tends to make these people succumb to the strange delusion that they are stepping into a world which is actually larger and more varied than their own. The best way that a man could test his readiness to encounter the common variety of mankind would be to climb down a chimney into any house at random, and get on as well as possible with the people inside. And that is essentially what each one of us did on the day that he was born.

This is, indeed, the sublime and special romance of the family. It is romantic because it is a toss-up. It is romantic because it is everything that its enemies call it. It is romantic because it is arbitrary. It is romantic because it is there. So long as you have groups of men chosen rationally, you have some special or sectarian atmosphere. It is when you have groups of men chosen irrationally that you have men. The element of adventure begins to exist; for an adventure is, by its nature, a thing that comes to us. It is a thing that chooses us, not a thing that we choose. Falling in love has been often regarded as the supreme adventure, the supreme romantic accident. In so much as there is in it something outside ourselves, something of a sort of merry fatalism, this is very true. Love does take us and transfigure and torture us. It does break our hearts with an unbearable beauty, like the unbearable beauty of music. But in so far as we have certainly something to do with the matter; in so far as we are in some sense prepared to fall in love and in some sense jump into it; in so far as we do to some extent choose and to some extent even judge—in all this falling in love is not truly romantic, is not truly adventurous at all. In this degree the supreme adventure is not falling in love. The supreme adventure is being born. There we do walk suddenly into a splendid and startling trap. There we do see something of which we have not dreamed before. Our father and mother do lie in wait for us and leap out on us, like brigands from a bush. Our uncle is a surprise. Our aunt is, in the beautiful common expression, a bolt from the blue. When we step into the family, by the act of being born, we do step into a world which is incalculable, into a world which has its own strange laws, into a world which could do without us, into a world that we have not made. In other words, when we step into the family we step into a fairy-tale.

This colour as of a fantastic narrative ought to cling to the family and to our relations with it throughout life. Romance is the deepest thing in life; romance is deeper even than reality. For even if reality could be proved to be misleading, it still could not be proved to be unimportant or unimpressive. Even if the facts are false, they are still very strange. And this strangeness of life, this unexpected and even perverse element of things as they fall out, remains incurably interesting. The circumstances we can regulate may become tame or pessimistic; but the "circumstances over which we have no control" remain god-like to those who, like Mr. Micawber, can call on them and renew their strength. People wonder why the novel is the most popular form of literature; people wonder why it is read more than books of science or books of metaphysics. The reason is very simple; it is merely that the novel is more true than they are. Life may sometimes legitimately appear as a book of science. Life may sometimes appear, and with a much greater legitimacy, as a book of metaphysics. But life is always a novel. Our existence may cease to be a song; it may cease even to be a beautiful lament. Our existence may not be an intelligible justice, or even a recognizable wrong. But our existence is still a story. In the fiery alphabet of every sunset is written, "to be continued in our next." If we have sufficient intellect, we can finish a philosophical and exact deduction, and be certain that we are finishing it right. With the adequate brain-power we could finish any scientific discovery, and be certain that we were finishing it right. But not with the most gigantic intellect could we finish the simplest or silliest story, and be certain that we were finishing it right. That is because a story has behind it, not merely intellect which is partly mechanical, but will, which is in its essence divine. The narrative writer can send his hero to the gallows if he likes in the last chapter but one. He can do it by the same divine caprice whereby he, the author, can go to the gallows himself, and to hell afterwards if he chooses. And the same civilisation, the chivalric European civilisation which asserted freewill in the thirteenth century, produced the thing called "fiction" in the eighteenth. When Thomas Aquinas asserted the spiritual liberty of man, he created all the bad novels in the circulating libraries.

But in order that life should be a story or romance to us, it is necessary that a great part of it, at any rate, should be settled for us without our permission. If we wish life to be a system, this may be a nuisance; but if we wish it to be a drama, it is an essential. It may often happen, no doubt, that a drama may be written by somebody else which we like very little. But we should like it still less if the author came before the curtain every hour or so, and forced on us the whole trouble of inventing the next act. A man has control over many things in his life; he has control over enough things to be the hero of a novel. But if he had control over everything, there would be so much hero that there would be no novel. And the reason why the lives of the rich are at bottom so tame and uneventful is simply that they can choose the events. They are dull because they are omnipotent. They fail to feel adventures because they can make the adventures. The thing which keeps life romantic and full of fiery possibilities is the existence of these great plain limitations which force all of us to meet the things we do not like or do not expect. It is vain for the supercilious moderns to talk of being in uncongenial surroundings. To be in a romance is to be in uncongenial surroundings. To be born into this earth is to be born into uncongenial surroundings, hence to be born into a romance. Of all these great limitations and frameworks which fashion and create the poetry and variety of life, the family is the most definite and important. Hence it is misunderstood by the moderns, who imagine that romance would exist most perfectly in a complete state of what they call liberty. They think that if a man makes a gesture it would be a startling and romantic matter that the sun should fall from the sky. But the startling and romantic thing about the sun is that it does not fall from the sky. They are seeking under every shape and form a world where there are no limitations—that is, a world where there are no outlines; that is, a world where there are no shapes. There is nothing baser than that infinity. They say they wish to be as strong as the universe, but they really wish the whole universe as weak as themselves.

On Running After One's Hat

All Things Considered, 1908

I feel an almost savage envy on hearing that London has been flooded in my absence, while I am in the mere country. My own Battersea has been, I understand, particularly favoured as a meeting of the waters. Battersea was already, as I need hardly say, the most beautiful of human localities. Now that it has the additional splendour of great sheets of water, there must be something quite incomparable in the landscape (or waterscape) of my own romantic town. Battersea must be a vision of Venice. The boat that brought the meat from the butcher's must have shot along those lanes of rippling silver with the strange smoothness of the gondola. The greengrocer who brought cabbages to the corner of the Latchmere Road must have leant upon the oar with the unearthly grace of the gondolier. There is nothing so perfectly poetical as an island; and when a district is flooded it becomes an archipelago.

Some consider such romantic views of flood or fire slightly lacking in reality. But really this romantic view of such inconveniences is quite as practical as the other. The true optimist who sees in such things an opportunity for enjoyment is quite as logical and much more sensible than the ordinary "Indignant Ratepayer" who sees in them an opportunity for grumbling. Real pain, as in the case of being burnt at Smithfield or having a toothache, is a positive thing; it can be supported, but scarcely enjoyed. But, after all, our toothaches are the exception, and as for being burnt at Smithfield it only happens to us at the very longest intervals. And most of the inconveniences that make men swear or women cry are really sentimental or imaginative inconveniences—things altogether of the mind. For instance, we often hear grown-up people complaining of having to hang about a railway station and wait for a train. Did you ever hear a small boy complain of having to hang about a railway station and wait for a train? No, for to him to be inside a railway station is to be inside a cavern of wonder and a palace of poetical pleasures. Because to him the red light and the green light on the signal are like a new sun and a new moon. Because to him when the wooden arm of the signal falls down suddenly, it is as if a great king had thrown down his staff as a signal and started a shrieking tournament of trains. I myself am of little boys' habit in this matter. They also serve who only stand and wait for the two fifteen. Their meditations may be full of rich and fruitful things. Many of the most purple hours of my life have been passed at Clapham Junction, which is now, I suppose, under water. I have been there in many moods so fixed and mystical that the water might well have come up to my waist before I noticed it particularly. But in the case of all such annoyances, as I have said, everything depends upon the emotional point of view. You can safely apply the test to almost every one of the things that are currently talked of as the typical nuisance of daily life.

For instance, there is a current impression that it is unpleasant to have to run after one's hat. Why should it be unpleasant to the well-ordered and pious mind? Not merely because it is running, and running exhausts one. The same people run much faster in games and sports. The same people run much more eagerly after an uninteresting little leather ball than they will after a nice silk hat. There is an idea that it is humiliating to run after one's hat; and when people say it is humiliating they mean that it is comic. It certainly is comic; but man is a very comic creature, and most of the things he does are comic—eating, for instance. And the most comic things of all are exactly the things that are most worth doing—such as making love. A man running after a hat is not half so ridiculous as a man running after a wife.

Now a man could, if he felt rightly in the matter, run after his hat with the manliest ardour and the most sacred joy. He might regard himself as a jolly huntsman pursuing a wild animal, for certainly no animal could be wilder. In fact, I am inclined to believe that hat-hunting on windy days will be the sport of the upper classes in the future. There will be a meet of ladies and gentlemen on some high ground on a gusty morning. They will be told that the professional attendants have started a hat in such-and-such a thicket, or whatever be the technical term. Notice that this employment will in the fullest degree combine sport with humanitarianism. The hunters would feel that they were not inflicting pain. Nay, they would feel that they were inflicting pleasure, rich, almost riotous pleasure, upon the people who were looking on. When last I saw an old gentleman running after his hat in Hyde Park I told him that a heart so benevolent as his ought to be filled with peace and thanks at the thought of how much unaffected pleasure his every gesture and bodily attitude were at that moment giving to the crowd.

The same principle can be applied to every other typical domestic worry. A gentleman trying to get a fly out of the milk or a piece of cork out of his glass of wine often imagines himself to be irritated. Let him think for a moment of the patience of anglers sitting by dark pools, and let his soul be immediately irradiated with gratification and repose. Again, I have known some people of very modern views driven by their distress to the use of theological terms to which they attached no doctrinal significance, merely because a drawer was jammed tight and they could not pull it out. A friend of mine was particularly afflicted in this way. Every day his drawer was jammed, and every day in consequence it was something else that rhymes to it. But I pointed out to him that this sense of wrong was really subjective and relative; it rested entirely upon the assumption that the drawer could, should, and would come out easily. "But if," I said, "you picture to yourself that you are pulling against some powerful and oppressive enemy the struggle will become merely exciting and not exasperating. Imagine that you are tugging up a lifeboat out of the sea. Imagine that you are roping up a fellow-creature out of an Alpine crevasse. Imagine even that you are a boy again and engaged in a tug-of-war between French and English." Shortly after saying this I left him; but I have no doubt at all that my words bore the best possible fruit. I have no doubt that every day of his life he hangs on to the handle of that drawer with a flushed face and eyes bright with battle, uttering encouraging shouts to himself, and seeming to hear all round him the roar of an applauding ring.

So I do not think that it is altogether fanciful or incredible to suppose that even the floods in London may be accepted and enjoyed poetically. Nothing beyond inconvenience seems really to have been caused by them; and inconvenience, as I have said, is only one aspect, and that the most unimaginative and accidental aspect of a really romantic situation. An adventure is only an inconvenience rightly considered. An inconvenience is only an adventure wrongly considered. The water that girdled the houses and shops of London must, if anything, have only increased their previous witchery and wonder. For as the Roman Catholic priest in the story said: "Wine is good with everything except water," and on a similar principle water is good with everything except wine.

Woman

All Things Considered, 1908

A correspondent has written me an able and interesting letter in the matter of some allusions of mine to the subject of communal kitchens. He defends communal kitchens. He defends communal kitchens very lucidly from the standpoint of the calculating collectivist; but, like many of his school, he cannot apparently grasp that there is another test of the whole matter, with which such calculation has nothing at all to do. He knows it would be cheaper if a number of us ate at the same time, so as to use the same table. So it would. It would also be cheaper if a number of us slept at different times, so as to use the same pair of trousers. But the question is not how cheap are we buying a thing, but what are we buying? It is cheap to own a slave. And it is cheaper still to be a slave.

My correspondent also says that the habit of dining out in restaurants, etc., is growing. So, I believe, is the habit of committing suicide. I do not desire to connect the two facts together. It seems fairly clear that a man could not dine at a restaurant because he had just committed suicide; and it would be extreme perhaps, to suggest that he commits suicide because he has just dined at a restaurant. But the two cases when put side by side, are enough to indicate the falsity and poltroonery of this eternal modern argument from what is in fashion. The question for brave men is not whether a certain thing is increasing; the question is whether we are increasing it. I dine very often in restaurants because the nature of my trade makes it convenient: but if I thought that by dining in restaurants I was working for the creation of communal meals, I would never enter a restaurant again; I would carry bread and cheese in my pocket or eat chocolate out of automatic machines. For the personal element in some things is sacred. I heard Mr. Will Crooks put it perfectly the other day: "The most sacred thing is to be able to shut your own door."

My correspondent says, "Would not our women be spared the drudgery of cooking and all its attendant worries, leaving them free for higher culture?" The first thing that occurs to me to say about this is very simple, and is, I imagine, a part of all our experience. If my correspondent can find any way of preventing women from worrying, he will indeed be a remarkable man. I think the matter is a much deeper one. First of all, my correspondent overlooks a distinction which is elementary in our human nature. Theoretically, I suppose, every one would like to be freed from worries. But nobody in the world would always like to be freed from worrying occupations. I should very much like (as far as my feelings at the moment go) to be free from the consuming nuisance of writing this article. But it does not follow that I should like to be free from the consuming nuisance of being a journalist. Because we are worried about a thing, it does not follow that we are not interested in it. The truth is the other way. If we are not interested, why on earth should we be worried? Women are worried about housekeeping, but those that are most interested are the most worried. Women are still more worried about their husbands and their children. And I suppose if we strangled the children and pole-axed the husbands it would leave women free for higher culture. That is, it would leave them free to begin to worry about that. For women would worry about higher culture as much as they worry about everything else.

I believe this way of talking about women and their higher culture is almost entirely a growth of the classes which (unlike the journalistic class to which I belong) have always a reasonable amount of money. One odd thing I specially notice. Those who write like this seem entirely to forget the existence of the working and wage-earning classes. They say eternally, like my correspondent, that the ordinary woman is always a drudge. And what, in the name of the Nine Gods, is the ordinary man? These people seem to think that the ordinary man is a Cabinet Minister. They are always talking about man going forth to wield power, to carve his own way, to stamp his individuality on the world, to command and to be obeyed. This may be true of a certain class. Dukes, perhaps, are not drudges; but, then, neither are Duchesses. The Ladies and Gentlemen of the Smart Set are quite free for the higher culture, which consists chiefly of motoring and Bridge. But the ordinary man who typifies and constitutes the millions that make up our civilisation is no more free for the higher culture than his wife is.

Indeed, he is not so free. Of the two sexes the woman is in the more powerful position. For the average woman is at the head of something with which she can do as she likes; the average man has to obey orders and do nothing else. He has to put one dull brick on another dull brick, and do nothing else; he has to add one dull figure to another dull figure, and do nothing else. The woman's world is a small one, perhaps, but she can alter it. The woman can tell the tradesman with whom she deals some realistic things about himself. The clerk who does this to the manager generally gets the sack, or shall we say (to avoid the vulgarism), finds himself free for higher culture. Above all, as I said in my previous article, the woman does work which is in some small degree creative and individual. She can put the flowers or the furniture in fancy arrangements of her own. I fear the bricklayer cannot put the bricks in fancy arrangements of his own, without disaster to himself and others. If the woman is only putting a patch into a carpet, she can choose the thing with regard to colour. I fear it would not do for the office boy dispatching a parcel to choose his stamps with a view to colour; to prefer the tender mauve of the sixpenny to the crude scarlet of the penny stamp. A woman cooking may not always cook artistically; still she can cook artistically. She can introduce a personal and imperceptible alteration into the composition of a soup. The clerk is not encouraged to introduce a personal and imperceptible alteration into the figures in a ledger.

The trouble is that the real question I raised is not discussed. It is argued as a problem in pennies, not as a problem in people. It is not the proposals of these reformers that I feel to be false so much as their temper and their arguments. I am not nearly so certain that communal kitchens are wrong as I am that the defenders of communal kitchens are wrong. Of course, for one thing, there is a vast difference between the communal kitchens of which I spoke and the communal meal (*monstrum horrendum, informe*) which the darker and wilder mind of my correspondent diabolically calls up. But in both the trouble is that their defenders will not defend them humanly as human institutions. They will not interest themselves in the staring psychological fact that there are some things that a man or a woman, as the case may be, wishes to do for himself or herself. He or she must do it inventively, creatively, artistically, individually—in a word, badly. Choosing your wife (say) is one of these things. Is choosing your husband's dinner one of these things? That is the whole question: it is never asked.

And then the higher culture. I know that culture. I would not set any man free for it if I could help it. The effect of it on the rich men who are free for it is so horrible that it is worse than any of the other amusements of the millionaire—worse than gambling, worse even than philanthropy. It means thinking the smallest poet in Belgium greater than the greatest poet of England. It means losing every democratic sympathy. It means being unable to talk to a navvy about sport, or about beer, or about the Bible, or about the Derby, or about patriotism or about anything whatever that he, the navvy, wants to talk about. It means taking literature seriously, a very amateurish thing to do. It means pardoning indecency only when it is gloomy indecency. Its disciples will call a spade a spade: but only when it is a grave-digger's spade. The higher culture is sad, cheap, impudent, unkind, without honesty, and without ease. In short, it is "high." That abominable word (also applied to game) admirably describes it.

No; if you were setting women free for something else I might be more melted. If you can assure me, privately and gravely, that you are setting women free to dance on the mountains like Maenads, or to worship some monstrous goddess, I will make a note of your request. If you are quite sure that the ladies in Brixton, the moment they give up cooking, will beat great gongs and blow horns to Mumbo Jumbo, then I will agree that the occupation is at least human and is more or less entertaining. Women have been set free to be Bacchantes; they have been set free to be Virgin Martyrs; they have been set free to be Witches. Do not ask them now to sink so low as the higher culture.

I have my own little notions of the possible emancipation of women; but I suppose I should not be taken very seriously if I propounded them. I should favour anything that would increase the present enormous authority of women and their creative action in their own homes. The average woman, as I have said, is a despot; the average man is a serf. I am for any scheme that any one can suggest that will make the average woman more of a despot. So far from wishing her to get her cooked meals from outside, I should like her to cook more wildly and at her own will than she does. So far from getting always the same meals from the same place, let her invent, if she likes, a new dish every day of her life. Let woman be more of a maker, not less. We are right to talk about "Woman": only blackguards talk about women. Yet all men talk about men, and that is the whole difference. Men represent the deliberative and democratic element in life. Woman represents the despotic.

A Piece of Chalk

Tremendous Trifles, 1909

I remember one splendid morning, all blue and silver, in the summer holidays when I reluctantly tore myself away from the task of doing nothing in particular, and put on a hat of some sort and picked up a walking-stick, and put six very bright-coloured chalks in my pocket. I then went into the kitchen (which, along with the rest of the house, belonged to a very square and sensible old woman in a Sussex village), and asked the owner and occupant of the kitchen if she had any brown paper. She had a great deal; in fact, she had too much; and she mistook the purpose and the rationale of the existence of brown paper. She seemed to have an idea that if a person wanted brown paper he must be wanting to tie up parcels; which was the last thing I wanted to do; indeed, it is a thing which I have found to be beyond my mental capacity. Hence she dwelt very much on the varying qualities of toughness and endurance in the material. I explained to her that I only wanted to draw pictures on it, and that I did not want them to endure in the least; and that from my point of view, therefore, it was a question, not of tough consistency, but of responsive surface, a thing comparatively irrelevant in a parcel. When she understood that I wanted to draw she offered to overwhelm me with note-paper, apparently supposing that I did my notes and correspondence on old brown paper wrappers from motives of economy.

I then tried to explain the rather delicate logical shade, that I not only liked brown paper, but liked the quality of brownness in paper, just as I liked the quality of brownness in October woods, or in beer, or in the peat-streams of the North.

Brown paper represents the primal twilight of the first toil of creation, and with a bright-coloured chalk or two you can pick out points of fire in it, sparks of gold, and blood-red, and sea-green, like the first fierce stars that sprang out of divine darkness. All this I said (in an off-hand way) to the old woman; and I put the brown paper in my pocket along with the chalks, and possibly other things. I suppose everyone must have reflected how primeval and how poetical are the things that one carries in one's pocket; the pocket-knife, for instance, the type of all human tools, the infant of the sword. Once I planned to write a book of poems entirely about the things in my pockets. But I found it would be too long; and the age of the great epics is past.

With my stick and my knife, my chalks and my brown paper, I went out on to the great downs. I crawled across those colossal contours that express the best quality of England, because they are at the same time soft and strong. The smoothness of them has the same meaning as the smoothness of great cart-horses, or the smoothness of the beech-tree; it declares in the teeth of our timid and cruel theories that the mighty are merciful. As my eye swept the landscape, the landscape was as kindly as any of its cottages, but for power it was like an earthquake. The villages in the immense valley were safe, one could see, for centuries; yet the lifting of the whole land was like the lifting of one enormous wave to wash them all away.

I crossed one swell of living turf after another, looking for a place to sit down and draw. Do not, for heaven's sake, imagine I was going to sketch from Nature. I was going to draw devils and seraphim, and blind old gods that men worshipped before the dawn of right, and saints in robes of angry crimson, and seas of strange green, and all the sacred or monstrous symbols that look so well in bright colours on brown paper. They are much better worth drawing than Nature; also they are much easier to draw. When a cow came slouching by in the field next to me, a mere artist might have drawn it; but I always get wrong in the hind legs of quadrupeds. So I drew the soul of the cow; which I saw there plainly walking before me in the sunlight; and the soul was all purple and silver, and had seven horns and the mystery that belongs to all the beasts. But though I could not with a crayon get the best out of the landscape, it does not follow that the landscape was not getting the best out of me. And this, I think, is the mistake that people make about the old poets who lived before Wordsworth, and were supposed not to care very much about Nature because they did not describe it much.

They preferred writing about great men to writing about great hills; but they sat on the great hills to write it. They gave out much less about Nature, but they drank in, perhaps, much more. They painted the white robes of their holy virgins with the blinding snow, at which they had stared all day. They blazoned the shields of their paladins with the purple and gold of many heraldic sunsets. The greenness of a thousand green leaves clustered into the live green figure of Robin Hood. The blueness of a score of forgotten skies became the blue robes of the Virgin. The inspiration went in like sunbeams and came out like Apollo.

But as I sat scrawling these silly figures on the brown paper, it began to dawn on me, to my great disgust, that I had left one chalk, and that a most exquisite and essential chalk, behind. I searched all my pockets, but I could not find any white chalk. Now, those who are acquainted with all the philosophy (nay, religion) which is typified in the art of drawing on brown paper, know that white is positive and essential. I cannot avoid remarking here upon a moral significance. One of the wise and awful truths which this brown-paper art reveals, is this, that white is a colour. It is not a mere absence of colour; it is a shining and affirmative thing, as fierce as red, as definite as black. When, so to speak, your pencil grows red-hot, it draws roses; when it grows white-hot, it draws stars. And one of the two or three defiant verities of the best religious morality, of real Christianity, for example, is exactly this same thing; the chief assertion of religious morality is that white is a colour. Virtue is not the absence of vices or the avoidance of moral dangers; virtue is a vivid and separate thing, like pain or a particular smell. Mercy does not mean not being cruel or sparing people revenge or punishment; it means a plain and positive thing like the sun, which one has either seen or not seen.

Chastity does not mean abstention from sexual wrong; it means something flaming, like Joan of Arc. In a word, God paints in many colours, but He never paints so gorgeously, I had almost said so gaudily, as when He paints in white. In a sense our age has realised this fact, and expressed it in our sullen costume. For if it were really true that white was a blank and colourless thing, negative and non-committal, then white would be used instead of black and grey for the funeral dress of this pessimistic period. We should see city gentlemen in frock coats of spotless silver linen, with top hats as white as wonderful arum lilies. Which is not the case.

Meanwhile, I could not find my chalk.

I sat on the hill in a sort of despair. There was no town nearer than Chichester at which it was even remotely probable that there would be such a thing as an artist's colourman. And yet, without white, my absurd little pictures would be as pointless as the world would be if there were no good people in it. I stared stupidly round, racking my brain for expedients. Then I suddenly stood up and roared with laughter, again and again, so that the cows stared at me and called a committee. Imagine a man in the Sahara regretting that he had no sand for his hour-glass. Imagine a gentleman in mid-ocean wishing that he had brought some salt water with him for his chemical experiments. I was sitting on an immense warehouse of white chalk. The landscape was made entirely out of white chalk. White chalk was piled more miles until it met the sky. I stooped and broke a piece off the rock I sat on: it did not mark so well as the shop chalks do; but it gave the effect. And I stood there in a trance of pleasure, realising that this Southern England is not only a grand peninsula, and a tradition and a civilisation; it is something even more admirable. It is a piece of chalk.

What I Found in My Pocket

Tremendous Trifles, 1909

Once when I was very young I met one of those men who have made the Empire what it is—a man in an astracan coat, with an astracan moustache—a tight, black, curly moustache. Whether he put on the moustache with the coat or whether his Napoleonic will enabled him not only to grow a moustache in the usual place, but also to grow little moustaches all over his clothes, I do not know. I only remember that he said to me the following words: "A man can't get on nowadays by banging about with his hands in his pockets." I made reply with the quite obvious flippancy that perhaps a man got on by having his hands in other people's pockets; whereupon he began to argue about Moral Evolution, so I suppose what I said had some truth in it. But the incident now comes back to me, and connects itself with another incident—if you can call it an incident—which happened to me only the other day.

I have only once in my life picked a pocket, and then (perhaps through some absentmindedness) I picked my own. My act can really with some reason be so described. For in taking things out of my own pocket I had at least one of the more tense and quivering emotions of the thief; I had a complete ignorance and a profound curiosity as to what I should find there. Perhaps it would be the exaggeration of eulogy to call me a tidy person. But I can always pretty satisfactorily account for all my possessions. I can always tell where they are, and what I have done with them, so long as I can keep them out of my pockets. If once anything slips into those unknown abysses, I wave it a sad Virgilian farewell. I suppose that the things that I have dropped into my pockets are still there; the same presumption applies to the things that I have dropped into the sea. But I regard the riches stored in both these bottomless chasms with the same reverent ignorance. They tell us that on the last day the sea will give up its dead; and I suppose that on the same occasion long strings of extraordinary things will come running out of my pockets. But I have quite forgotten what any of them are; and there is really nothing (excepting the money) that I shall be at all surprised at finding among them.

Such at least has hitherto been my state of innocence. I here only wish briefly to recall the special, extraordinary, and hitherto unprecedented circumstances which led me in cold blood, and being of sound mind, to turn out my pockets. I was locked up in a third-class carriage for a rather long journey. The time was towards evening, but it might have been anything, for everything resembling earth or sky or light or shade was painted out as if with a great wet brush by an unshifting sheet of quite colourless rain. I had no books or newspapers. I had not even a pencil and a scrap of paper with which to write a religious epic. There were no advertisements on the walls of the carriage, otherwise I could have plunged into the study of them, for any collection of printed words is quite enough to suggest infinite complexities of mental ingenuity. When I find myself opposite the words "Sunlight Soap" I can exhaust all the aspects of Sun Worship, Apollo, and Summer poetry before I go on to the less congenial subject of soap. But there was no printed word or picture anywhere; there was nothing but blank wood inside the carriage and blank wet without. Now I deny most energetically that anything is, or can be, uninteresting. So I stared at the joints of the walls and seats, and began thinking hard on the fascinating subject of wood. Just as I had begun to realise why, perhaps, it was that Christ was a carpenter, rather than a bricklayer, or a baker, or anything else, I suddenly started upright, and remembered my pockets. I was carrying about with me an unknown treasury. I had a British Museum and a South Kensington collection of unknown curios hung all over me in different places. I began to take the things out.

The first thing I came upon consisted of piles and heaps of Battersea tram tickets. There were enough to equip a paper chase. They shook down in showers like confetti. Primarily, of course, they touched my patriotic emotions, and brought tears to my eyes; also they provided me with the printed matter I required, for I found on the back of them some short but striking little scientific essays about some kind of pill. Comparatively speaking, in my then destitution, those tickets might be regarded as a small but well-chosen scientific library. Should my railway journey continue (which seemed likely at the time) for a few months longer, I could imagine myself throwing myself into the controversial aspects of the pill, composing replies and rejoinders pro and con upon the data furnished to me. But after all it was the symbolic quality of the tickets that moved me most. For as certainly as the cross of St. George means English patriotism, those scraps of paper meant all that municipal patriotism which is now, perhaps, the greatest hope of England.

The next thing that I took out was a pocket-knife. A pocket-knife, I need hardly say, would require a thick book full of moral meditations all to itself. A knife typifies one of the most primary of those practical origins upon which as upon low, thick pillows all our human civilisation reposes. Metals, the mystery of the thing called iron and of the thing called steel, led me off half-dazed into a kind of dream. I saw into the entrails of dim, damp wood, where the first man among all the common stones found the strange stone. I saw a vague and violent battle, in which stone axes broke and stone knives were splintered against something shining and new in the hand of one desperate man. I heard all the hammers on all the anvils of the earth. I saw all the swords of Feudal and all the weals of Industrial war. For the knife is only a short sword; and the pocket-knife is a secret sword. I opened it and looked at that brilliant and terrible tongue which we call a blade; and I thought that perhaps it was the symbol of the oldest of the needs of man. The next moment I knew that I was wrong; for the thing that came next out of my pocket was a box of matches. Then I saw fire, which is stronger even than steel, the old, fierce female thing, the thing we all love, but dare not touch.

The next thing I found was a piece of chalk; and I saw in it all the art and all the frescoes of the world. The next was a coin of a very modest value; and I saw in it not only the image and superscription of our own Caesar, but all government and order since the world began. But I have not space to say what were the items in the long and splendid procession of poetical symbols that came pouring out. I cannot tell you all the things that were in my pocket. I can tell you one thing, however, that I could not find in my pocket. I allude to my railway ticket.

On Lying in Bed

Tremendous Trifles, 1909

Lying in bed would be an altogether perfect and supreme experience if only one had a coloured pencil long enough to draw on the ceiling. This, however, is not generally a part of the domestic apparatus on the premises. I think myself that the thing might be managed with several pails of Aspinall and a broom. Only if one worked in a really sweeping and masterly way, and laid on the colour in great washes, it might drip down again on one's face in floods of rich and mingled colour like some strange fairy rain; and that would have its disadvantages. I am afraid it would be necessary to stick to black and white in this form of artistic composition. To that purpose, indeed, the white ceiling would be of the greatest possible use; in fact it is the only use I think of a white ceiling being put to.

But for the beautiful experiment of lying in bed I might never have discovered it. For years I have been looking for some blank spaces in a modern house to draw on. Paper is much too small for any really allegorical design; as Cyrano de Bergerac says, "Il me faut des géants." But when I tried to find these fine clear spaces in the modern rooms such as we all live in I was continually disappointed. I found an endless pattern and complication of small objects hung like a curtain of fine links between me and my desire. I examined the walls; I found them to my surprise to be already covered with wall-paper, and I found the wall-paper to be already covered with very uninteresting images, all bearing a ridiculous resemblance to each other. I could not understand why one arbitrary symbol (a symbol apparently entirely devoid of any religious or philosophical significance) should thus be sprinkled all over my nice walls like a sort of small-pox. The Bible must be referring to wall-papers, I think, when it says "Use not vain repetitions, as the Gentiles do." I found the Turkey carpet a mass of unmeaning colours, rather like the Turkish Empire, or like the sweetmeat called Turkish delight. I do not exactly know what Turkish delight really is; but I suppose it is Macedonian Massacres. Everywhere that I went forlornly, with my pencil or my paint brush, I found that others had unaccountably been before me, spoiling the walls, the curtains, and the furniture with their childish and barbaric designs.

Nowhere did I find a really clear place for sketching until this occasion when I prolonged beyond the proper limit the process of lying on my back in bed. Then the light of that white heaven broke upon my vision, that breadth of mere white which is indeed almost the definition of Paradise, since it means purity and also means freedom. But alas! like all heavens, now that it is seen it is found to be unattainable; it looks more austere and more distant than the blue sky outside the window. For my proposal to paint on it with the bristly end of a broom has been discouraged—never mind by whom; by a person debarred from all political rights—and even my minor proposal to put the other end of the broom into the kitchen fire and turn it into charcoal has not been conceded. Yet I am certain that it was from persons in my position that all the original inspiration came for covering the ceilings of palaces and cathedrals with a riot of fallen angels or victorious gods. I am sure that it was only because Michelangelo was engaged in the ancient and honourable occupation of lying in bed that he ever realised how the roof of the Sistine Chapel might be made into an awful imitation of a divine drama that could only be acted in the heavens.

The tone now commonly taken towards the practise of lying in bed is hypocritical and unhealthy. Of all the marks of modernity that seem to mean a kind of decadence, there is none more menacing and dangerous than the exaltation of very small and secondary matters of conduct at the expense of very great and primary ones, at the expense of eternal public and tragic human morality. If there is one thing worse than the modern weakening of major morals it is the modern strengthening of minor morals. Thus it is considered more withering to accuse a man of bad taste than of bad ethics. Cleanliness is not next to godliness nowadays, for cleanliness is made an essential and godliness is regarded as an offence. A playwright can attack the institution of marriage so long as he does not misrepresent the manners of society, and I have met Ibsenite pessimists who thought it wrong to take beer but right to take prussic acid. Especially this is so in matters of hygiene; notably such matters as lying in bed. Instead of being regarded, as it ought to be, as a matter of personal convenience and adjustment, it has come to be regarded by many as if it were a part of essential morals to get up early in the morning. It is upon the whole part of practical wisdom; but there is nothing good about it or bad about its opposite.

Misers get up early in the morning; and burglars, I am informed, get up the night before. It is the great peril of our society that all its mechanisms may grow more fixed while its spirit grows more fickle. A man's minor actions and arrangements ought to be free, flexible, creative; the things that should be unchangeable are his principles, his ideals. But with us the reverse is true; our views change constantly; but our lunch does not change. Now, I should like men to have strong and rooted conceptions, but as for their lunch, let them have it sometimes in the garden, sometimes in bed, sometimes on the roof, sometimes in the top of a tree. Let them argue from the same first principles, but let them do it in a bed, or a boat, or a balloon. This alarming growth of good habits really means a too great emphasis on those virtues which mere custom can misuse, it means too little emphasis on those virtues which custom can never quite ensure, sudden and splendid virtues of inspired pity or of inspired candour. If ever that abrupt appeal is made to us we may fail. A man can get used to getting up at five o'clock in the morning. A man cannot very well get used to being burnt for his opinions; the first experiment is commonly fatal. Let us pay a little more attention to these possibilities of the heroic and the unexpected. I daresay that when I get out of this bed I shall do some deed of an almost terrible virtue.

For those who study the great art of lying in bed there is one emphatic caution to be added. Even for those who can do their work in bed (like journalists), still more for those whose work cannot be done in bed (as, for example, the professional harpooner of whales), it is obvious that the indulgence must be very occasional. But that is not the caution I mean. The caution is this: if you do lie in bed, be sure you do it without any reason or justification at all. I do not speak, of course, of the seriously sick. But if a healthy man lies in bed, let him do it without a rag of excuse; then he will get up a healthy man. If he does it for some secondary hygienic reason, if he has some scientific explanation, he may get up a hypochondriac.

The Diabolist

Tremendous Trifles, 1909

Every now and then I have introduced into this column an element of truth. Things that really happened have been mentioned, such as meeting President Kruger or being thrown out of a cab. What I have now to relate really happened; yet there was no element in it of practical politics or of personal danger. It was simply a quiet conversation which I had with another man. But that quiet conversation was by far the most terrible thing that has ever happened to me in my life. It happened so long ago that I cannot be certain of the exact words of the dialogue, only of its main questions and answers; but there is one sentence in it for which I can answer absolutely and word for word. It was a sentence so awful that I could not forget it if I would. It was the last sentence spoken; and it was not spoken to me.

The thing befell me in the days when I was at an art school. An art school is different from almost all other schools or colleges in this respect: that, being of new and crude creation and of lax discipline, it presents a specially strong contrast between the industrious and the idle. People at an art school either do an atrocious amount of work or do no work at all. I belonged, along with other charming people, to the latter class; and this threw me often into the society of men who were very different from myself, and who were idle for reasons very different from mine. I was idle because I was very much occupied; I was engaged about that time in discovering, to my own extreme and lasting astonishment, that I was not an Atheist. But there were others also at loose ends who were engaged in discovering what Carlyle called (I think with needless delicacy) the fact that ginger is hot in the mouth.

I value that time, in short, because it made me acquainted with a good representative number of blackguards. In this connection there are two very curious things which the critic of human life may observe. The first is the fact that there is one real difference between men and women; that women prefer to talk in twos, while men prefer to talk in threes. The second is that when you find (as you often do) three young cads and idiots going about together and getting drunk together every day you generally find that one of the three cads and idiots is (for some extraordinary reason) not a cad and not an idiot. In those small groups devoted to a drivelling dissipation there is almost always one man who seems to have condescended to his company; one man who, while he can talk a foul triviality with his fellows, can also talk politics with a Socialist, or philosophy with a Catholic.

It was just such a man whom I came to know well. It was strange, perhaps, that he liked his dirty, drunken society; it was stranger still, perhaps, that he liked my society. For hours of the day he would talk with me about Milton or Gothic architecture; for hours of the night he would go where I have no wish to follow him, even in speculation. He was a man with a long, ironical face, and close and red hair; he was by class a gentleman, and could walk like one, but preferred, for some reason, to walk like a groom carrying two pails. He looked like a sort of Super-jockey; as if some archangel had gone on the Turf. And I shall never forget the half-hour in which he and I argued about real things for the first and the last time.

Along the front of the big building of which our school was a part ran a huge slope of stone steps, higher, I think, than those that lead up to St. Paul's Cathedral. On a black wintry evening he and I were wandering on these cold heights, which seemed as dreary as a pyramid under the stars. The one thing visible below us in the blackness was a burning and blowing fire; for some gardener (I suppose) was burning something in the grounds, and from time to time the red sparks went whirling past us like a swarm of scarlet insects in the dark. Above us also was gloom; but if one stared long enough at that upper darkness, one saw vertical stripes of grey in the black and then became conscious of the colossal façade of the Doric building, phantasmal, yet filling the sky, as if Heaven were still filled with the gigantic ghost of Paganism.

The man asked me abruptly why I was becoming orthodox. Until he said it, I really had not known that I was; but the moment he had said it I knew it to be literally true. And the process had been so long and full that I answered him at once, out of existing stores of explanation.

"I am becoming orthodox," I said, "because I have come, rightly or wrongly, after stretching my brain till it bursts, to the old belief that heresy is worse even than sin. An error is more menacing than a crime, for an error begets crimes. An Imperialist is worse than a pirate. For an Imperialist keeps a school for pirates; he teaches piracy disinterestedly and without an adequate salary. A Free Lover is worse than a profligate. For a profligate is serious and reckless even in his shortest love; while a Free Lover is cautious and irresponsible even in his longest devotion. I hate modern doubt because it is dangerous."

"You mean dangerous to morality," he said in a voice of wonderful gentleness. "I expect you are right. But why do you care about morality?"

I glanced at his face quickly. He had thrust out his neck as he had a trick of doing; and so brought his face abruptly into the light of the bonfire from below, like a face in the footlights. His long chin and high cheekbones were lit up infernally from underneath; so that he looked like a fiend staring down into the flaming pit. I had an unmeaning sense of being tempted in a wilderness; and even as I paused a burst of red sparks broke past.

"Aren't those sparks splendid?" I said.

"Yes," he replied.

"That is all that I ask you to admit," said I. "Give me those few red specks and I will deduce Christian morality. Once I thought like you, that one's pleasure in a flying spark was a thing that could come and go with that spark. Once I thought that the delight was as free as the fire. Once I thought that red star we see was alone in space. But now I know that the red star is only on the apex of an invisible pyramid of virtues. That red fire is only the flower on a stalk of living habits, which you cannot see. Only because your mother made you say 'Thank you' for a bun are you now able to thank Nature or chaos for those red stars of an instant or for the white stars of all time. Only because you were humble before fireworks on the fifth of November do you now enjoy any fireworks that you chance to see. You only like them being red because you were told about the blood of the martyrs; you only like them being bright because brightness is a glory. That flame flowered out of virtues, and it will fade with virtues. Seduce a woman, and that spark will be less bright. Shed blood, and that spark will be less red. Be really bad, and they will be to you like the spots on a wallpaper."

He had a horrible fairness of the intellect that made me despair of his soul. A common, harmless atheist would have denied that religion produced humility or humility a simple joy: but he admitted both. He only said, "But shall I not find in evil a life of its own? Granted that for every woman I ruin one of those red sparks will go out: will not the expanding pleasure of ruin . . ."

"Do you see that fire?" I asked. "If we had a real fighting democracy, some one would burn you in it; like the devil-worshipper that you are."

"Perhaps," he said, in his tired, fair way. "Only what you call evil I call good."

He went down the great steps alone, and I felt as if I wanted the steps swept and cleaned. I followed later, and as I went to find my hat in the low, dark passage where it hung, I suddenly heard his voice again, but the words were inaudible. I stopped, startled: then I heard the voice of one of the vilest of his associates saying "Nobody can possibly know." And then I heard those two or three words which I remember in every syllable and cannot forget. I heard the Diabolist say, "I tell you I have done everything else. If I do that I shan't know the difference between right and wrong." I rushed out without daring to pause; and as I passed the fire I did not know whether it was hell or the furious love of God.

I have since heard that he died: it may be said, I think, that he committed suicide; though he did it with tools of pleasure, not with tools of pain. God help him, I know the road he went; but I have never known or even dared to think what was that place at which he stopped and refrained.

The Twelve Men

Tremendous Trifles, 1909

The other day, while I was meditating on morality and Mr. H. Pitt, I was, so to speak, snatched up and put into a jury box to try people. The snatching took some weeks, but to me it seemed something sudden and arbitrary. I was put into this box because I lived in Battersea, and my name began with a C. Looking round me, I saw that there were also summoned and in attendance in the court whole crowds and processions of men, all of whom lived in Battersea, and all of whose names began with a C.

It seems that they always summon jurymen in this sweeping alphabetical way. At one official blow, so to speak, Battersea is denuded of all its C's, and left to get on as best it can with the rest of the alphabet. A Cumberpatch is missing from one street—a Chizzolpop from another—three Chucksterfields from Chucksterfield House; the children are crying out for an absent Cadgerboy; the woman at the street corner is weeping for her Coffintop, and will not be comforted. We settle down with a rollicking ease into our seats (for we are a bold, devil-may-care race, the C's of Battersea), and an oath is administered to us in a totally inaudible manner by an individual resembling an army surgeon in his second childhood. We understand, however, that we are to well and truly try the case between our sovereign lord the King and the prisoner at the bar, neither of whom has put in an appearance as yet.

Just when I was wondering whether the King and the prisoner were, perhaps, coming to an amicable understanding in some adjoining public-house, the prisoner's head appears above the barrier of the dock; he is accused of stealing bicycles, and he is the living image of a great friend of mine. We go into the matter of the stealing of the bicycles. We do well and truly try the case between the King and the prisoner in the affair of the bicycles. And we come to the conclusion, after a brief but reasonable discussion, that the King is not in any way implicated. Then we pass on to a woman who neglected her children, and who looks as if somebody or something had neglected her. And I am one of those who fancy that something had.

All the time that the eye took in these light appearances and the brain passed these light criticisms, there was in this heart a barbaric pity and fear which men have never been able to utter from the beginning, but which is the power behind half the poems of the world. The mood cannot even inadequately be suggested, except faintly by this statement that tragedy is the highest expression of the infinite value of human life. Never had I stood so close to pain; and never so far away from pessimism. Ordinarily, I should not have spoken of these dark emotions at all, for speech about them is too difficult; but I mention them now for a specific and particular reason to the statement of which I will proceed at once. I speak of these feelings because out of the furnace of them there came a curious realisation of a political or social truth. I saw with a queer and indescribable kind of clearness what a jury really is, and why we must never let it go.

The trend of our epoch up to this time has been consistently towards socialism and professionalism. We tend to have trained soldiers because they fight better, trained singers because they sing better, trained dancers because they dance better, specially instructed laughers because they laugh better, and so on and so on. The principle has been applied to law and politics by innumerable modern writers. Many Fabians have insisted that a greater part of our political work should be performed by experts. Many legalists have declared that the untrained jury should be altogether supplanted by the trained Judge.

Now, if this world of ours were really what is called reasonable, I do not know that there would be any fault to find with this. But the true result of all experience and the true foundation of all religion is this. That the four or five things that it is most practically essential that a man should know, are all of them what people call paradoxes. That is to say, that though we all find them in life to be mere plain truths, yet we cannot easily state them in words without being guilty of seeming verbal contradictions. One of them, for instance, is the unimpeachable platitude that the man who finds most pleasure for himself is often the man who least hunts for it. Another is a paradox of courage; the fact that the way to avoid death is not to have too much aversion to it. Whoever is careless enough of his bones to climb some hopeless cliff above the tide may save his bones by that carelessness. Whoever will lose his life, the same shall save it; an entirely practical and prosaic statement.

Now, one of these four or five paradoxes which should be taught to every infant prattling at his mother's knee is the following: That the more a man looks at a thing, the less he can see it, and the more a man learns a thing the less he knows it. The Fabian argument of the expert, that the man who is trained should be the man who is trusted, would be absolutely unanswerable if it were really true that a man who studied a thing and practised it every day went on seeing more and more of its significance. But he does not. He goes on seeing less and less of its significance. In the same way, alas! we all go on every day, unless we are continually goading ourselves into gratitude and humility, seeing less and less of the significance of the sky or the stones.

Now, it is a terrible business to mark a man out for the vengeance of men. But it is a thing to which a man can grow accustomed, as he can to other terrible things; he can even grow accustomed to the sun. And the horrible thing about all legal officials, even the best, about all judges, magistrates, barristers, detectives, and policemen, is not that they are wicked (some of them are good), not that they are stupid (several of them are quite intelligent), it is simply that they have got used to it.

Strictly they do not see the prisoner in the dock; all they see is the usual man in the usual place. They do not see the awful court of judgment; they only see their own workshop. Therefore, the instinct of Christian civilisation has most wisely declared that into their judgments there shall upon every occasion be infused fresh blood and fresh thoughts from the streets. Men shall come in who can see the court and the crowd, and the coarse faces of the policemen and the professional criminals, the wasted faces of the wastrels, the unreal faces of the gesticulating counsel, and see it all as one sees a new picture or a ballet hitherto unvisited.

Our civilisation has decided, and very justly decided, that determining the guilt or innocence of men is a thing too important to be trusted to trained men. It wishes for light upon that awful matter, it asks men who know no more law than I know, but who can feel the things that I felt in the jury box. When it wants a library catalogued, or the solar system discovered, or any trifle of that kind it uses up its specialists. But when it wishes anything done which is really serious, it collects twelve of the ordinary men standing round. The same thing was done, if I remember right, by the Founder of Christianity.

The Shop of Ghosts

Tremendous Trifles, 1909

Nearly all the best and most precious things in the universe you can get for a halfpenny. I make an exception, of course, of the sun, the moon, the earth, people, stars, thunderstorms, and such trifles. You can get them for nothing. But the general principle will be at once apparent. In the street behind me, for instance, you can now get a ride on an electric tram for a halfpenny. To be on an electric tram is to be on a flying castle in a fairy tale. You can get quite a large number of brightly coloured sweets for a halfpenny.

But if you want to see what a vast and bewildering array of valuable things you can get at a halfpenny each, you should do as I was doing last night. I was gluing my nose against the glass of a very small and dimly lit toy shop in one of the greyest and leanest of the streets of Battersea. But dim as was that square of light, it was filled (as a child once said to me) with all the colours God ever made. Those toys of the poor were like the children who buy them; they were all dirty; but they were all bright. For my part, I think brightness more important than cleanliness; since the first is of the soul, and the second of the body. You must excuse me; I am a democrat; I know I am out of fashion in the modern world.

As I looked at that palace of pigmy wonders, at small green omnibuses, at small blue elephants, at small black dolls, and small red Noah's arks, I must have fallen into some sort of unnatural trance. That lit shop-window became like the brilliantly lit stage when one is watching some highly coloured comedy. I forgot the grey houses and the grimy people behind me as one forgets the dark galleries and the dim crowds at a theatre. It seemed as if the little objects behind the glass were small, not because they were toys, but because they were objects far away. The green omnibus was really a green omnibus, a green Bayswater omnibus, passing across some huge desert on its ordinary way to Bayswater. The blue elephant was no longer blue with paint; he was blue with distance. The black doll was really a Negro relieved against passionate tropic foliage in the land where every weed is flaming and only man is black. The red Noah's ark was really the enormous ship of earthly salvation riding on the rain-swollen sea, red in the first morning of hope.

Every one, I suppose, knows such stunning instants of abstraction, such brilliant blanks in the mind. In such moments one can see the face of one's own best friend as an unmeaning pattern of spectacles or moustaches. They are commonly marked by the two signs of the slowness of their growth and the suddenness of their termination. The return to real thinking is often as abrupt as bumping into a man. Very often indeed (in my case) it is bumping into a man. But in any case the awakening is always emphatic and, generally speaking, it is always complete. Now, in this case, I did come back with a shock of sanity to the consciousness that I was, after all, only staring into a dingy little toy-shop; but in some strange way the mental cure did not seem to be final. There was still in my mind an unmanageable something that told me that I had strayed into some odd atmosphere, or that I had already done some odd thing. I felt as if I had worked a miracle or committed a sin. It was as if I had (at any rate) stepped across some border in the soul.

To shake off this dangerous and dreamy sense I went into the shop and tried to buy wooden soldiers. The man in the shop was very old and broken, with confused white hair covering his head and half his face, hair so startlingly white that it looked almost artificial. Yet though he was senile and even sick, there was nothing of suffering in his eyes; he looked rather as if he were gradually falling asleep in a not unkindly decay. He gave me the wooden soldiers, but when I put down the money he did not at first seem to see it; then he blinked at it feebly, and then he pushed it feebly away.

"No, no," he said vaguely. "I never have. I never have. We are rather old-fashioned here."

"Not taking money," I replied, "seems to me more like an uncommonly new fashion than an old one."

"I never have," said the old man, blinking and blowing his nose; "I've always given presents. I'm too old to stop."

"Good heavens!" I said. "What can you mean? Why, you might be Father Christmas."

"I am Father Christmas," he said apologetically, and blew his nose again.

The lamps could not have been lighted yet in the street outside. At any rate, I could see nothing against the darkness but the shining shop-window. There were no sounds of steps or voices in the street; I might have strayed into some new and sunless world. But something had cut the chords of common sense, and I could not feel even surprise except sleepily. Something made me say, "You look ill, Father Christmas."

"I am dying," he said.

I did not speak, and it was he who spoke again.

"All the new people have left my shop. I cannot understand it. They seem to object to me on such curious and inconsistent sort of grounds, these scientific men, and these innovators. They say that I give people superstitions and make them too visionary; they say I give people sausages and make them too coarse. They say my heavenly parts are too heavenly; they say my earthly parts are too earthly; I don't know what they want, I'm sure. How can heavenly things be too heavenly, or earthly things too earthly? How can one be too good, or too jolly? I don't understand. But I understand one thing well enough. These modern people are living and I am dead."

"You may be dead," I replied. "You ought to know. But as for what they are doing—do not call it living."

A silence fell suddenly between us which I somehow expected to be unbroken. But it had not fallen for more than a few seconds when, in the utter stillness, I distinctly heard a very rapid step coming nearer and nearer along the street. The next moment a figure flung itself into the shop and stood framed in the doorway. He wore a large white hat tilted back as if in impatience; he had tight black old-fashioned pantaloons, a gaudy old-fashioned stock and waistcoat, and an old fantastic coat. He had large, wide-open, luminous eyes like those of an arresting actor; he had a pale, nervous face, and a fringe of beard. He took in the shop and the old man in a look that seemed literally a flash and uttered the exclamation of a man utterly staggered.

"Good lord!" he cried out; "it can't be you! It isn't you! I came to ask where your grave was."

"I'm not dead yet, Mr. Dickens," said the old gentleman, with a feeble smile; "but I'm dying," he hastened to add reassuringly.

"But, dash it all, you were dying in my time," said Mr. Charles Dickens with animation; "and you don't look a day older."

"I've felt like this for a long time," said Father Christmas.

Mr. Dickens turned his back and put his head out of the door into the darkness.

"Dick," he roared at the top of his voice; "he's still alive."

Another shadow darkened the doorway, and a much larger and more full-blooded gentleman in an enormous periwig came in, fanning his flushed face with a military hat of the cut of Queen Anne. He carried his head well back like a soldier, and his hot face had even a look of arrogance, which was suddenly contradicted by his eyes, which were literally as humble as a dog's. His sword made a great clatter, as if the shop were too small for it.

"Indeed," said Sir Richard Steele, "'tis a most prodigious matter, for the man was dying when I wrote about Sir Roger de Coverley and his Christmas Day."

My senses were growing dimmer and the room darker. It seemed to be filled with newcomers.

"It hath ever been understood," said a burly man, who carried his head humorously and obstinately a little on one side—I think he was Ben Jonson—"It hath ever been understood, consule Jacobo, under our King James and her late Majesty, that such good and hearty customs were fallen sick, and like to pass from the world. This grey beard most surely was no lustier when I knew him than now."

And I also thought I heard a green-clad man, like Robin Hood, say in some mixed Norman French, "But I saw the man dying."

"I have felt like this a long time," said Father Christmas, in his feeble way again.

Mr. Charles Dickens suddenly leant across to him.

"Since when?" he asked. "Since you were born?"

"Yes," said the old man, and sank shaking into a chair. "I have been always dying."

Mr. Dickens took off his hat with a flourish like a man calling a mob to rise.

"I understand it now," he cried, "you will never die."

The Romantic in the Rain

A Miscellany of Men, 1912

The middle classes of modern England are quite fanatically fond of washing; and are often enthusiastic for teetotalism. I cannot therefore comprehend why it is that they exhibit a mysterious dislike of rain. Rain, that inspiring and delightful thing, surely combines the qualities of these two ideals with quite a curious perfection. Our philanthropists are eager to establish public baths everywhere. Rain surely is a public bath; it might almost be called mixed bathing. The appearance of persons coming fresh from this great natural lustration is not perhaps polished or dignified; but for the matter of that, few people are dignified when coming out of a bath. But the scheme of rain in itself is one of an enormous purification. It realises the dream of some insane hygienist: it scrubs the sky. Its giant brooms and mops seem to reach the starry rafters and starless corners of the cosmos; it is a cosmic spring-cleaning.

If the Englishman is really fond of cold baths, he ought not to grumble at the English climate for being a cold bath. In these days we are constantly told that we should leave our little special possessions and join in the enjoyment of common social institutions and a common social machinery. I offer the rain as a thoroughly Socialistic institution. It disregards that degraded delicacy which has hitherto led each gentleman to take his shower-bath in private. It is a better shower-bath, because it is public and communal; and, best of all, because somebody else pulls the string.

As for the fascination of rain for the water drinker, it is a fact the neglect of which I simply cannot comprehend. The enthusiastic water drinker must regard a rainstorm as a sort of universal banquet and debauch of his own favourite beverage. Think of the imaginative intoxication of the wine drinker if the crimson clouds sent down claret or the golden clouds hock. Paint upon primitive darkness some such scenes of apocalypse, towering and gorgeous skyscapes in which champagne falls like fire from heaven or the dark skies grow purple and tawny with the terrible colours of port. All this must the wild abstainer feel, as he rolls in the long soaking grass, kicks his ecstatic heels to heaven, and listens to the roaring rain. It is he, the water drinker, who ought to be the true bacchanal of the forests; for all the forests are drinking water. Moreover, the forests are apparently enjoying it: the trees rave and reel to and fro like drunken giants; they clash boughs as revellers clash cups; they roar undying thirst and howl the health of the world.

All around me as I write is a noise of Nature drinking; and Nature makes a noise when she is drinking, being by no means refined. If I count it Christian mercy to give a cup of cold water to a sufferer, shall I complain of these multitudinous cups of cold water handed round to all living things; a cup of water for every shrub; a cup of water for every weed? I would be ashamed to grumble at it. As Sir Philip Sidney said, their need is greater than mine—especially for water.

There is a wild garment that still carries nobly the name of a wild Highland clan: a clan come from those hills where rain is not so much an incident as an atmosphere. Surely every man of imagination must feel a tempestuous flame of Celtic romance spring up within him whenever he puts on a mackintosh. I could never reconcile myself to carrying an umbrella; it is a pompous Eastern business, carried over the heads of despots in the dry, hot lands. Shut up, an umbrella is an unmanageable walking-stick; open, it is an inadequate tent. For my part, I have no taste for pretending to be a walking pavilion; I think nothing of my hat, and precious little of my head. If I am to be protected against wet, it must be by some closer and more careless protection, something that I can forget altogether. It might be a Highland plaid. It might be that yet more Highland thing, a mackintosh.

And there is really something in the mackintosh of the military qualities of the Highlander. The proper cheap mackintosh has a blue and white sheen as of steel or iron; it gleams like armour. I like to think of it as the uniform of that ancient clan in some of its old and misty raids. I like to think of all the Macintoshes, in their mackintoshes, descending on some doomed Lowland village, their wet waterproofs flashing in the sun or moon. For indeed this is one of the real beauties of rainy weather, that while the amount of original and direct light is commonly lessened, the number of things that reflect light is unquestionably increased. There is less sunshine; but there are more shiny things; such beautifully shiny things as pools and puddles and mackintoshes. It is like moving in a world of mirrors.

And indeed this is the last and not the least gracious of the casual works of magic wrought by rain: that while it decreases light, yet it doubles it. If it dims the sky, it brightens the earth. It gives the roads (to the sympathetic eye) something of the beauty of Venice. Shallow lakes of water reiterate every detail of earth and sky; we dwell in a double universe. Sometimes walking upon bare and lustrous pavements, wet under numerous lamps, a man seems a black blot on all that golden looking-glass, and could fancy he was flying in a yellow sky. But wherever trees and towns hang head downwards in a pigmy puddle, the sense of Celestial topsy-turvydom is the same. This bright, wet, dazzling confusion of shape and shadow, of reality and reflection, will appeal strongly to any one with the transcendental instinct about this dreamy and dual life of ours. It will always give a man the strange sense of looking down at the skies.

The Mad Official

A Miscellany of Men, 1912

Going mad is the slowest and dullest business in the world. I have very nearly done it more than once in my boyhood, and so have nearly all my friends, born under the general doom of mortals, but especially of moderns; I mean the doom that makes a man come almost to the end of thinking before he comes to the first chance of living.

But the process of going mad is dull, for the simple reason that a man does not know that it is going on. Routine and literalism and a certain dry-throated earnestness and mental thirst, these are the very atmosphere of morbidity. If once the man could become conscious of his madness, he would cease to be man. He studies certain texts in Daniel or cryptograms in Shakespeare through monstrously magnifying spectacles, which are on his nose night and day. If once he could take off the spectacles he would smash them. He deduces all his fantasies about the Sixth Seal or the Anglo-Saxon Race from one unexamined and invisible first principle. If he could once see the first principle, he would see that it is not there.

This slow and awful self-hypnotism of error is a process that can occur not only with individuals, but also with whole societies. It is hard to pick out and prove; that is why it is hard to cure. But this mental degeneration may be brought to one test, which I truly believe to be a real test. A nation is not going mad when it does extravagant things, so long as it does them in an extravagant spirit. Crusaders not cutting their beards till they found Jerusalem, Jacobins calling each other Harmodius and Epaminondas when their names were Jacques and

Jules: these are wild things, but they were done in wild spirits at a wild moment.

But whenever we see things done wildly, but taken tamely, then the State is growing insane. For instance, I have a gun license. For all I know, this would logically allow me to fire off fifty-nine enormous field-guns day and night in my back garden. I should not be surprised at a man doing it; for it would be great fun. But I should be surprised at the neighbours putting up with it, and regarding it as an ordinary thing merely because it might happen to fulfil the letter of my license.

Or, again, I have a dog license; and I may have the right (for all I know) to turn ten thousand wild dogs loose in Buckinghamshire. I should not be surprised if the law were like that; because in modern England there is practically no law to be surprised at. I should not be surprised even at the man who did it; for a certain kind of man, if he lived long under the English landlord system, might do anything. But I should be surprised at the people who consented to stand it. I should, in other words, think the world a little mad if the incident were received in silence.

Now things every bit as wild as this are being received in silence every day. All strokes slip on the smoothness of a polished wall. All blows fall soundless on the softness of a padded cell. For madness is a passive as well as an active state: it is a paralysis, a refusal of the nerves to respond to the normal stimuli, as well as an unnatural stimulation. There are commonwealths, plainly to be distinguished here and there in history, which pass from prosperity to squalor, or from glory to insignificance, or from freedom to slavery, not only in silence, but with serenity. The face still smiles while the limbs, literally and loathsomely, are dropping from the body. These are peoples that have lost the power of astonishment at their own actions. When they give birth to a fantastic fashion or a foolish law, they do not start or stare at the monster they have brought forth. They have grown used to their own unreason; chaos is their cosmos; and the whirlwind is the breath of their nostrils. These nations are really in danger of going off their heads *en masse*; of becoming one vast vision of imbecility, with toppling cities and crazy countrysides, all dotted with industrious lunatics. One of these countries is modern England.

Now here is an actual instance, a small case of how our social conscience really works: tame in spirit, wild in result, blank in realisation; a thing without the light of mind in it. I take this paragraph from a daily paper:—

> At Epping, yesterday, Thomas Woolbourne, a Lambourne labourer, and his wife were summoned for neglecting their five children. Dr. Alpin said he was invited by the inspector of the N.S.P.C.C. to visit defendants' cottage. Both the cottage and the children were dirty. The children looked exceedingly well in health, but the conditions would be serious in case of illness. Defendants were stated to be sober. The man was discharged. The woman, who said she was hampered by the cottage having no water supply and that she was ill, was sentenced to six weeks' imprisonment. The sentence caused surprise, and the woman was removed crying, "Lord save me!"

I know no name for this but Chinese. It calls up the mental picture of some archaic and changeless Eastern Court, in which men with dried faces and stiff ceremonial costumes perform some atrocious cruelty to the accompaniment of formal proverbs and sentences of which the very meaning has been forgotten. In both cases the only thing in the whole farrago that can be called real is the wrong. If we apply the lightest touch of reason to the whole Epping prosecution it dissolves into nothing.

I here challenge any person in his five wits to tell me what that woman was sent to prison for. Either it was for being poor, or it was for being ill. Nobody could suggest, nobody will suggest, nobody, as a matter of fact, did suggest, that she had committed any other crime. The doctor was called in by a Society for the Prevention of Cruelty to Children. Was this woman guilty of cruelty to children? Not in the least. Did the doctor say she was guilty of cruelty to children? Not in the least. Was there any evidence even remotely bearing on the sin of cruelty? Not a rap. The worse that the doctor could work himself up to saying was that though the children were "exceedingly" well, the conditions would be serious in case of illness. If the doctor will tell me any conditions that would be comic in case of illness, I shall attach more weight to his argument. Now this is the worst effect of modern worry. The mad doctor has gone mad. He is literally and practically mad; and still he is quite literally and practically a doctor. The only question is the old one, *Quis docebit ipsum doctorem*? Now cruelty to children is an utterly unnatural thing; instinctively accursed of earth and heaven. But neglect of children is a natural thing; like neglect of any other duty. It is a mere difference of degree that divides extending arms and legs in calisthenics and extending them on the rack. It is a mere difference of degree that separates any operation from any torture. The thumb-screw can easily be called Manicure. Being pulled about by wild horses can easily be called Massage. The modern problem is not so much what people will endure as what they will not endure. But I fear I interrupt. . . . The boiling oil is boiling; and the Tenth Mandarin is already reciting the "Seventeen Serious Principles and the Fifty-three Virtues of the Sacred Emperor."

The Mystagogue

A Miscellany of Men, 1912

Whenever you hear of things being unutterable and indefinable and impalpable and unnamable and subtly indescribable, then elevate your aristocratic nose towards heaven and snuff up the smell of decay. It is perfectly true that there is something in all good things that is beyond all speech or figure of speech. But it is also true that there is in all good things a perpetual desire for expression and concrete embodiment; and though the attempt to embody it is always inadequate, the attempt is always made. If the idea does not seek to be the word, the chances are that it is an evil idea. If the word is not made flesh it is a bad word.

Thus Giotto or Fra Angelico would have at once admitted theologically that God was too good to be painted; but they would always try to paint Him. And they felt (very rightly) that representing Him as a rather quaint old man with a gold crown and a white beard, like a king of the elves, was less profane than resisting the sacred impulse to express Him in some way. That is why the Christian world is full of gaudy pictures and twisted statues which seem, to many refined persons, more blasphemous than the secret volumes of an atheist. The trend of good is always towards Incarnation. But, on the other hand, those refined thinkers who worship the Devil, whether in the swamps of Jamaica or the *salons* of Paris, always insist upon the shapelessness, the wordlessness, the unutterable character of the abomination. They call him "horror of emptiness," as did the black witch in Stevenson's *Dynamiter*; they worship him as the unspeakable name, as the unbearable silence.

They think of him as the void in the heart of the whirlwind; the cloud on the brain of the maniac; the toppling turrets of vertigo or the endless corridors of nightmare. It was the Christians who gave the Devil a grotesque and energetic outline, with sharp horns and spiked tail. It was the saints who drew Satan as comic and even lively. The Satanists never drew him at all.

And as it is with moral good and evil, so it is also with mental clarity and mental confusion. There is one very valid test by which we may separate genuine, if perverse and unbalanced, originality and revolt from mere impudent innovation and bluff. The man who really thinks he has an idea will always try to explain that idea. The charlatan who has no idea will always confine himself to explaining that it is much too subtle to be explained. The first idea may really be very *outrée* or specialist; it may really be very difficult to express to ordinary people. But because the man is trying to express it, it is most probable that there is something in it, after all. The honest man is he who is always trying to utter the unutterable, to describe the indescribable; but the quack lives not by plunging into mystery, but by refusing to come out of it.

Perhaps this distinction is most comically plain in the case of the thing called Art, and the people called Art Critics. It is obvious that an attractive landscape or a living face can only half express the holy cunning that has made them what they are. It is equally obvious that a landscape painter expresses only half of the landscape; a portrait painter only half of the person; they are lucky if they express so much. And again it is yet more obvious that any literary description of the pictures can only express half of them, and that the less important half. Still, it does express something; the thread is not broken that connects God with Nature, or Nature with men, or men with critics. The "Mona Lisa" was in some respects (not all, I fancy) what God meant her to be. Leonardo's picture was, in some respects, like the lady. And Walter Pater's rich description was, in some respects, like the picture. Thus we come to the consoling reflection that even literature, in the last resort, can express something other than its own unhappy self.

Now the modern critic is a humbug, because he professes to be entirely inarticulate. Speech is his whole business; and he boasts of being speechless. Before Botticelli he is mute. But if there is any good in Botticelli (there is much good, and much evil too) it is emphatically the critic's business to explain it; to translate it from terms of painting into terms of diction. Of course, the rendering will be inadequate—but so is Botticelli. It is a fact he would be the first to admit. But anything which has been intelligently received can at least be intelligently suggested. Pater does suggest an intelligent cause for the cadaverous colour of Botticelli's "Venus Rising from the Sea." Ruskin does suggest an intelligent motive for Turner destroying forests and falsifying landscapes. These two great critics were far too fastidious for my taste; they urged to excess the idea that a sense of art was a sort of secret to be patiently taught and slowly learnt. Still, they thought it could be taught: they thought it could be learnt. They constrained themselves, with considerable creative fatigue, to find the exact adjectives which might parallel in English prose what has been done in Italian painting. The same is true of Whistler and R.A.M. Stevenson and many others in the exposition of

Velasquez. They had something to say about the pictures; they knew it was unworthy of the pictures, but they said it.

Now the eulogists of the latest artistic insanities (Cubism and Post-Impressionism and Mr. Picasso) are eulogists and nothing else. They are not critics; least of all creative critics. They do not attempt to translate beauty into language; they merely tell you that it is untranslatable—that is, unutterable, indefinable, indescribable, impalpable, ineffable, and all the rest of it. The cloud is their banner; they cry to chaos and old night. They circulate a piece of paper on which Mr. Picasso has had the misfortune to upset the ink and tried to dry it with his boots, and they seek to terrify democracy by the good old anti-democratic muddlements: that "the public" does not understand these things; that "the likes of us" cannot dare to question the dark decisions of our lords.

I venture to suggest that we resist all this rubbish by the very simple test mentioned above. If there were anything intelligent in such art, something of it at least could be made intelligible in literature. Man is made with one head, not with two or three. No criticism of Rembrandt is as good as Rembrandt; but it can be so written as to make a man go back and look at his pictures. If there is a curious and fantastic art, it is the business of the art critics to create a curious and fantastic literary expression for it; inferior to it, doubtless, but still akin to it. If they cannot do this, as they cannot; if there is nothing in their eulogies, as there is nothing except eulogy—then they are quacks or the high-priests of the unutterable. If the art critics can say nothing about the artists except that they are good it is because the artists are bad. They can explain nothing because they have found nothing; and they have found nothing because there is nothing to be found.

The Architect of Spears

A Miscellany of Men, 1912

The other day, in the town of Lincoln, I suffered an optical illusion which accidentally revealed to me the strange greatness of the Gothic architecture. Its secret is not, I think, satisfactorily explained in most of the discussions on the subject. It is said that the Gothic eclipses the classical by a certain richness and complexity, at once lively and mysterious. This is true; but Oriental decoration is equally rich and complex, yet it awakens a widely different sentiment. No man ever got out of a Turkey carpet the emotions that he got from a cathedral tower. Over all the exquisite ornament of Arabia and India there is the presence of something stiff and heartless, of something tortured and silent. Dwarfed trees and crooked serpents, heavy flowers and hunchbacked birds accentuate by the very splendour and contrast of their colour the servility and monotony of their shapes. It is like the vision of a sneering sage, who sees the whole universe as a pattern. Certainly no one ever felt like this about Gothic, even if he happens to dislike it. Or, again, some will say that it is the liberty of the Middle Ages in the use of the comic or even the coarse that makes the Gothic more interesting than the Greek. There is more truth in this; indeed, there is real truth in it. Few of the old Christian cathedrals would have passed the Censor of Plays. We talk of the inimitable grandeur of the old cathedrals; but indeed it is rather their gaiety that we do not dare to imitate. We should be rather surprised if a chorister suddenly began singing "Bill Bailey" in church. Yet that would be only doing in music what the mediævals did in sculpture. They put into a Miserere seat the very scenes that we put into a music-hall song: comic domestic scenes similar to the spilling of the beer and the banging out of the washing. But though the gaiety of Gothic is one of its features, it also is not the secret of its unique effect. We see a domestic topsy-turvydom in many Japanese sketches. But delightful as these are, with their fairy tree-tops, paper houses, and toddling, infantile inhabitants, the pleasure they give is of a kind quite different from the joy and energy of the gargoyles. Some have even been so shallow and illiterate as to maintain that our pleasure in mediæval building is a mere pleasure in what is barbaric, in what is rough, shapeless, or crumbling like the rocks. This can be dismissed after the same fashion; South Sea idols, with painted eyes and radiating bristles, are a delight to the eye; but they do not affect it in at all the same way as Westminster Abbey. Some again (going to another and almost equally foolish extreme) ignore the coarse and comic in mediævalism; and praise the pointed arch only for its utter purity and simplicity, as of a saint with his hands joined in prayer. Here, again, the uniqueness is missed. There are Renaissance things (such as the ethereal silvery drawings of Raphael), there are even pagan things (such as the Praying Boy) which express as fresh and austere a piety. None of these explanations explain. And I never saw what was the real point about Gothic till I came into the town of Lincoln, and saw it behind a row of furniture-vans.

I did not know they were furniture-vans; at the first glance and in the smoky distance I thought they were a row of cottages. A low stone wall cut off the wheels, and the vans were somewhat of the same colour as the yellowish clay or stone of the buildings around them. I had come across that interminable Eastern plain which is like the open sea, and all the more so because the one small hill and tower of Lincoln stands up in it like a lighthouse. I had climbed the sharp, crooked streets up to this ecclesiastical citadel; just in front of me was a flourishing and richly coloured kitchen garden; beyond that was the low stone wall; beyond that the row of vans that looked like houses; and beyond and above that, straight and swift and dark, light as a flight of birds, and terrible as the Tower of Babel, Lincoln Cathedral seemed to rise out of human sight.

As I looked at it I asked myself the questions that I have asked here; what was the soul in all those stones? They were varied, but it was not variety; they were solemn, but it was not solemnity; they were farcical, but it was not farce. What is it in them that thrills and soothes a man of our blood and history, that is not there in an Egyptian pyramid or an Indian temple or a Chinese pagoda? All of a sudden the vans I had mistaken for cottages began to move away to the left. In the start this gave to my eye and mind I really fancied that the Cathedral was moving towards the right. The two huge towers seemed to start striding across the plain like the two legs of some giant whose body was covered with the clouds. Then I saw what it was.

The truth about Gothic is, first, that it is alive, and second, that it is on the march. It is the Church Militant; it is the only fighting architecture. All its spires are spears at rest; and all its stones are stones asleep in a catapult. In that instant of illusion, I could hear the arches clash like swords as they crossed each other. The mighty and numberless columns seemed to go swinging by like the huge feet of imperial elephants. The graven foliage wreathed and blew like banners going into battle; the silence was deafening with all the mingled noises of a military march; the great bell shook down, as the organ shook up its thunder. The thirsty-throated gargoyles shouted like trumpets from all the roofs and pinnacles as they passed; and from the lectern in the core of the cathedral the eagle of the awful evangelist crashed his wings of brass.

And amid all the noises I seemed to hear the voice of a man shouting in the midst like one ordering regiments hither and thither in the fight; the voice of the great half-military master-builder; the architect of spears. I could almost fancy he wore armour while he made that church; and I knew indeed that, under a scriptural figure, he had borne in either hand the trowel and the sword.

I could imagine for the moment that the whole of that house of life had marched out of the sacred East, alive and interlocked, like an army. Some Eastern nomad had found it solid and silent in the red circle of the desert. He had slept by it as by a world-forgotten pyramid; and been woke at midnight by the wings of stone and brass, the tramping of the tall pillars, the trumpets of the waterspouts. On such a night every snake or sea-beast must have turned and twisted in every crypt or corner of the architecture. And the fiercely coloured saints marching eternally in the flamboyant windows would have carried their glorioles like torches across dark lands and distant seas; till the whole mountain of music and darkness and lights descended roaring on the lonely Lincoln hill. So for some hundred and sixty seconds I saw the battle-beauty of the Gothic; then the last furniture-van shifted itself away; and I saw only a church tower in a quiet English town, round which the English birds were floating.

Don't*

Daily News, May 7, 1910

I have republished all these old articles of mine because they cover a very controversial period, in which I was in nearly all the controversies, whether I was visible there or no. And I wish to gather up into this last article a valedictory violence about all such things; and then pass to where, beyond these voices, there is peace—or in other words, to the writing of Penny Dreadfuls; a noble and much-needed work. But before I finally desert the illusions of rationalism for the actualities of romance, I should very much like to write one last roaring, raging book telling all the rationalists not to be so utterly irrational. The book would be simply a string of violent vetoes, like the Ten Commandments. I would call it "Don'ts for Dogmatists; or Things I am Tired Of."

This book of intellectual etiquette, like most books of etiquette, would begin with superficial things; but there would be, I fancy, a wailing imprecation in the words that could not be called artificial; it might begin thus:—

(1) Don't use a noun and then an adjective that crosses out the noun. An adjective qualifies, it cannot contradict. Don't say, "Give me a patriotism that is free from all boundaries." It is like saying, "Give me a pork pie with no pork in it." Don't say, "I look forward to that larger religion that shall have no special dogmas." It is like saying, "I look forward to that larger quadruped who shall have no feet." A quadruped means something with four feet; and a religion means something that commits a man to some

* "Don't" is the original title of this essay when it was first published in the *Daily News*, May 7, 1910. It was collected in *A Miscellany of Men* under the title "The Author: His Farewell".

doctrine about the universe. Don't let the meek substantive be absolutely murdered by the joyful, exuberant adjective.

(2) Don't say you are not going to say a thing, and then say it. This practise is very flourishing and successful with public speakers. The trick consists of first repudiating a certain view in unfavourable terms, and then repeating the same view in favourable terms. Perhaps the simplest form of it may be found in a landlord of my neighbourhood, who said to his tenants in an election speech, "Of course I'm not going to threaten you, but if this Budget passes the rents will go up." The thing can be done in many forms besides this. "I am the last man to mention party politics; but when I see the Empire rent in pieces by irresponsible Radicals," etc. "In this hall we welcome all creeds. We have no hostility against any honest belief; but only against that black priestcraft and superstition which can accept such a doctrine as," etc. "I would not say one word that could ruffle our relations with Germany. But this I will say; that when I see ceaseless and unscrupulous armament," etc. Please don't do it. Decide to make a remark or not to make a remark. But don't fancy that you have somehow softened the saying of a thing by having just promised not to say it.

(3) Don't use secondary words as primary words. "Happiness" (let us say) is a primary word. You know when you have the thing, and you jolly well know when you haven't. "Progress" is a secondary word; it means the degree of one's approach to happiness, or to some such solid ideal. But modern controversies constantly turn on asking, "Does Happiness help Progress?" Thus, I see in the *New Age* this week a letter from Mr. Egerton Swann, in which he warns the world against me and my friend Mr. Belloc, on the ground that our democracy is "spasmodic" (whatever that means); while our "reactionism is settled and permanent." It never strikes Mr. Swann that democracy means something in itself; while "reactionism" means nothing—except in connection with democracy. You cannot react except from some-

thing. If Mr. Swann thinks I have ever reacted from the doctrine that the people should rule, I wish he would give me the reference.

(4) Don't say, "There is no true creed; for each creed believes itself right and the others wrong." Probably one of the creeds is right and the others are wrong. Diversity does show that most of the views must be wrong. It does not by the faintest logic show that they all must be wrong. I suppose there is no subject on which opinions differ with more desperate sincerity than about which horse will win the Derby. There are certainly solemn convictions; men risk ruin for them. The man who puts his shirt on Potosi must believe in that animal, and each of the other men putting their last garments upon other quadrupeds must believe in them quite as sincerely. They are all serious, and most of them are wrong. But one of them is right. One of the faiths is justified; one of the horses does win; not always even the dark horse which might stand for Agnosticism, but often the obvious and popular horse of Orthodoxy. Democracy has its occasional victories; and even the Favourite has been known to come in first.

But the point here is that something comes in first. That there were many beliefs does not destroy the fact that there was one well-founded belief. I believe (merely upon authority) that the world is round. That there may be tribes who believe it to be triangular or oblong does not alter the fact that it is certainly some shape, and therefore not any other shape. Therefore I repeat, with the wail of imprecation, don't say that the variety of creeds prevents you from accepting any creed. It is an unintelligent remark.

(5) Don't (if any one calls your doctrine mad, which is likely enough), don't answer that madmen are only the minority and the sane only the majority. The sane are sane because they are the corporate substance of mankind; the insane are not a minority because they are not a mob. Then man who thinks himself a man thinks the next man a man; he reckons his neighbour as

himself. But the man who thinks he is a chicken does not try to look through the man who thinks he is glass. The man who thinks himself Jesus Christ does not quarrel with the man who thinks himself Rockefeller; as would certainly happen if the two had ever met. But madmen never meet. It is the only thing they cannot do. They can talk, they can inspire, they can fight, they can found religions; but they cannot meet. Maniacs can never be the majority; for the simple reason that they can never be even a minority. If two madmen had ever agreed they might have conquered the world.

(6) Don't say that the idea of human equality is absurd, because some men are tall and some short, some clever and some stupid. At the height of the French Revolution it was noticed that Danton was tall and Marat short. In the wildest popular excitement of America it is known that Rockefeller is stupid and that Bryan is clever. The doctrine of human equality reposes upon this: that there is no man really clever who has not found that he is stupid. That there is no big man who has not felt small. Some men never feel small; but these are the few men who are.

(7) Don't say (O don't say) that Primitive Man knocked down a woman with a club and carried her away. Why on earth should he? Does the male sparrow knock down the female sparrow with a twig? Does the male giraffe knock down the female giraffe with a palm tree? Why should the male have had to use any violence at any time in order to make the female a female? Why should the woman roll herself in the mire lower than the sow or the she-bear; and profess to have been a slave where all these creatures were creators; where all these beasts were gods? Do not talk such bosh. I implore you, I supplicate you not to talk such bosh. Utterly and absolutely abolish all such bosh—and we may yet begin to discuss these public questions properly. But I fear my list of protests grows too long; and I know it could grow longer for ever. The reader must forgive my elongations and elaborations. I fancied for the moment that I was writing a book.

The Mystery of the Mystics

(Review of Eleanor Gregory's *An Introduction to Christian Mysticism*)

Daily News, August 30, 1901

Miss Eleanor Gregory has written a decidedly lucid and interesting account of the great mystics, in which there is perhaps little fault to be found, except that she falls into the common and natural error of regarding mysticism as something mysterious. Among all the various versions of mysticism upon which she dwells, there is probably no school which would differ from the general definition that mysticism is the art of seeing everything as supernatural, of seeing every material object encircled with a halo from a secret sun. In other words, mysticism consists in seeing the material universe as a thing so defective as to suggest perfection, a thing inspiringly imperfect. To the mystic, the merely physical version of the universe is like a cow with three legs, or a man with one eye. To speak more strictly, it is like a geometrical problem in which two straight lines converge and almost collide together, but vanish into darkness an instant before they collide. Thus mysticism is a sense of that outrageous and crying imperfection which involves perfection. The rationalist of the ordinary modern type will never do justice to the mystic until he realises that the mystic finds himself in the presence, not of the clockwork chaos which science reveals, but of the fragments of a larger law. The mystic seeks a version of the universe in which everything becomes orderly, in which monsters become natural, and grasses supernatural, in which the mammoth is as mild as the primrose, and the lion lies down with the lamb.

As I have noted above, Miss Gregory tends too much, like all other mystics, to exaggerate what one may call the mysticism of mysticism. Mysticism in its noblest sense, mysticism as it existed in St. John, and Plato, and Paraceleus, and Sir Thomas Browne, is not an exceptionally dark and secret thing, but an exceptionally luminous and open thing. It is in reality too clear for most of us to comprehend, and too obvious for most of us to see. Such an utterance as the utterance that "God is Love" does in reality overwhelm us like an immeasurable landscape on a clear day, like the light of an intolerable summer sun. We may call it a dark saying; but we have an inward knowledge all the time that it is we who are dark.

It is remarkable to notice even in daily life how constant is this impression of the essential rationality of mysticism. If we went up to a man in the street who happened to be standing opposite a lamppost and addressed him playfully with the words, "Whence did this strange object spring? How did this lean Cyclops with the eye of fire start out of unbegotten night?" it may generally be inferred, with every possible allowance for the temperament of the individual, that he would not regard our remarks as particularly cogent and practical. And yet our surprise at the lamppost would be entirely rational; his habit of taking lampposts for granted would be merely a superstition. The power that makes men accept material phenomena of this universe, its cities, civilisations, and solar systems, is merely a vulgar prejudice, like the prejudice which made them accept cock-fights or the Inquisition. It is the mystic to whom every star is like a sudden rocket, every flower an earthquake of the dust, who is the clear-minded man. Mysticism, or a sense of the mystery of things, is simply the most gigantic form of common-sense. We should not have to complain of any materialism if common-sense were only common.

The object of Miss Gregory's book is to discuss the character of Christian mysticism, and this object has, to my mind, a very genuine value. Christian mysticism has by its very nature one seriously important difference from other mysticism—the fact that it is democratic, while all other mysticism tends to be aristocratic. Pagan mysticism draws a line between the mystical and the material; Christian mysticism, if it is worthy of its name, should refuse to admit that anything is not mystical. This distinction Miss Gregory ignores, and even to a certain extent invalidates, by insisting at great length upon the falsity of such doctrines as the doctrine of Pantheism. Surely the whole question of Pantheism is so large that it matters very little. If the God of the Pantheists is false, it only means that He is one of the facets of divinity, included with hundreds of gods of wood and stone in the infinity of the central existence. If God accepts the worship of savages He can scarcely refuse that of metaphysicians; and when we have destroyed any philosophic conception we are still bound to admit that it remains as true as every deity from Zeus to Mumbo Jumbo. God includes all the gods; and if the Christian has any quarrel with the pantheistic deity it can only be because the abstract spirit which inspires every weed and whirlwind still remains limited; because the word "impersonal" remains a negative word. There is a far deeper and more essential trait which should characterise Christian mysticism than those which Miss Gregory considers. It can only be realised if we consider what are the peculiar characteristics of that modern mysticism which deliberately ignores Christianity and founds itself upon Egyptian and Indian mythologies, worshipping in ruined temples and invoking forgotten gods. It seems strange that men who freely admit that all mythologies are merely symbols should seek out the symbols which are most remote and most fallen and most emptied of significance. It is curious that men who hold all things to be a part of divinity should begin by trampling and ignoring the things which millions of their own blood and civilisation have unceasingly reckoned as divine. But whatever we may think of the fact, the fact unquestionably remains that a large part of modern mysticism goes back to Pagan and even to non-Aryan inspiration. Such a fact demands serious study from the point of view of the Christian mystic, and if properly studied can scarcely fail, I think, to reveal the unique and essential point in which Christian mysticism stands alone.

The curse of modern mysticism, the mysticism of the neo-Buddhists and the neo-Egyptians, is the aristocratic spirit. It is that fretful and ungrateful search for the best which has in all ages been the worst enemy of the good. The modern neophyte is possessed with the idea of rising in the spiritual world. It is an ambition only fit for a grocer who wishes to be made a Baronet. In the spiritual world it is he that abaseth himself that shall be exalted. There is too much of this kind of mystical snobbishness running through the whole of the mystical language about preparation and purification and initiation. The whole is a desire to steal a march on others to obtain possession of truth, not because it is obvious, but because it is secret. Compared with all this paraphernalia of tests and consummations, this numbered and ticketed natural history of the invisible world, there was an enormous truth in the democracy of Christianity against which so much has been said. In the material world there are inequalities, gaps between the poet and the ploughman, between the prophet and the child. But in the spiritual world one all-embracing mystery knocks everything flat as with the blow of a hammer. In comparison with the infinite goodness, all differences between Shakespeare and a toadstool sink into relative insignificance, for both Shakespeare and the toadstool exist and neither know why. Socialism is the very essence of the spiritual commonwealth; it stands in the presence of something before whose path every valley is exalted and every mountain and hill is brought low. This bitter and bracing kindliness of the old Christian conception is immeasurably sounder and more wholesome than the planes and the initiations and the esoteric doctrines and all the metaphysical tuft-hunting of latter-day mysticism. That so many modern students of transcendentalism have even the desire to belong to a spiritual aristocracy, to sit on thrones which have to be competed for like so many posts under Government, is a single and sufficient proof that they have not in themselves even the rudiments of spirituality. True spirituality is as humble as a lover and as careless as a school-boy.

If any order of mysticism might be expected to denounce and counteract this evil aristocratic tendency in the modern mystic, it would be that to which Miss Gregory devotes her book. Christian mysticism should at least stand for the principle that the moral life is not an egotistical scramble in which the devil catches the hindmost, but a great fellowship in which the devil generally catches the most confident person. When a man reaches, as St. Francis reached, the highest plane of spirituality the fact is signalised by his calling his own beast of burden "my brother the ass." Miss Gregory rightly insists that self-surrender is one of the essential points of true mysticism, but self-surrender, which is a plain and deliberate act, may easily in some cases be more insolently selfish than selfishness itself. The true key of Christian mysticism is not so much self-surrender, which is a painful and complex thing, as self-forgetfulness, which we all fall into in the presence of a splendid sunrise or a little child, and which is to our highest nature as natural as singing to a bird.

A Much Repeated Repetition

Daily News, March 26, 1904

He must have been a man with a very dim and strange mind who said, "History repeats itself." Of course, there is a grain of veracity in it, but surely the correct way of stating the matter would be, "The Universe repeats itself, with the possible exception of history." Of all earthly studies history is the only one that does not repeat itself. This is the very definition of the divinity of man. Astronomy repeats itself; botany repeats itself; trigonometry repeats itself; mechanics repeats itself; compound long division repeats itself. Every sum if worked out in the same way at any time will bring out the same answer. But it is the peculiarity and fascination of the sums of history that with the most perfect calculation the sum comes out with a slight mysterious difference every time. There is a certain amount of the divine in every government or society. In most governments and societies it is a very small amount indeed; but there is just enough of it to do the noble and needful work; there is just enough, that is to say, to make that government or society go where it doesn't want to go, and produce something entirely different from what it had intended.

A great many moderns say that history is a science; if so it occupies a solitary and splendid elevation among the sciences; it is the only science the conclusions of which are always wrong. History has filled itself with many and bewildering crimes. It has consumed continents; it has destroyed nations and empires and civilisations; it has given birth to men who seemed to be like demons let loose, like monsters from an immoral planet. But there is one unendurable thing that it has never done;

there is one unpardonable sin that it has never committed. It has never repeated itself. It has never asked to agonise once more with precisely the same agony; it has never asked us to look again upon the same living and hateful face. Carlyle said admirably of the Court chaplains who spoke of Louis XV as having "fallen asleep in the Lord" that after all the main matter was that he did fall asleep. "Curtained in thick night, under what keeping we ask not, he at least will never, through unending ages, insult the face of the sun any more."

The life of man is a terrible thing at many times and in many places: he has much to put up with in any case. But he has not to put up with the horror of history repeating itself. That is the freedom and glory of the god which he has bought by so much suffering. That is what he has won by giving up the Nirvans of the Cabbages; by surrendering the perfect heaven of matter. When a man has struck a tyrant dead he does not have to say, "A precise replica of this tyrant will be standing in this spot a year hence. I have only cut down a poppy." When a man takes the trouble to go mad and break down and lay waste a temple, he does not have to say, "An exact reproduction of this temple will grow out of the ground in twelve months. I have only plucked a blade of grass." To man is spared the hideous and frantic and violent farce of repetition. Politicians do not come again like the flowers of spring. Eminent public persons do not rise again like the sun.

Imagine what it would be if things were so! A perfect Chamberlain, with eyeglass and orchid, would grow out of the ground at regular seasons; there might be clusters, nay, there might be fields full of them. There would be a regular month for them. They would be sowed and reaped and all that sort of thing. But fortunately for us, things do not in history happen in that way. In history a thing recurs, but it never recurs quite exactly. It comes back, but it is never quite the same. Mr. Chamberlain, for instance, will undoubtedly repeat himself. He will come back in human history; or the type of man he is will come back; but he will not be quite the same in every detail. The differences might be many. Personally, I believe he will have red whiskers and will understand the nature of war. But no one can prophesy.

I need scarcely insist further upon the fearful prospect if history really repeated itself. There is something about the actual demeanour of mankind, as I perceive it, which leads me to believe that they do not think the Flood will repeat itself. There is something about the demeanour of the ruling classes which leads me to believe that they do not think that the French Revolution will repeat itself. There is an indefinable air about the splendid, hardy, victorious Anglo-Saxon generals of our age which leads me to believe that they do not think that Napoleon will repeat himself. Everybody really assumes in human affairs and in human relations that everything that comes will be something that has never exactly come before; it may be good, it may be bad, it may be excellent, it may be atrocious, but it will at least be new. Novelty is the one element which we demand of all human things. It is the one element that we always have. Even the awful blow which awaits us all at last has one great human peculiarity; it is mysterious. It awakens regret, terror, and curiosity.

All this is the origin of the one distinctly human thing—the story. There can be as good science about a turnip as about a man. There can be, properly considered, as good philosophy about a turnip as about a man. There can be, I should strongly, though reverently, suspect, as good theology about a turnip as about a man. There can be, without any question at all, as good higher mathematics about a turnip as about a man. But I do not think, though I speak in a manner somewhat tentative, that there could be as good a novel written about a turnip as about a man. I am not sure; there may be a quiet, silvery school of fiction, to which a turnip would lend itself.

But I think, on the whole, that even in the most quiet and silvery school there would be needed a certain swell and ebb of events. No; in this matter of the story comes in the real supremacy of man. Of a mechanical thing we have a full knowledge. Of a living thing we have a divine ignorance; and a divine ignorance may be called the definition of romance. The Christian gospel is not a system; a system is fit for turnips. The Christian gospel is literally a story; that is, a thing in which one does not know what is to happen next. This thing, called Fiction, then, is the main fact of our human supremacy. If you want to know what is our human kinship with Nature, with the brutes, and with the stars, you can find cartloads of big philosophical volumes to show it you. You will find our kinship with Nature in books on geology and books on metaphysics. But if you want to find our isolation and divinity, you must pick up a penny novelette.

The Maxims of Maxim

Daily News, February 25, 1905

Sir Hiram Maxim, the distinguished inventor, has been, like certain humbler persons, getting himself mixed up with the controversy about the modern position of Christianity. It is not, however, on the larger question (justly dreaded by the editor of this paper) that I have a crow to pick (a dove to pick, let us say, if so we may express the utter meekness of my intentions), but a minor matter touching the type and temper of the man of science. Sir Hiram Maxim has written a letter to "To-Day" replying to some attacks upon a former contribution to that paper, which begins in the following somewhat impressive manner:

> Sir,—I have only just received copies of "To-Day" containing criticisms of my letter. I am in no way surprised to find that these criticisms are not only unfair but misleading in the extreme. They are misleading in so far that anyone reading them would be led to believe the exact opposite of the truth. It is quite possible that I, an old and trained engineer and chronic experimenter, should put an undue value upon truth; but this is common to all scientific men. As nothing but the truth is of any value to them, they naturally dislike things that are not true. But I am not blaming Colonel Acklom or any of the religious parties who criticised my letter. While my training has, perhaps, warped my mind so that I put an undue value upon truth, their training has been such as to cause them to abhor exact truth and logic. My last letter—the one that appeared in "To-Day"—was totally logical.

Now if Sir Hiram Maxim really were logical, I think this haughty tone would be a little calculated to exasperate the reader. If his boast were well-founded, it would be irritating. But the reader need have no fear. Sir Hiram Maxim is a genuine and typical example of the man of science, romantic, excitable, full of real but somewhat obvious poetry, a little hazy in logic and philosophy, but full of a hearty enthusiasm and an honourable simplicity. He is, as he expresses it, "an old and trained engineer," and is like all of the old and trained engineers I have happened to come across, a man who indemnifies himself for the superhuman or inhuman concentration required for physical science by a vague and dangerous romanticism about everything else. In that paragraph which I have quoted can be clearly seen the essential trait of the controversial scientist of our time, his boyish delight in the grim and unapproachable pose of the realist. Later on in his letter he says blandly about the people who venture to differ from him, that in dealing with his religious opponents he knew "how difficult it was for these people to tell the truth." This is not, as you might suppose at a hurried glance, an indecent insult. It is only a romantic posture.

Some attention is still, perhaps, due to the venerable and extraordinary idea which Sir Hiram here represents and champions; I mean the idea that the man of science is in controversial, philosophical, or moral matters likely to care for truth more than another man. Why did anyone ever imagine that a man of science was more truthful than anyone else? You might as well say that every soap-boiler was full of a wild desire of cleanliness and a passionate demand for the utter purity of the body. You might as well say that every florist was a poet and a lover of nature, or that every butcher was a man of blood and a mighty hunter before the Lord. Of course, the scientific man, when he is engaged in his own particular work, thinks observation and accuracy very necessary; so does every other man, when engaged in his particular work, think observation and accuracy very necessary. A man of science knows it is very important not to mistake eight grains for nine grains, just as a money-changer knows that it is very important not to mistake eight shillings for nine shillings, just as a hatter sending off large parcels and executing large orders knows it is very important not to mistake eight hats for nine hats. But I never heard that the man who changes money for you at Charing-cross set up as an austere amorist of truth or said that his love of verity had warped his soul. I never heard that a wealthy hatter said in general conversation that he knew hard it was for people who were not hatters to tell the truth.

The man of science loves truth exactly as often as the hatter loves truth—that is to say, when he happens to be that sort of man. The man of science is truthful when, and when only (as I have no doubt is the case in the case of Sir Hiram Maxim), he happens to be an honourable man. Huxley, for instance, had a genuine and positive love of honesty and actuality, precisely because he was an old-fashioned English gentleman inheriting those traditions which encourage such a moral attitude. Sir Hiram Maxim, I dare say, does the same thing for the same cause. But if he imagines that he has any strange and subtle love for mere reality, his own letter disproves it. For he denounces the Christian belief in devils as a "debasing belief." He might as well denounce the belief in hydrophobia as a debasing belief. That the existence of evil influences in the mental or spiritual world is a depressing fact has nothing to do with whether it is a fact. But poets like Sir Hiram are always anxious to preserve the paradise of illusion.

Although Sir Hiram Maxim groups "truth" and "logic" together, it was not necessary that he should fail in both, nor would he, I think, have fallen into these separate disasters but for the excess of the romantic in his temperament. Logic and truth, as a matter of fact, have very little to do with each other. Logic is concerned merely with the fidelity and accuracy with which a certain process is performed, a process which can be performed with any materials, with any assumptions. You can be as logical about griffins and basilisks as about sheep and pigs. On the assumption that a man has two ears, it is good logic that three men have six ears; but on the assumption that a man has four ears it is equally good logic that three men have twelve. And the power of seeing how many ears the average man, as a fact, possesses, the power of counting a gentleman's ears accurately and without mathematical confusion is not a logical thing, but a primary and direct experience, like a physical sense, like a religious vision. The power of seeing ears may be limited by a blow on the head; it may be disturbed and even augmented by two bottles of champagne; but it cannot be affected by argument. Logic has again and again been exposed and expended most brilliantly and effectively on things that do not exist at all. There is far more logic, more sustained consistency of the mind, in the science of heraldry than in the science of biology. Heraldry has plenty of impossible creatures, but it has no unaccountable creature. It has dancing dragons and leopards made of gold; but it has no Missing Link.

Nor did this combination of logic and fantasy, of mathematical madness, die with heraldry and the labyrinthine sciences of the later Middle Ages. There are many modern things in which the spirit of the dancing dragon, who is yet a disciplined dragon, reappears. There is more logic, for instance, in "Alice in Wonderland" than in the Statute Books or the Blue Books. The relations of logic to truth depend then, not upon its perfection as logic, but upon certain pre-logical faculties and certain pre-logical discoveries, upon the possession of those faculties, upon the power of making these discoveries. If a man start with certain assumptions he may be a good logician and a good citizen, a wise man, a successful figure. If he start with certain other assumptions he may be an equally good logician and a bankrupt, a criminal, a raving lunatic. Logic, then, is not necessarily an instrument for finding truth; on the contrary, truth is necessarily an instrument for using logic, for using it, that is, for the discovery of further truth and for the profit of humanity. Briefly, you can only find truth with logic if you have already found truth without it.

The Book of Job

GKC as MC, 1929

The Book of Job is among the other Old Testament Books both a philosophical riddle and a historical riddle. It is the philosophical riddle that concerns us in such an introduction as this; so we may dismiss first the few words of general explanation or warning which should be said about the historical aspect. Controversy has long raged about which parts of this epic belong to its original scheme and which are interpolations of considerably later date. The doctors disagree, as it is the business of doctors to do; but upon the whole the trend of investigation has always been in the direction of maintaining that the parts interpolated, if any, were the prose prologue and epilogue and possibly the speech of the young man who comes in with an apology at the end. I do not profess to be competent to decide such questions. But whatever decision the reader may come to concerning them, there is a general truth to be remembered in this connection. When you deal with any ancient artistic creation do not suppose that it is anything against it that it grew gradually. The Book of Job may have grown gradually just as Westminster Abbey grew gradually. But the people who made the old folk poetry, like the people who made Westminster Abbey, did not attach that importance to the actual date and the actual author, that importance which is entirely the creation of the almost insane individualism of modern times. We may put aside the case of Job, as one complicated with religious difficulties, and take any other, say the case of the Iliad. Many people have maintained the characteristic formula of modern scepticism, that Homer was not written by Homer, but by another person of the same name. Just in the same way many have maintained that Moses was not Moses but another person called Moses. But the thing really to be remembered in the matter of the Iliad is that if other people did interpolate the passages, the thing did not create the same sense of shock as would be created by such proceedings in these individualistic times. The creation of the tribal epic was to some extent regarded as a tribal work, like the building of the tribal temple. Believe then, if you will, that the prologue of Job and the epilogue and the speech of Elihu are things inserted after the original work was composed. But do not suppose that such insertions have that obvious and spurious character which would belong to any insertions in a modern individualistic book. Do not regard the insertions as you would regard a chapter in George Meredith which you afterwards found had not been written by George Meredith, or half a scene in Ibsen which you found had been cunningly sneaked in by Mr. William Archer. Remember that this old world which made these old poems like the Iliad and Job, always kept the tradition of what it was making. A man could almost leave a poem to his son to be finished as he would have finished it, just as a man could leave a field to his son, to be reaped as he would have reaped it. What is called Homeric unity may be a fact or not. The Iliad may have been written by one man. It may have been written by a hundred men. But let us remember that there was more unity in those times in a hundred men than there is unity now in one man. Then a city was like one man. Now one man is like a city in civil war.

Without going, therefore, into questions of unity as understood by the scholars, we may say of the scholarly riddle that the book has unity in the sense that all great traditional creations have unity; in the sense that Canterbury Cathedral has unity. And the same is broadly true of what I have called the philosophical riddle. There is a real sense in which the Book of Job stands apart from most of the books included in the canon of the Old Testament. But here again those are wrong who insist on the entire absence of unity. Those are wrong who maintain that the Old Testament is a mere loose library; that it has no consistency or aim. Whether the result was achieved by some supernal spiritual truth, or by a steady national tradition, or merely by an ingenious selection in after times, the books of the Old Testament have a quite perceptible unity. To attempt to understand the Old Testament without realising this main idea is as absurd as it would be to study one of Shakespeare's plays without realising that the author of them had any philosophical object at all. It is as if a man were to read the history of Hamlet, Prince of Denmark, thinking all the time that he was reading what really purported to be the history of an old Danish pirate prince. Such a reader would not realise at all that Hamlet's procrastination was on the part of the poet intentional. He would merely say, "How long Shakespeare's hero does take to kill his enemy." So speak the Bible smashers, who are unfortunately always at bottom Bible worshippers. They do not understand the special tone and intention of the Old Testament; they do not understand its main idea, which is the idea of all men being merely the instruments of a higher power.

Those, for instance, who complain of the atrocities and treacheries of the judges and prophets of Israel have really got a notion in their head that has nothing to do with the subject. They are too Christian. They are reading back into the pre-Christian scriptures a purely Christian idea—the idea of saints, the idea that the chief instruments of God are very particularly good men. This is a deeper, a more daring, and a more interesting idea than the old Jewish one. It is the idea that innocence has about it something terrible which in the long run makes and re-makes empires and the world. But the Old Testament idea was much more what may be called the common-sense idea, that strength is strength, that cunning is cunning, that worldly success is worldly success, and that Jehovah uses these things for His own ultimate purpose, just as He uses natural forces or physical elements. He uses the strength of a hero as He uses that of a Mammoth—without any particular respect for the Mammoth. I cannot comprehend how it is that so many simple-minded sceptics have read such stories as the fraud of Jacob and supposed that the man who wrote it (whoever he was) did not know that Jacob was a sneak just as well as we do. The primeval human sense of honour does not change so much as that. But these simple-minded sceptics are, like the majority of modern sceptics, Christians. They fancy that the patriarchs must be meant for patterns; they fancy that Jacob was being set up as some kind of saint; and in that case I do not wonder that they are a little startled. That is not the atmosphere of the Old Testament at all. The heroes of the Old Testament are not the sons of God, but the slaves of God, gigantic and terrible slaves, like the genii, who were the slaves of Aladdin.

The central idea of the great part of the Old Testament may be called the idea of the loneliness of God. God is not only the chief character of the Old Testament; God is properly the only character in the Old Testament. Compared with His clearness of purpose all the other wills are heavy and automatic, like those of animals; compared with His actuality all the sons of flesh are shadows. Again and again the note is struck, "With whom hath he taken counsel?" "I have trodden the wine press alone, and of the peoples there was no man with me." All the patriarchs and prophets are merely His tools or weapons; for the Lord is a man of war. He uses Joshua like an axe or Moses like a measuring-rod. For Him Samson is only a sword and Isaiah a trumpet. The saints of Christianity are supposed to be like God, to be, as it were, little statuettes of Him. The Old Testament hero is no more supposed to be of the same nature as God than a saw or a hammer is supposed to be of the same shape as the carpenter. This is the main key and characteristic of the Hebrew scriptures as a whole. There are, indeed, in those scriptures innumerable instances of the sort of rugged humour, keen emotion, and powerful individuality which is never wanting in great primitive prose and poetry. Nevertheless the main characteristic remains; the sense not merely that God is stronger than man, not merely that God is more secret than man, but that He means more, that He knows better what He is doing, that compared with Him we have something of the vagueness, the unreason, and the vagrancy of the beasts that perish. "It is He that sitteth above the earth, and the inhabitants thereof are as grasshoppers." We might almost put it thus. The book is so intent upon asserting the personality of God that it almost asserts the impersonality of man. Unless this gigantic cosmic brain has conceived a thing, that thing is insecure and void; man has not enough tenacity to ensure its continuance. "Except the Lord build the house their labour is but lost that build it. Except the Lord keep the city the watchman watcheth but in vain."

Everywhere else, then, the Old Testament positively rejoices in the obliteration of man in comparison with the divine purpose. The Book of Job stands definitely alone because the Book of Job definitely asks, "But what is the purpose of God?" Is it worth the sacrifice even of our miserable humanity? Of course it is easy enough to wipe out our own paltry wills for the sake of a will that is grander and kinder. But is it grander and kinder? Let God use His tools; let God break His tools. But what is He doing and what are they being broken for? It is because of this question that we have to attack as a philosophical riddle the riddle of the Book of Job.

The present importance of the Book of Job cannot be expressed adequately even by saying that it is the most interesting of ancient books. We may almost say of the Book of

Job that it is the most interesting of modern books. In truth, of course, neither of the two phrases covers the matter, because fundamental human religion and fundamental human irreligion are both at once old and new; philosophy is either eternal or it is not philosophy. The modern habit of saying, "This is my opinion, but I may be wrong," is entirely irrational. If I say that it may be wrong I say that it is not my opinion. The modern habit of saying, "Every men has a different philosophy; this is my philosophy and it suits me": the habit of saying this is mere weak-mindedness. A cosmic philosophy is not constructed to fit a man; a cosmic philosophy is constructed to fit a cosmos. A man can no more possess a private religion than he can possess a private sun and moon.

The first of the intellectual beauties of the Book of Job is that it is all concerned with this desire to know the actuality; the desire to know what is, and not merely what seems. If moderns were writing the book we should probably find that Job and his comforters got on quite well together by the simple operation of referring their differences to what is called the temperament, saying that the comforters were by nature "optimists" and Job by nature a "pessimist." And they would be quite comfortable, as people can often be, for some time at least, by agreeing to say what is obviously untrue. For if the word "pessimist" means anything at all, then emphatically Job is not a pessimist. His case alone is sufficient to refute the modern absurdity of referring everything to physical temperament. Job does not in any sense look at life in a gloomy way. If wishing to be happy and being quite ready to be happy constitute an optimist, Job is an optimist; he is an outraged and insulted optimist. He wishes the universe to justify itself, not because he wishes it to be caught out, but because he really wishes it to be justified. He demands an explanation from God, but he does not do it at all in the spirit in which Hampden might demand an explanation from Charles I. He does it in the spirit in which a wife might demand an explanation from her husband whom she really respected. He remonstrates with his Maker because he is proud of his Maker. He even speaks of the Almighty as his enemy, but he never doubts, at the back of his mind, that his enemy has some kind of a case which he does not understand. In a fine and famous blasphemy he says, "Oh, that mine adversary had written a book!" It never really occurs to him that it could possibly be a bad book. He is anxious to be convinced, that is, he thinks that God could convince him. In short, we may say again that if the word optimist means anything (which I doubt) Job is an optimist. He shakes the pillars of the world and strikes insanely at the heavens; he lashes the stars, but it is not to silence them; it is to make them speak.

In the same way we may speak of the official optimists, the Comforters of Job. Again, if the word pessimist means anything (which I doubt) the comforters of Job may be called pessimists rather than optimists. All that they really believe is not that God is good but that God is so strong that it is much more judicious to call Him good. It would be the exaggeration of censure to call them evolutionists; but they have something of the vital error of the evolutionary optimist. They will keep on saying that everything in the universe fits into everything else: as if there were anything comforting about a number of nasty things all fitting into each other. We shall see later how God in the great climax of the poem turns this particular argument altogether upside down.

When, at the end of the poem, God enters (somewhat abruptly), is struck the sudden and splendid note which makes the thing as great as it is. All the human beings through the story, and Job especially, have been asking questions of God. A more trivial poet would have made God enter in some sense or other in order to answer the questions. By a touch truly to be called inspired, when God enters, it is to ask a number more questions on His own account. In this drama of scepticism God Himself takes up the role of sceptic. He does what all the great voices defending religion have always done. He does, for instance, what Socrates did. He turns rationalism against itself. He seems to say that if it comes to asking questions, He can ask some questions which will fling down and flatten out all conceivable human questioners. The poet by an exquisite intuition has made God ironically accept a kind of controversial equality with His accusers. He is willing to regard it as if it were a fair intellectual duel: "Gird up now thy loins like a man; for I will demand of thee, and answer thou me." The everlasting adopts an enormous and sardonic humility. He is quite willing to be prosecuted. He only asks for the right which every prosecuted person possesses; He asks to be allowed to cross-examine the witness for the prosecution. And He carries yet further the correctness of the legal parallel. For the first question, essentially speaking, which He asks of Job is the question that any criminal accused by Job would be most entitled to ask. He asks Job who he is. And Job, being a man of candid intellect, takes a little time to consider, and comes to the conclusion that he does not know.

This is the first great fact to notice about the speech of God, which is the culmination of the inquiry. It represents all human sceptics routed by a higher scepticism. It is this method, used sometimes by supreme and sometimes by mediocre minds, that has ever since been the logical weapon of the true mystic. Socrates, as I have said, used it when he showed that if you only allowed him enough sophistry he could destroy all the sophists. Jesus Christ used it when He reminded the Sadducees, who could not imagine the nature of marriage in heaven, that if it came to that they had not really imagined the nature of marriage at all. In the break up of Christian theology in the eighteenth century, Butler used it, when he pointed out that rationalistic arguments could be used as much against vague religion as against doctrinal religion, as much against rationalist ethics as against Christian ethics. It is the root and reason of the fact that men who have religious faith have also philosophic doubt, like Cardinal Newman, Mr. Balfour, or Mr. Mallock. These are the small streams of the delta; the Book of Job is the first great cataract that creates the river. In dealing with the arrogant asserter of doubt, it is not the right method to tell him to stop doubting. It is rather the right method to tell him to go on doubting, to doubt a little more, to doubt every day newer and wilder things in the universe, until at last, by some strange enlightenment, he may begin to doubt himself.

This, I say, is the first fact touching the speech; the fine inspiration by which God comes in at the end, not to answer riddles, but to propound them. The other great fact which, taken together with this one, makes the whole work religious instead of merely philosophical, is that other great surprise which makes Job suddenly satisfied with the mere presentation of something impenetrable. Verbally speaking the enigmas of Jehovah seem darker and more desolate than the enigmas of Job; yet Job was comfortless before the speech of Jehovah and is comforted after it. He has been told nothing, but he feels the terrible and tingling atmosphere of something which is too good to be told. The refusal of God to explain His design is itself a burning hint of His design. The riddles of God are more satisfying than the solutions of man.

Thirdly, of course, it is one of the splendid strokes that God rebukes alike the man who accused, and the men who defended Him; that He knocks down pessimists and optimists with the same hammer. And it is in connection with the mechanical and supercilious comforters of Job that there occurs the still deeper and finer inversion of which I have spoken. The mechanical optimist endeavours to justify the universe avowedly upon the ground that it is a rational and consecutive pattern. He points out that the fine thing about the world is that it can all be explained. That is one point, if I may put it so, on which God, in return, is explicit to the point of violence. God says, in effect, that if there is one fine thing about the world, as far as men are concerned, it is that it cannot be explained. He insists on the inexplicableness of everything; "Hath the rain a father? . . . Out of whose womb came the ice?" He goes farther, and insists on the positive and palpable unreason of things: "Hast thou sent the rain upon the desert where no man is, and upon the wilderness wherein there is no man?" God will make man see things, if it is only against the black background of nonentity. God will make Job see a startling universe if He can only do it by making Job see an idiotic universe. To startle man God becomes for an instant a blasphemer; one might almost say that God becomes for an instant an atheist. He unrolls before Job a long panorama of created things, the horse, the eagle, the raven, the wild ass, the peacock, the ostrich, the crocodile. He so describes each of them that it sounds like a monster walking in the sun. The whole is a sort of psalm or rhapsody of the sense of wonder. The maker of all things is astonished at the things He has Himself made.

This we may call the third point. Job puts forward a note of interrogation; God answers with a note of exclamation. Instead of proving to Job that it is an explicable world, He insists that is a much stranger world than Job ever thought it was. Lastly, the poet has achieved in this speech, with that unconscious artistic accuracy found in so many of the simpler epics, another and much more delicate thing. Without once relaxing the rigid impenetrability of Jehovah in His deliberate declaration, he has contrived to let fall here and there in the metaphors, in the parenthetical imagery, sudden and splendid suggestions that the secret of God is a bright and not a sad one—semi-accidental suggestions, like light seen for an instant through the cracks of a closed door. It would be difficult to praise too highly, in a purely poetical sense, the instinctive exactitude and ease with which these more optimistic insinuations are let fall in other connections, as if the Almighty Himself were scarcely aware that He was letting them out. For instance, there is that famous passage where Jehovah, with devastating sarcasm, asks Job where he was when the foundations of the world were laid, and then (as if merely fixing a date) mentions the time when the sons of God shouted for joy. One cannot help feeling, even upon this meagre information, that they must have had something to shout about. Or again, when God is speaking of snow and hail in the mere catalogue of the physical cosmos, He speaks of them as a treasury that He has laid up against the day of battle—a hint of some huge Armageddon in which evil shall be at last overthrown.

Nothing could be better, artistically speaking, than this optimism breaking through agnosticism like fiery gold round the edges of a black cloud. Those who look superficially at the barbaric origin of the epic may think it fanciful to read so much artistic significance into its casual similes or accidental phrases. But no one who is well acquainted with great examples of semi-barbaric poetry, as in the Song of Roland or the old ballads, will fall into this mistake. No one who knows what primitive poetry is, can fail to realise that while its conscious form is simple some of its finer effects are subtle. The Iliad contrives to express the idea that Hector and Sarpedon have a certain tone or tint of sad and chivalrous resignation, not bitter enough to be called pessimism and not jovial enough to be called optimism; Homer could never have said this in elaborate words. But somehow he contrives to say it in simple words. The Song of Roland contrives to express the idea that Christianity imposes upon its heroes a paradox: a paradox of great humility in the matter of their sins combined with great ferocity in the matter of their ideas. Of course the Song of Roland could not say this; but it conveys this. In the same way the Book of Job must be credited with many subtle effects which were in the author's soul without being, perhaps, in the author's mind. And of these by far the most important remains even yet to be stated. I do not know, and I doubt whether even scholars know, if the Book of Job had a great effect or had any effect upon the after development of Jewish thought. But if it did have any effect it may have saved them from an enormous collapse and decay. Here in this Book the question is really asked whether God invariably punishes vice with terrestrial punishment and rewards virtue with terrestrial prosperity. If the Jews had answered that question wrong they might have lost all their after influence in human history. They might have sunk even down to the level of modern well educated society. For when once people have begun to believe that prosperity is the reward of virtue their next calamity is obvious. If prosperity is regarded as the reward of virtue it will be regarded as the symptom of virtue. Men will leave off the heavy task of making good men successful. They will adopt the easier task of making our successful men good. This, which has happened throughout modern commerce and journalism, is the ultimate Nemesis of the wicked optimism of the comforters of Job. If the Jews could be saved from it, the Book of Job saved them. The Book of Job is chiefly remarkable, as I have insisted throughout, for the fact that it does not end in a way that is conventionally satisfactory. Job is not told that his misfortunes were due to his sins or a part of any plan for his improvement. But in the prologue we see Job tormented not because he was the worst of men, but because he was the best. It is the lesson of the whole work that man is most comforted by paradoxes; and it is by all human testimony the most reassuring. I need not suggest what a high and strange history awaited this paradox of the best man in the worst fortune. I need not say that in the freest and most philosophical sense there is one Old Testament figure who is truly a type; or say what is pre-figured in the wounds of Job.

Cheese

Alarms and Discursions, 1910

My forthcoming work in five volumes, "The Neglect of Cheese in European Literature," is a work of such unprecedented and laborious detail that it is doubtful if I shall live to finish it. Some overflowings from such a fountain of information may therefore be permitted to sprinkle these pages. I cannot yet wholly explain the neglect to which I refer. Poets have been mysteriously silent on the subject of cheese. Virgil, if I remember right, refers to it several times, but with too much Roman restraint. He does not let himself go on cheese. The only other poet I can think of just now who seems to have had some sensibility on the point was the nameless author of the nursery rhyme which says: "If all the trees were bread and cheese"—which is, indeed, a rich and gigantic vision of the higher gluttony. If all the trees were bread and cheese there would be considerable deforestation—in any part of England where I was living. Wild and wide woodlands would reel and fade before me as rapidly as they ran after Orpheus. Except Virgil and this anonymous rhymer, I can recall no verse about cheese. Yet it has every quality which we require in exalted poetry. It is a short, strong word; it rhymes to "breeze" and "seas" (an essential point); that it is emphatic in sound is admitted even by the civilisation of the modern cities. For their citizens, with no apparent intention except emphasis, will often say, "Cheese it!" or even "Quite the cheese." The substance itself is imaginative. It is ancient—sometimes in the individual case, always in the type and custom. It is simple, being directly derived from milk, which is one of the ancestral drinks, not lightly to be corrupted with soda-water. You know, I hope (though I myself have only just thought of it), that the four rivers of Eden were milk, water, wine, and ale. Aerated waters only appeared after the Fall.

But cheese has another quality, which is also the very soul of song. Once in endeavouring to lecture in several places at once, I made an eccentric journey across England, a journey of so irregular and even illogical shape that it necessitated my having lunch on four successive days in four roadside inns in four different counties. In each inn they had nothing but bread and cheese; nor can I imagine why a man should want more than bread and cheese, if he can get enough of it. In each inn the cheese was good; and in each inn it was different. There was a noble Wensleydale cheese in Yorkshire, a Cheshire cheese in Cheshire, and so on. Now, it is just here that true poetic civilisation differs from that paltry and mechanical civilisation which holds us all in bondage. Bad customs are universal and rigid, like modern militarism. Good customs are universal and varied, like native chivalry and self-defence. Both the good and bad civilisation cover us as with a canopy, and protect us from all that is outside. But a good civilisation spreads over us freely like a tree, varying and yielding because it is alive. A bad civilisation stands up and sticks out above us like an umbrella—artificial, mathematical in shape; not merely universal, but uniform. So it is with the contrast between the substances that vary and the substances that are the same wherever they penetrate. By a wise doom of heaven men were commanded to eat cheese, but not the same cheese. Being really universal it varies from valley to valley. But if, let us say, we compare cheese with soap (that vastly inferior substance), we shall see that soap tends more and more to be merely Smith's Soap or Brown's Soap, sent automatically all over the world. If the Red Indians have soap it is Smith's Soap. If the Grand Lama has soap it is Brown's soap. There is nothing subtly and strangely Buddhist, nothing tenderly Tibetan, about his soap. I fancy the Grand Lama does not eat cheese (he is not worthy), but if he does it is probably a local cheese, having some real relation to his life and outlook. Safety matches, tinned foods, patent medicines are sent all over the world; but they are not produced all over the world. Therefore there is in them a mere dead identity, never that soft play of slight variation which exists in things produced everywhere out of the soil, in the milk of the kine, or the fruits of the orchard. You can get a whisky and soda at every outpost of the Empire: that is why so many Empire-builders go mad. But you are not tasting or touching any environment, as in the cider of Devonshire or the grapes of the Rhine. You are not approaching Nature in one of her myriad tints of mood, as in the holy act of eating cheese.

When I had done my pilgrimage in the four wayside public-houses I reached one of the great northern cities, and there I proceeded, with great rapidity and complete inconsistency, to a large and elaborate restaurant, where I knew I could get many other things besides bread and cheese. I could get that also, however; or at least I expected to get it; but I was sharply reminded that I had entered Babylon, and left England behind. The waiter brought me cheese, indeed, but cheese cut up into contemptibly small pieces; and it is the awful fact that, instead of Christian bread, he brought me biscuits. Biscuits—to one who had eaten the cheese of four great countrysides! Biscuits—to one who had proved anew for himself the sanctity of the ancient wedding between cheese and bread! I addressed the waiter in warm and moving terms. I asked him who he was that he should put asunder those whom Humanity had joined. I asked him if he did not feel, as an artist, that a solid but yielding substance like cheese went naturally with a solid, yielding substance like bread; to eat it off biscuits is like eating it off slates. I asked him if, when he said his prayers, he was so supercilious as to pray for his daily biscuits. He gave me generally to understand that he was only obeying a custom of Modern Society. I have therefore resolved to raise my voice, not against the waiter, but against Modern Society, for this huge and unparalleled modern wrong.

On Gargoyles

Alarms and Discursions, 1910

Alone at some distance from the wasting walls of a disused abbey I found half sunken in the grass the grey and goggle-eyed visage of one of those graven monsters that made the ornamental water-spouts in the cathedrals of the Middle Ages. It lay there, scoured by ancient rains or striped by recent fungus, but still looking like the head of some huge dragon slain by a primeval hero. And as I looked at it, I thought of the meaning of the grotesque, and passed into some symbolic reverie of the three great stages of art.

I

Once upon a time there lived upon an island a merry and innocent people, mostly shepherds and tillers of the earth. They were republicans, like all primitive and simple souls; they talked over their affairs under a tree, and the nearest approach they had to a personal ruler was a sort of priest or white witch who said their prayers for them. They worshipped the sun, not idolatrously, but as the golden crown of the god whom all such infants see almost as plainly as the sun.

Now this priest was told by his people to build a great tower, pointing to the sky in salutation of the Sun-god; and he pondered long and heavily before he picked his materials. For he was resolved to use nothing that was not almost as clear and exquisite as sunshine itself; he would use nothing that was not washed as white as the rain can wash the heavens, nothing that did not sparkle as spotlessly as that crown of God. He would have nothing grotesque or obscure; he would not have even anything emphatic or even anything mysterious. He would have all the arches as light as laughter and as candid as logic. He built the temple in three concentric courts, which were cooler and more exquisite in substance each than the other. For the outer wall was a hedge of white lilies, ranked so thick that a green stalk was hardly to be seen; and the wall within that was of crystal, which smashed the sun into a million stars. And the wall within that, which was the tower itself, was a tower of pure water, forced up in an everlasting fountain; and upon the very tip and crest of that foaming spire was one big and blazing diamond, which the water tossed up eternally and caught again as a child catches a ball.

"Now," said the priest, "I have made a tower which is a little worthy of the sun."

II

But about this time the island was caught in a swarm of pirates; and the shepherds had to turn themselves into rude warriors and seamen; and at first they were utterly broken down in blood and shame; and the pirates might have taken the jewel flung up for ever from their sacred fount. And then, after years of horror and humiliation, they gained a little and began to conquer because they did not mind defeat. And the pride of the pirates went sick within them after a few unexpected foils; and at last the invasion rolled back into the empty seas and the island was delivered. And for some reason after this men began to talk quite differently about the temple and the sun. Some, indeed, said, "You must not touch the temple; it is classical; it is perfect, since it admits no imperfections." But the others answered, "In that it differs from the sun, that shines on the evil and the good and on mud and monsters everywhere. The temple is of the noon; it is made of white marble clouds and sapphire sky. But the sun is not always of the noon. The sun dies daily; every night he is crucified in blood and fire."

Now the priest had taught and fought through all the war, and his hair had grown white, but his eyes had grown young. And he said, "I was wrong and they are right. The sun, the symbol of our father, gives life to those earthly things that are full of ugliness and energy. All the exaggerations are right, if they exaggerate the right thing. Let us point to heaven with tusks and horns and fins and trunks and tails so long as they all point to heaven. The ugly animals praise God as much as the beautiful. The frog's eyes stand out of his head because he is staring at heaven. The giraffe's neck is long because he is stretching towards heaven. The donkey has ears to hear—let him hear."

And under the new inspiration they planned a gorgeous cathedral in the Gothic manner, with all the animals of the earth crawling over it, and all the possible ugly things making up one common beauty, because they all appealed to the god. The columns of the temple were carved like the necks of giraffes; the dome was like an ugly tortoise; and the highest pinnacle was a monkey standing on his head with his tail pointing at the sun. And yet the whole was beautiful, because it was lifted up in one living and religious gesture as a man lifts his hands in prayer.

III

But this great plan was never properly completed. The people had brought up on great wagons the heavy tortoise roof and the huge necks of stone, and all the thousand and one oddities that made up that unity, the owls and the efts and the crocodiles and the kangaroos, which hideous by themselves might have been magnificent if reared in one definite proportion and dedicated to the sun. For this was Gothic, this was romantic, this was Christian art; this was the whole advance of Shakespeare upon Sophocles. And that symbol which was to crown it all, the ape upside down, was really Christian; for man is the ape upside down.

But the rich, who had grown riotous in the long peace, obstructed the thing, and in some squabble a stone struck the priest on the head and he lost his memory. He saw piled in front of him frogs and elephants, monkeys and giraffes, toadstools and sharks, all the ugly things of the universe which he had collected to do honour to God. But he forgot why he had collected them. He could not remember the design or the object. He piled them all wildly into one heap fifty feet high; and when he had done it all the rich and influential went into a passion of applause and cried, "This is real art! This is Realism! This is things as they really are!"

That, I fancy, is the only true origin of Realism. Realism is simply Romanticism that has lost its reason. This is so not merely in the sense of insanity but of suicide. It has lost its reason; that is its reason for existing. The old Greeks summoned godlike things to worship their god. The mediæval Christians summoned all things to worship theirs, dwarfs and pelicans, monkeys and madmen. The modern realists summon all these million creatures to worship their god; and then have no god for them to worship. Paganism was in art a pure beauty; that was the dawn. Christianity was a beauty created by controlling a million monsters of ugliness; and that in my belief was the zenith and the noon. Modern art and science practically mean having the million monsters and being unable to control them; and I will venture to call that the disruption and the decay. The finest lengths of the Elgin marbles consist of splendid horses going to the temple of a virgin. Christianity, with its gargoyles and grotesques, really amounted to saying this: that a donkey could go before all the horses of the world when it was really going to the temple. Romance means a holy donkey going to the temple. Realism means a lost donkey going nowhere.

The fragments of futile journalism or fleeting impression which are here collected are very like the wrecks and riven blocks that were piled in a heap round my imaginary priest of the sun. They are very like that grey and gaping head of stone that I found overgrown with the grass. Yet I will venture to make even of these trivial fragments the high boast that I am a mediævalist and not a modern. That is, I really have a notion of why I have collected all the nonsensical things there are. I have not the patience nor perhaps the constructive intelligence to state the connecting link between all these chaotic papers. But it could be stated. This row of shapeless and ungainly monsters which I now set before the reader does not consist of separate idols cut out capriciously in lonely valleys or various islands. These monsters are meant for the gargoyles of a definite cathedral. I have to carve the gargoyles, because I can carve nothing else; I leave to others the angels and the arches and the spires. But I am very sure of the style of the architecture and of the consecration of the church.

The Fading Fireworks

Alarms and Discursions, 1910

In the frosty grey of winter twilight there comes a crackle and spurt of bluish fire; it is waved for an instant in a sort of weak excitement, and then fizzles out into darkness: and by the blue flash I can just see some little boys lurching by with a limp bolster and a loose flapping mask. They attempt to light another firework, but it emits only a kind of crackle; and then they fade away in the dark; while all around the frosted trees stand up indifferent and like candelabras of iron. It is the last Guy; perhaps the last in all England; for the custom has been dwindling to nothing in all parts of the country. It is as sad as the last oracle. For with it passes the great positive Protestant faith which was for three centuries a real religion of the English. The burning of that image has been as central and popular as the jubilee procession, as serious as the Funeral of the King. Guido of Vaux has taken three hundred years to burn to ashes; for much of the time the flare of him lit up the whole vault of heaven, and good men as well as bad, saints as well as statesmen, warmed their hands at that gigantic fire. But now the last gleam of red dies in the grey ashes: and leaves English men in that ancient twilight of agnosticism, which is so natural to men—and so depressing to them. The echo of the last oracle still lingers in my ears. For though I am neither a Protestant nor a Pagan, I cannot see without sadness the flame of vesta extinguished, nor the fires of the Fifth of November: I cannot but be touched a little to see Paganism merely a cold altar and Protestantism only a damp squib.

The old Protestant English who sustained this strange festival for three centuries, were at least so far Christian that they tended to be Frivolous. They were still sufficiently at one with the old religious life of Europe to exhibit one of its most notable peculiarities; the slow extraction of pleasurable associations from terrible or even painful dates and names. Nothing so stamps the soul of Christendom as the strange subconscious gaiety which can make farces out of tragedies, which can turn instruments of torture into toys. So in the Catholic dramas the Devil was always the comic character; so in the great Protestant drama of Punch and Judy, the gallows and the coffin are the last and best of the jokes. So it is also with even the nobler solemnities. St. Valentine was a priest and denied himself the love of women; but his feast has been turned into a day for love-making. In certain indifferent lands and epochs this has doubtless gone too far; there are too many people who connect Good Friday only with hot cross buns; there are many who at Michaelmas think only of the wings of a goose, and never of the wings of an Archangel. But broadly speaking, this tendency is a real tribute to the healthful and invigorating quality in the Christian faith. For if the tender mercies of the wicked are cruel, even the terrors of the good can grow kindly. And there is certainly no stronger instance of the thing than this quaint English survival; which has interpreted the most hideous of deaths in terms of a hilarious half-holiday; and has changed the fires of Smithfield into fireworks.

Quaintly enough, among the fireworks that light up this Protestant festival, there are some that have almost papistical names; but they also bear witness to the mystical levity which turns gibbets and faggots into playthings. When little boys dance with delight at the radiant rotation of a Catherine wheel, they seldom (I imagine) suppose themselves to be looking at the frightful torments of a virgin martyr celebrated in Catholic art; yet this must surely be the origin of the title. We might imagine a symbolic pageant of the faiths and philosophies of mankind carried in this vivid art or science of coloured fires;

in such a procession Confucianism, I suppose, would be typified by Chinese crackers; but surely there would be little doubt of the significance of Roman candles. They are at least somewhat singular things to brandish when one is renouncing the Pope and all his works; unless we do it on the principle of the man who expressed his horror of cigars by burning them one at a time.

And, indeed, speaking of Confucianism, I have heard it said that the whole art of fireworks came first from the land of Confucius. There is something not inappropriate in such an origin. The art of coloured glass can truly be called the most typically Christian of all arts or artifices. The art of coloured lights is as essentially Confucian as the art of coloured windows is Christian. Æsthetically, they produce somewhat the same impression on the fancy; the impression of something glowing and magical; something at once mysterious and transparent. But the difference between their substance and structure is the whole difference between the great western faith and the great eastern agnosticism. The Christian windows are solid and human, made of heavy lead, of hearty and characteristic colours; but behind them is the light. The colours of the fireworks are as festive and as varied; but behind them is the darkness. They themselves are their only illumination; even as in that stern philosophy, man is his own star. The rockets of ruby and sapphire fade away slowly upon the dome of hollowness and darkness. But the kings and saints in the old Gothic windows, dusky and opaque in this hour of midnight, still contain all their power of full flamboyance, and await the rising of the sun.

The Furrows

Alarms and Discursions, 1910

As I see the corn grow green all about my neighbourhood, there rushes on me for no reason in particular a memory of the winter. I say "rushes," for that is the very word for the old sweeping lines of the ploughed fields. From some accidental turn of a train-journey or a walking tour, I saw suddenly the fierce rush of the furrows. The furrows are like arrows; they fly along an arc of sky. They are like leaping animals; they vault an inviolable bill and roll down the other side. They are like battering battalions; they rush over a bill with flying squadrons and carry it with a cavalry charge. They have all the air of Arabs sweeping a desert, of rockets sweeping the sky, of torrents sweeping a watercourse. Nothing ever seemed so living as those brown lines as they shot sheer from the height of a ridge down to their still whirl of the valley. They were swifter than arrows, fiercer than Arabs, more riotous and rejoicing than rockets. And yet they were only thin straight lines drawn with difficulty, like a diagram, by painful and patient men. The men that ploughed tried to plough straight; they had no notion of giving great sweeps and swirls to the eye. Those cataracts of cloven earth; they were done by the grace of God. I had always rejoiced in them; but I had never found any reason for my joy. There are some very clever people who cannot enjoy the joy unless they understand it. There are other and even cleverer people who say that they lose the joy the moment they do understand it. Thank God I was never clever, and could always enjoy things when I understood them and when I didn't. I can enjoy the orthodox Tory, though I could never understand him. I can also enjoy the orthodox Liberal, though I understand him only too well.

But the splendour of furrowed fields is this: that like all brave things they are made straight, and therefore they bend. In everything that bows gracefully there must be an effort at stiffness. Bows are beautiful when they bend only because they try to remain rigid; and sword-blades can curl like silver ribbons only because they are certain to spring straight again. But the same is true of every tough curve of the tree-trunk, of every strong-backed bend of the bough; there is hardly any such thing in Nature as a mere droop of weakness. Rigidity yielding a little, like justice swayed by mercy, is the whole beauty of the earth. The cosmos is a diagram just bent beautifully out of shape. Everything tries to be straight; and everything just fortunately fails.

The foil may curve in the lunge; but there is nothing beautiful about beginning the battle with a crooked foil. So the strict aim, the strong doctrine, may give a little in the actual fight with facts; but that is no reason for beginning with a weak doctrine or a twisted aim. Do not be an opportunist; try to be theoretic at all the opportunities; fate can be trusted to do all the opportunist part of it. Do not try to bend, any more than the trees try to bend. Try to grow straight, and life will bend you.

Alas! I am giving the moral before the fable; and yet I hardly think that otherwise you could see all that I mean in that enormous vision of the ploughed hills. These great furrowed slopes are the oldest architecture of man: the oldest astronomy was his guide, the oldest botany his object. And for geometry, the mere word proves my case.

But when I looked at those torrents of ploughed parallels, that great rush of rigid lines, I seemed to see the whole huge achievement of democracy. Here was mere equality: but equality seen in bulk is more superb than any supremacy. Equality free and flying, equality rushing over hill and dale, equality charging the world—that was the meaning of those military furrows, military in their identity, military in their energy. They sculptured hill and dale with strong curves merely because they did not mean to curve at all. They made the strong lines of landscape with their stiffly driven swords of the soil. It is not only nonsense, but blasphemy, to say that man has spoilt the country. Man has created the country; it was his business, as the image of God. No hill, covered with common scrub or patches of purple heath, could have been so sublimely hilly as that ridge up to which the ranked furrows rose like aspiring angels. No valley, confused with needless cottages and towns, can have been so utterly valleyish as that abyss into which the down-rushing furrows raged like demons into the swirling pit.

It is the hard lines of discipline and equality that mark out a landscape and give it all its mould and meaning. It is just because the lines of the furrow are ugly and even that the landscape is living and superb. As I think I have remarked before, the Republic is founded on the plough.

The Meaning of Dreams

Lunacy and Letters, 1958

In the earlier part of the Victorian era, when rationalism was at its height and retained at least the traces of rationality, the phenomena of dreams were very much used in connection with the phenomena of religion. It was proudly boasted in those days by the hilarious sceptic that for the most part all the mighty Churches and arresting creeds of mankind could be traced to an origin so mean and obvious as that of dreams. Nowadays we may be inclined to ask whether they could be traced to an origin more mysterious or more sublime. For the truth is that there will always be religions so long as certain primeval facts of life remain inexplicable and therefore religious. Such things as birth and death and dreams are at once so impenetrable and so provocative that to ask men to put them on one side, and have no hopes or theories about them, is like asking them not to look at a comet or not to look out the answer of a riddle. Around these elemental acrostics human hypothesis has circled and will always continue to circle. Even in an empire of atheists the dead man is always sacred. The grave, like a tilled field, brings forth crop after crop of creeds and mythologies. If we adopt the too common modern theory that the history of man commenced with the publication of the *Descent of Man* we may be able to treat this whole tendency as superstition. But if we take a large and lucid view of the main history of mankind we shall be driven to the conclusion that nothing is upon the whole so natural as supernaturalism.

This sacredness is, as I have said, everywhere predicated to the dead man. It is a strange and amusing fact that even the materialists who believe that death does nothing except turn a fellow-creature into refuse, only begin to reverence a fellow-creature at the moment that he has been turned into refuse. Now, by a very accurate parallel, a parallel enshrined in the old Greek saying about Death and his brother, men have come generally to this conclusion, that some portion at least of the sacredness of the dead man belongs to the sleeping man. Nor is this without a very real meaning. The greatest act of faith that a man can perform is the act that we perform every night. We abandon our identity, we turn our soul and body into chaos and old night. We uncreate ourselves as if at the end of the world: for all practical purposes we become dead men, in the sure and certain hope of a glorious resurrection. After that it is in vain for us to call ourselves pessimists when we have this trust in the laws of nature, when we let them keep an armed and omnipotent watch over our cradle. It is in vain for us to say that we think the ultimate power evil when every twelve hours or so we give our soul and body back to God without security. This is the essential sanctity of sleep, and the sound and sufficient reason why all tribes and ages have found in it and its phenomena a source of religious speculation. In this sudden and astonishing trance which we call sleep we are carried away without our choice or will and shown prodigious landscapes, sensational incidents, and the fragments of half-decipherable stories. Men have in all ages based a great many creeds and speculations upon this fact. With considerable confidence it may be said that they would have been great fools if they had not.

There is a great deal in dreams which is very beautiful, very happy, and even very triumphant. But, alike in happiness and in unhappiness, there is a peculiar element of thwarting and insecurity. We find marvellous things in dreamland—things often more precious and splendid than anything that is made under the sun. But the one thing that we never find is the thing we are looking for. A strange strand of eternal pathos runs through dreams which comes from the very loom of life itself. Dreams are, if I may so express it, like life only more so. Dreams, like life, are full of nobility and joy, but of a nobility and joy utterly arbitrary and incalculable. We have gratitude, but never certainty.

Of course, an absolutely accurate view of dreams is impossible. For dreams are functions of the human soul, and the human soul is the only thing that we cannot properly study, because it is at once both the study and the student. We can analyse a beetle by looking through a microscope, but we cannot analyse a beetle by looking through a beetle. But, though in the last resort the discovery of the truth about dreams is as impossible as the whole science of psychology, it is possible to arrive at certain general underlying laws of dreamland.

One of the most widespread and fundamental elements in the dream-world, it seems to me, is the element of the divorce between the appearance proper to one thing and the emotions proper to another. In real life we are frightened of vipers and decorate ourselves with flowers. In dreams we are quite capable of being afraid of flowers and decorating ourselves with vipers. In dreams we think violets nauseous, sewers fragrant, toads beautiful, stars ugly, a street with three lampposts exquisite, a pole with a white rag horrible. It is a commonplace how we attribute emotional qualities to the things that happen in dreams, how we believe a string of idiotic words to be superlative poetry, how we permit a perfectly trumpery set of events to overwhelm us with indescribable passions. The real point is, as it appears to me, that all this amounts simply to the conclusion that in dreams is revealed the elemental truth that it is the spiritual essence behind a thing that is important, not its material form. Spiritual forces, abroad in the world, simply disguise themselves under material forms. A good force disguises itself as a rose in bloom, a bad force disguises itself as an attack of chicken-pox. But in the world of subconscious speculation, where all superficial ornaments are shattered and only the essentials remain intact, everything but the ultimate meaning is altered. The spiritual forces, in their nocturnal holiday, have, like lovers on a Bank Holiday, changed hats.

All the outrageous topsy-turvydom of dreams is sufficiently represented by saying that angel and devil have changed hats, or, to speak more accurately, have changed heads. In a dream we love pestilence and hate the sunrise. In a dream we shatter temples and worship mud. The whole explanation is to be found in the conception that there is something mystical and undefined behind all the things which we love and hate, which makes us love and hate them. The metaphysicians of the Middle Ages, who talked a great deal more sense than they are nowadays given credit for, had a theory that every object had two parts: its accidents and its substance. Thus a pig was not only fat and four-legged and grunting and belonging to a particular zoological order, and pink and sagacious and absurd—beyond all this he was a pig. Dreams give a great deal of support to this conception; in a dream a thing might have the substance of a pig, while retaining all the external qualities of a boiled cod. The mediæval doctors, of course, applied this principle most strongly to the idea of Transubstantiation, maintaining that a thing might be in its accidents bread, while being in its substance divine. Whether it be reasonable or not for a waking man to worship a wafer of bread, it is quite certain that a dreaming man would worship a wafer of bread, or a pair of boots, or a sack of potatoes, or a pint of castor oil. It all depends upon what disguise the highest spiritual power took in appearing to him, the incognito in which the King chose to travel.

On Being Moved

Lunacy and Letters, 1958

I am sitting and trying to write this article in a room with nothing in it except a dining-room table, a kitchen chair, and a dislocated bookcase. There are no carpets, but plenty of dust. I write with an old chalk pencil on such pieces of wall-paper, etc., as I can find lying about. I try to imagine myself to be a starving genius in a bare garret, a man brilliant, indeed, but (alas!) embittered against his kind. The illusion is periodically disturbed by the entrance of enormous men with green baize aprons who tramp in and out, taking things away. They would take my chair away but for the formidable necessity of carrying me away in it; a task from which the most enormous shrink. But sideboards and pianos melt away at their lightest gesture and bedsteads simply flee before them. Like some landslide, chair by chair ... what is it that Tennyson says in the pretty lyric about Amphion? I get up and go to the dislocated bookcase to verify the quotation. But there is no dislocated bookcase. They have taken it away. I come back to my writing table and sit down again.

I wonder what the dickens I shall write about (I am not the Dickens who could write about anything); I get up again and go to the window. A white morning mist chokes either end of the road and veils Battersea Park, which I love and leave; making it like the ghost of a greenwood. I am glad it is not what people call fine weather; there is something merciful and proper in this cloud and twilight on the borderland between two lives. For the modern fate is fallen on me; I am moving into the country; I am going into exile; into England.

I am going ... if, indeed, I go, for all my mind is clouded with a doubt ... why am I haunted with scraps of Tennyson, especially now that they have taken away the bookcase, and I cannot spell the island valley of Avilion? Avilion is a very nice place, situated in Buckinghamshire; but, like Arthur after his last battle, I feel it fitting that a vapour should veil the moment of passing; the slipping through from state to state ... Tennyson again. Hades, the place of shadows of which the pagan poets sang, is not our state after death; it is simply death itself, the instant of transition and dissolution. In the end the dim beneficent powers will take the cosmos to pieces all round me, as my house is being taken to pieces now. I am glad that a cloud sits on Battersea to cover this monstrous transformation.

I go back to my writing table; at least I do not exactly go back to it, because they have taken it away, with silent treachery, while I was meditating on death at the window. I sit down on the chair and try to write on my knee—which is really difficult, especially when one has nothing to write about. I feel strangely grateful to the noble wooden quadruped on which I sit. Who am I that the children of men should have shaped and carved for me four extra wooden legs besides the two that were given me by the gods? For it is the point of all deprivation that it sharpens the idea of value; and, perhaps, this is, after all, the reason of the riddle of death. In a better world, perhaps, we may permanently possess, and permanently be astonished at possession. In some strange estate beyond the stars we may manage at once to have and to enjoy. But in this world, through some sickness at the root of psychology, we have to be reminded that a thing is ours by its power of disappearance. With us the prize of life is one great, glorious cry of the dying; it is always "morituri te salutant." ["We about to die salute you."] At the four corners of our human temple of happiness stand a lame man pointing to one road, and a blind man worshipping the sun, a deaf man listening for the birds, and a dead man thanking God for his creation.

I begin to be moved; I perceive that there are many mysteries concealed in that kitchen chair. That kitchen chair may truly be called (as they say in the colleges) the Chair of Philosophy. I stride up and down the room, rejoicing in the divine meaning of chairs. I wave away, with wild gestures, that merely dingy and spiteful democracy which consists in declaring that every throne is only a chair. The true democracy consists in declaring that every chair is a throne. I return rapturously to the chair; but I do not sit down in it. Wisely; because it is not there. It has been taken away. I sit down on the floor, which the enormous workmen assure me (with elephantine courtesy) they will not want for the present.

What is it, then, that makes it impossible to write anything connected or intelligible to-day? It is not mere interruption: I wrote my first criticisms of books in an office with two typewriters going at once and clerks rushing in and out every five minutes. It is not mere discomfort; I have in my youth written articles in the middle of the night, leaning against the stall of a hot-potato man. It is not for me to say that the articles were good, but they were as good as anything else I have ever written. No; I know what it is ... it is Battersea. I have the strongest and most sensible reasons in the world for going into the country. Going into the country is a joyful thing: but leaving London is a sad one. Here at least you have a harmless alphabetical paradox; one admitted by the souls of all sane men and women. It is glorious to become a man; but pathetic to leave off being a child. It is jolly to become a married man; yet it is depressing to leave off being a bachelor. Permit to us who pass from one state to another something of the pathos that is to be permitted to those that approach to death. We are happy to go into the country, but we are unhappy to leave the town. I am leaving the most living part of London, the most romantic, the most realistic, the borough that has led the people. I am leaving the borough of Battersea. I cannot write of that; and I cannot write of anything else. When I forget thee, O Jerusalem, may my right hand forget its cunning; that is, let it forget how to write, in blue chalk on old wall-paper, an article about nothing at all.

The Pickwick Papers

Appreciations and Criticisms of the Works of Charles Dickens, 1911

There are those who deny with enthusiasm the existence of a God and are happy in a hobby which they call the Mistakes of Moses. I have not studied their labours in detail, but it seems that the chief mistake of Moses was that he neglected to write the Pentateuch. The lesser errors, apparently, were not made by Moses, but by another person equally unknown. These controversialists cover the very widest field, and their attacks upon Scripture are varied to the point of wildness. They range from the proposition that the unexpurgated Bible is almost as unfit for an American girls' school as is an unexpurgated Shakespeare; they descend to the proposition that kissing the Book is almost as hygienically dangerous as kissing the babies of the poor. A superficial critic might well imagine that there was not one single sentence left of the Hebrew or Christian Scriptures which this school had not marked with some ingenious and uneducated comment. But there is one passage at least upon which they have never pounced, at least to my knowledge; and in pointing it out to them I feel that I am, or ought to be, providing material for quite a multitude of Hyde Park orations. I mean that singular arrangement in the mystical account of the Creation by which light is created first and all the luminous bodies afterwards. One could not imagine a process more open to the elephantine logic of the Bible-smasher than this: that the sun should be created after the sunlight. The conception that lies at the back of the phrase is indeed profoundly antagonistic to much of the modern point of view.

To many modern people it would sound like saying that foliage existed before the first leaf; it would sound like saying that childhood existed before a baby was born. The idea is, as I have said, alien to most modern thought, and like many other ideas which are alien to most modern thought, it is a very subtle and a very sound idea. Whatever be the meaning of the passage in the actual primeval poem, there is a very real metaphysical meaning in the idea that light existed before the sun and stars. It is not barbaric; it is rather Platonic. The idea existed before any of the machinery which made manifest the idea. Justice existed when there was no need of judges, and mercy existed before any man was oppressed.

However this may be in the matter of religion and philosophy, it can be said with little exaggeration that this truth is the very key of literature. The whole difference between construction and creation is exactly this: that a thing constructed can only be loved after it is constructed; but a thing created is loved before it exists, as the mother can love the unborn child. In creative art the essence of a book exists before the book or before even the details or main features of the book; the author enjoys it and lives in it with a kind of prophetic rapture. He wishes to write a comic story before he has thought of a single comic incident. He desires to write a sad story before he has thought of anything sad. He knows the atmosphere before he knows anything. There is a low priggish maxim sometimes uttered by men so frivolous as to take humour seriously—a maxim that a man should not laugh at his own jokes. But the great artist not only laughs at his own jokes; he laughs at his own jokes before he has made them. In the case of a man really humorous we can see humour in his eye before he has thought of any amusing words at all. So the creative writer laughs at his comedy before he creates it, and he has tears for his tragedy before he knows what it is. When the symbols and the fulfilling facts do come to him, they come generally in a manner very fragmentary and inverted, mostly in irrational glimpses of crisis or consummation. The last page comes before the first; before his romance has begun, he knows that it has ended well. He sees the wedding before the wooing; he sees the death before the duel. But most of all he sees the colour and character of the whole story prior to any possible events in it. This is the real argument for art and style, only that the artists and the stylists have not the sense to use it. In one very real sense style is far more important than either character or narrative. For a man knows what style of book he wants to write when he knows nothing else about it.

Pickwick is in Dickens's career the mere mass of light before the creation of sun or moon. It is the splendid, shapeless substance of which all his stars were ultimately made. You might split up Pickwick into innumerable novels as you could split up that primeval light into innumerable solar systems. The *Pickwick Papers* constitute first and foremost a kind of wild promise, a pre-natal vision of all the children of Dickens. He had not yet settled down into the plain, professional habit of picking out a plot and characters, of attending to one thing at a time, of writing a separate, sensible novel and sending it off to his publishers. He is still in the youthful whirl of the kind of world that he would like to create. He has not yet really settled what story he will write, but only what sort of story he will write. He tries to tell ten stories at once; he pours into the pot all the chaotic fancies and crude experiences of his boyhood; he sticks in irrelevant short stories shamelessly, as into a scrap-book; he adopts designs and abandons them, begins episodes and leaves them unfinished; but from the first page to the last there is a nameless and elemental ecstasy—that of the man who is doing the kind of thing that he can do. Dickens, like every other honest and effective writer, came at last to some degree of care and self-restraint. He learned how to make his *dramatis personae* assist his drama; he learned how to write stories which were full of rambling and perversity, but which were stories. But before he wrote a single real story, he had a kind of vision. It was a vision of the Dickens world—a maze of white roads, a map full of fantastic towns, thundering coaches, clamorous marketplaces, uproarious inns, strange and swaggering figures. That vision was *Pickwick*.

It must be remembered that this is true even in connection with the man's contemporaneous biography. Apart from anything else about it, *Pickwick* was his first great chance. It was a big commission given in some sense to an untried man, that he might show what he could do. It was in a strict sense a sample. And just as a sample of leather can be only a piece of leather, or a sample of coal a lump of coal, so this book may most properly be regarded as simply a lump of Dickens. He was anxious to show all that was in him. He was more concerned to prove that he could write well than to prove that he could write this particular book well. And he did prove this, at any rate. No one ever sent such a sample as the sample of Dickens. His roll of leather blocked up the street; his lump of coal set the Thames on fire.

The book originated in the suggestion of a publisher; as many more good books have done than the arrogance of the man of letters is commonly inclined to admit. Very much is said in our time about Apollo and Admetus, and the impossibility of asking genius to work within prescribed limits or assist an alien design. But after all, as a matter of fact, some of the greatest geniuses have done it, from Shakespeare botching up bad comedies and dramatising bad novels down to Dickens writing a masterpiece as the mere framework for a Mr. Seymour's sketches. Nor is the true explanation irrelevant to the spirit and power of Dickens. Very delicate, slender, and *bizarre* talents are indeed incapable of being used for an outside purpose, whether of public good or of private gain. But about very great and rich talent there goes a certain disdainful generosity which can turn its hand to anything. Minor poets cannot write to order; but very great poets can write to order. The larger the man's mind, the wider his scope of vision, the more likely it will be that anything suggested to him will seem significant and promising; the more he has a grasp of everything the more ready he will be to write anything. It is very hard (if that is the question) to throw a brick at a man and ask him to write an epic; but the more he is a great man the more able he will be to write about the brick. It is very unjust (if that is all) to point to a hoarding of Colman's mustard and demand a flood of philosophical eloquence; but the greater the man is the more likely he will be to give it to you. So it was proved, not for the first time, in this great experiment of the early employment of Dickens. Messrs. Chapman and Hall came to him with a scheme for a string of sporting stories to serve as the context, and one might almost say the excuse, for a string of sketches by Seymour, the sporting artist. Dickens made some modifications in the plan, but he adopted its main feature; and its main feature was Mr. Winkle. To think of what Mr. Winkle might have been in the hands of a dull *farceur*, and then to think of what he is, is to experience the feeling that Dickens made a man out of rags and refuse. Dickens was to work splendidly and successfully in many fields, and to send forth many brilliant books and brave figures. He was destined to have the applause of continents like a statesman, and to dictate to his publishers like a despot; but perhaps he never worked again so supremely well as here, where he worked in chains. It may well be questioned whether his one hack book is not his masterpiece.

Of course it is true that as he went on his independence increased, and he kicked quite free of the influences that had suggested his story. So Shakespeare declared his independence of the original chronicle of Hamlet, Prince of Denmark, eliminating altogether (with some wisdom) another uncle called Wiglerus. At the start the Nimrod Club of Chapman and Hall may have even had equal chances with the Pickwick Club of young Mr. Dickens; but the Pickwick Club became something much better than any publisher had dared to dream of. Some of the old links were indeed severed by accident or extraneous trouble; Seymour, for whose sake the whole had perhaps been planned, blew his brains out before he had drawn ten pictures. But such things were trifles compared to *Pickwick* itself. It mattered little now whether Seymour blew his brains out, so long as Charles Dickens blew his brains in. The work became systematically and progressively more powerful and masterly. Many critics have commented on the somewhat discordant and inartistic change between the earlier part of *Pickwick* and the later; they have pointed out, not without good sense, that the character of Mr. Pickwick changes from that of a silly buffoon to that of a solid merchant. But the case, if these critics had noticed it, is much stronger in the minor characters of the great company. Mr. Winkle, who has been an idiot (even, perhaps, as Mr. Pickwick says, "an impostor"), suddenly becomes a romantic and even reckless lover, scaling a forbidden wall and planning a bold elopement. Mr. Snodgrass, who has behaved in a ridiculous manner in all serious positions, suddenly finds himself in a ridiculous position—that of a gentleman surprised in a secret love affair—and behaves in a manner perfectly manly, serious, and honourable. Mr. Tupman alone has no serious emotional development, and for this reason it is, presumably, that we hear less and less of Mr. Tupman towards the end of the book. Dickens has by this time got into a thoroughly serious mood—a mood expressed indeed by extravagant incidents, but none the less serious for that; and into this Winkle and Snodgrass, in the character of romantic lovers, could be made to fit. Mr. Tupman had to be left out of the love affairs; therefore Mr. Tupman is left out of the book.

Much of the change was due to the entrance of the greatest character in the story. It may seem strange at the first glance to say that Sam Weller helped to make the story serious. Nevertheless, this is strictly true. The introduction of Sam Weller had, to begin with, some merely accidental and superficial effects. When Samuel Weller had appeared, Samuel Pickwick was no longer the chief farcical character. Weller became the joker and Pickwick in some sense the butt of his jokes. Thus it was obvious that the more simple, solemn, and really respectable this butt could be made the better. Mr. Pickwick had been the figure capering before the footlights. But with the advent of Sam, Mr. Pickwick had become a sort of black background and had to behave as such. But this explanation, though true as far as it goes, is a mean and unsatisfactory one, leaving the great elements unexplained. For a much deeper and more righteous reason Sam Weller introduces the more serious tone of Pickwick. He introduces it because he introduces something which it was the chief business of Dickens to preach throughout his life—something which he never preached so well as when he preached it unconsciously. Sam Weller introduces the English people.

Sam Weller is the great symbol in English literature of the populace peculiar to England. His incessant stream of sane nonsense is a wonderful achievement of Dickens: but it is no great falsification of the incessant stream of sane nonsense as it really exists among the English poor. The English poor live in an atmosphere of humour; they think in humour. Irony is the very air that they breathe. A joke comes suddenly from time to time into the head of a politician or a gentleman, and then as a rule he makes the most of it; but when a serious word comes into the mind of a coster it is almost as startling as a joke. The word "chaff" was, I suppose, originally applied to badinage to express its barren and unsustaining character; but to the English poor chaff is as sustaining as grain. The phrase that leaps to their lips is the ironical phrase. I remember once being driven in a hansom cab down a street that turned out to be a *cul de sac*, and brought us bang up against a wall. The driver and I simultaneously said something. But I said: "This'll never do!" and he said: "This is all right!" Even in the act of pulling back his horse's nose from a brick wall, that confirmed satirist thought in terms of his highly trained and traditional satire; while I, belonging to a duller and simpler class, expressed my feelings in words as innocent and literal as those of a rustic or a child.

This eternal output of divine derision has never been so truly typified as by the character of Sam; he is a grotesque fountain which gushes the living waters for ever. Dickens is accused of exaggeration and he is often guilty of exaggeration; but here he does not exaggerate: he merely symbolises and sublimates like any other great artist. Sam Weller does not exaggerate the wit of the London street arab one atom more than Colonel Newcome, let us say, exaggerates the stateliness of an ordinary soldier and gentleman, or than Mr. Collins exaggerates the fatuity of a certain kind of country clergyman. And this breath from the boisterous brotherhood of the poor lent a special seriousness and smell of reality to the whole story. The unconscious follies of Winkle and Tupman are blown away like leaves before the solid and conscious folly of Sam Weller. Moreover, the relations between Pickwick and his servant Sam are in some ways new and valuable in literature. Many comic writers had described the clever rascal and his ridiculous dupe; but here, in a fresh and very human atmosphere, we have a clever servant who was not a rascal and a dupe who was not ridiculous. Sam Weller stands in some ways for a cheerful knowledge of the world; Mr. Pickwick stands for a still more cheerful ignorance of the world. And Dickens responded to a profound human sentiment (the sentiment that has made saints and the sanctity of children) when he made the gentler and less-travelled type—the type which moderates and controls. Knowledge and innocence are both excellent things, and they are both very funny. But it is right that knowledge should be the servant and innocence the master.

The sincerity of this study of Sam Weller has produced one particular effect in the book which I wonder that critics of Dickens have never noticed or discussed. Because it has no Dickens "pathos," certain parts of it are truly pathetic. Dickens, realising rightly that the whole tone of the book was fun, felt that he ought to keep out of it any great experiments in sadness and keep within limits those that he put in. He used this restraint in order not to spoil the humour; but (if he had known himself better) he might well have used it in order not to spoil the pathos. This is the one book in which Dickens was, as it were, forced to trample down his tender feelings; and for that very reason it is the one book where all the tenderness there is is quite unquestionably true. An admirable example of what I mean may be found in the scene in which Sam Weller goes down to see his bereaved father after the death of his stepmother. The most loyal admirer of Dickens can hardly prevent himself from giving a slight shudder when he thinks of what Dickens might have made of that scene in some of his more expansive and maudlin moments. For all I know old Mrs. Weller might have asked what the wild waves were saying; and for all I know old Mr. Weller might have told her. As it is, Dickens, being forced to keep the tale taut and humorous, gives a picture of humble respect and decency which is manly, dignified, and really sad. There is no attempt made by these simple and honest men, the father and son, to pretend that the dead woman was anything greatly other than she was; their respect is for death, and for the human weakness and mystery which it must finally cover. Old Tony Weller does not tell his shrewish wife that she is already a white-winged angel; he speaks to her with an admirable good nature and good sense:

"'Susan,' I says, 'you've been a wery good vife to me altogether: keep a good heart, my dear, and you'll live to see me punch that 'ere Stiggins's 'ead yet.' She smiled at this, Samivel . . . but she died arter all."

That is perhaps the first and the last time that Dickens ever touched the extreme dignity of pathos. He is restraining his compassion, and afterwards he let it go. Now laughter is a thing that can be let go; laughter has in it a quality of liberty. But sorrow has in it by its very nature a quality of confinement; pathos by its very nature fights with itself. Humour is expansive; it bursts outwards; the fact is attested by the common expression, "holding one's sides." But sorrow is not expansive; and it was afterwards the mistake of Dickens that he tried to make it expansive. It is the one great weakness of Dickens as a great writer, that he did try to make that sudden sadness, that abrupt pity, which we call pathos, a thing quite obvious, infectious, public, as if it were journalism or the measles. It is pleasant to think that in this supreme masterpiece, done in the dawn of his career, there is not even this faint fleck upon the sun of his just splendour. Pickwick will always be remembered as the great example of everything that made Dickens great; of the solemn conviviality of great friendships, of the erratic adventures of old English roads, of the hospitality of old English inns, of the great fundamental kindliness and honour of old English manners. First of all, however, it will always be remembered for its laughter, or, if you will, for its folly. A good joke is the one ultimate and sacred thing which cannot be criticised. Our relations with a good joke are direct and even divine relations. We speak of "seeing" a joke just as we speak of "seeing" a ghost or a vision. If we have seen it, it is futile to argue with us; and we have seen the vision of *Pickwick*. *Pickwick* may be the top of Dickens's humour; I think upon the whole it is. But the broad humour of *Pickwick* he broadened over many wonderful kingdoms; the narrow pathos of *Pickwick* he never found again.

The Bluff of the Big Shops

The Outline of Sanity, 1926

Twice in my life has an editor told me in so many words that he dared not print what I had written, because it would offend the advertisers in his paper. The presence of such pressure exists everywhere in a more silent and subtle form. But I have a great respect for the honesty of this particular editor; for it was evidently as near to complete honesty as the editor of an important weekly magazine can possibly go. He told the truth about the falsehood he had to tell.

On both those occasions he denied me liberty of expression because I said that the widely advertised stores and large shops were really worse than little shops. That, it may be interesting to note, is one of the things that a man is now forbidden to say; perhaps the only thing he is really forbidden to say. If it had been an attack on Government, it would have been tolerated. If it had been an attack on God, it would have been respectfully and tactfully applauded. If I had been abusing marriage or patriotism or public decency, I should have been heralded in headlines and allowed to sprawl across Sunday newspapers. But the big newspaper is not likely to attack the big shop; being itself a big shop in its way and more and more a monument of monopoly. But it will be well if I repeat here in a book what I found it impossible to repeat in an article. I think the big shop is a bad shop. I think it bad not only in a moral but a mercantile sense; that is, I think shopping there is not only a bad action but a bad bargain. I think the monster emporium is not only vulgar and insolent, but incompetent and uncomfortable; and I deny that its large organisation is efficient. Large organisation is loose organisation, nay, it would be almost as true to say that organisation is always disorganisation. The only thing perfectly organic is an organism; like that grotesque and obscure organism called a man. He alone can be quite certain of doing what he wants; beyond him, every extra man may be an extra mistake. As applied to things like shops, the whole thing is an utter fallacy. Some things like armies *have* to be organised; and therefore do their very best to be well organised. You must have a long rigid line stretched out to guard a frontier; and therefore you stretch it tight. But it is not true that you must have a long rigid line of people trimming hats or tying bouquets, in order that they may be trimmed or tied neatly. The work is much more likely to be neat if it is done by a particular craftsman for a particular customer with particular ribbons and flowers. The person told to trim the hat will never do it quite suitably to the person who wants it trimmed; and the hundredth person told to do it will do it badly; as he does. If we collected all the stories from all the housewives and householders about the big shops sending the wrong goods, smashing the right goods, forgetting to send any sort of goods, we should behold a welter of inefficiency. There are far more blunders in a big shop than ever happen in a small shop, where the individual customer can curse the individual shopkeeper. Confronted with modern efficiency the customer is silent; well aware of that organisation's talent for sacking the wrong man. In short, organisation is a necessary evil—which in this case is not necessary.

I have begun these notes with a note on the big shops because they are things near to us and familiar to us all. I need not dwell on other and still more entertaining claims made for the colossal combination of departments. One of the funniest is the statement that it is convenient to get everything in the same shop. That is to say, it is convenient to walk the length of the street, so long as you walk indoors or more frequently underground, instead of walking the same distance in the open air from one little shop to another. The truth is that the monopolists' shops are really very convenient—to the monopolist. They have all the advantage of concentrating business as they concentrate wealth, in fewer and fewer of the citizens. Their wealth sometimes permits them to pay tolerable wages; their wealth also permits them to buy up better businesses and advertise worse goods. But that their own goods are better nobody has ever even begun to show; and most of us know any number of concrete cases where they are definitely worse. Now I expressed this opinion of my own (so shocking to the magazine editor and his advertisers) not only because it is an example of my general thesis that small properties should be revived, but because it is essential to the realisation of another and much more curious truth. It concerns the psychology of all these things: of mere size, of mere wealth, of mere advertisement and arrogance. And it gives us the first working model of the way in which things are done to-day and the way in which (please God) they may be undone to-morrow.

There is one obvious and enormous and entirely neglected general fact to be noted before we consider the laws chiefly needed to renew the State. And that is the fact that one considerable revolution could be made without any laws at all. It does not concern any existing law, but rather an existing superstition. And the curious thing is that its upholders boast that it is a superstition. The other day I saw and very thoroughly enjoyed a popular play called *It Pays to Advertise*; which is all about a young business man who tries to break up the soap monopoly of his father, a more old-fashioned business man, by the wildest application of American theories of the psychology of advertising. One thing that struck me as rather interesting about it was this. It was quite good comedy to give the old man and the young man our sympathy in turn.

It was quite good farce to make the old man and the young man each alternately look a fool. But nobody seemed to feel what I felt to be the most outstanding and obvious points of folly. They scoffed at the old man because he was old; because he was old-fashioned; because he himself was healthy enough to scoff at the monkey tricks of their mad advertisements. But nobody really criticised him for having made a corner, for which he might once have stood in a pillory. Nobody seemed to have enough instinct for independence and human dignity to be irritated at the idea that one purse-proud old man could prevent us all from having an ordinary human commodity if he chose. And as with the old man, so it was with the young man. He had been taught by his American friend that advertisement can hypnotize the human brain; that people are dragged by a deadly fascination into the doors of a shop as into the mouth of a snake; that the subconscious is captured and the will paralysed by repetition; that we are all made to move like mechanical dolls when a Yankee advertiser says, "Do It Now." But it never seemed to occur to anybody to resent this. Nobody seemed sufficiently alive to be annoyed. The young man was made game of because he was poor; because he was bankrupt; because he was driven to the shifts of bankruptcy; and so on. But he did not seem to know he was something much worse than a swindler: a sorcerer. He did not know he was by his own boast a mesmerist and a mystagogue; a destroyer of reason and will; an enemy of truth and liberty.

I think such people exaggerate the extent to which it pays to advertise; even if there is only the devil to pay. But in one sense this psychological case for advertising is of great practical importance to any programme of reform. The American advertisers have got hold of the wrong end of the stick; but it is a stick that can be used to beat something else besides their own absurd big drum. It is a stick that can be used also to beat their own absurd business philosophy. They are always telling us that the success of modern commerce depends on creating an atmosphere, on manufacturing a mentality, on assuming a point of view. In short they insist that their commerce is not merely commercial, or even economic or political, but purely psychological. I hope they will go on saying it; for then some day everybody may suddenly see that it is true.

For the success of big shops and such things really is psychology; not to say psychoanalysis; or, in other words, nightmare. It is not real and, therefore, not reliable. This point concerns merely our immediate attitude, at the moment and on the spot, towards the whole plutocratic occupation of which such publicity is the gaudy banner. The very first thing to do, before we come to any of our proposals that are political and legal, is something that really is (to use their beloved word) entirely psychological. The very first thing to do is to tell these American poker-players that they do not know how to play poker. For they not only bluff, but they boast that they are bluffing. In so far as it really is a question of an instant psychological method, there must be, and there is, an immediate psychological answer. In other words, because they are admittedly bluffing, we can call their bluff.

I said recently that any practical programme for restoring normal property consists of two parts, which current cant would call destructive and constructive; but which might more truly be called defensive and offensive. The first is stopping the mere mad stampede towards monopoly, before the last traditions of property and liberty are lost. It is with that preliminary problem of resisting the world's trend towards being more monopolist, that I am first of all dealing here. Now, when we ask what we can do, here and now, against the actual growth of monopoly, we are always given a very simple answer. We are told that we can do nothing. By a natural and inevitable operation the large things are swallowing the small, as large fish might swallow little fish. The trust can absorb what it likes, like a dragon devouring what it likes, because it is already the largest creature left alive in the land. Some people are so finally resolved to accept this result that they actually condescend to regret it. They are so convinced that it is fate that they will even admit that it is fatality. The fatalists almost become sentimentalists when looking at the little shop that is being bought up by the big company. They are ready to weep, so long as it is admitted that they weep because they weep in vain. They are willing to admit that the loss of the little toy-shop of their childhood, or a little tea-shop of their youth, is even in the true sense a tragedy. For a tragedy means always a man's struggle with that which is stronger than man. And it is the feet of the gods themselves that are here trampling on our traditions; it is death and doom themselves that have broken our little toys like sticks; for against the stars of destiny none shall prevail. It is amazing what a little bluff will do in this world.

For they go on saying that the big fish eats the little fish, without asking whether little fish swim up to big fish and ask to be eaten. They accept the devouring dragon without wondering whether a fashionable crowd of princesses ran after the dragon to be devoured. They have never heard of a fashion; and do not know the difference between fashion and fate. The necessitarians have here carefully chosen the one example of something that is certainly not necessary, whatever else is necessary. They have chosen the one thing that does happen still to be free, as a proof of the unbreakable chains in which all things are bound. Very little is left free in the modern world; but private buying and selling are still supposed to be free; and indeed still are free; if anyone has a will free enough to use his freedom. Children may be driven by force to a particular school. Men may be driven by force away from a public-house. All sorts of people, for all sorts of new and nonsensical reasons, may be driven by force to a prison. But nobody is yet driven by force to a particular shop.

I shall deal later with some practical remedies and reactions against the rush towards rings and corners. But even before we consider these, it is well to have paused a moment on the moral fact which is so elementary and so entirely ignored. Of all things in the world, the rush to the big shops is the thing that could be most easily stopped—by the people who rush there. We do not know what may come later; but they cannot be driven there by bayonets just yet. American business enterprise, which has already used British soldiers for purposes of advertisement, may doubtless in time use British soldiers for purposes of coercion. But we cannot yet be dragooned by guns and sabres into Yankee shops or international stores. The alleged economic attraction, with which I will deal in due course, is quite a different thing: I am merely pointing out that if we came to the conclusion that big shops ought to be boycotted, we could boycott them as easily as we should (I hope) boycott shops selling instruments of torture or poisons for private use in the home. In other words, this first and fundamental question is not a question of necessity but of will. If we chose to make a vow, if we chose to make a league, for dealing only with little local shops and never with large centralized shops, the campaign could be every bit as practical as the Land Campaign in Ireland. It would probably be nearly as successful. It will be said, of course, that people will go to the best shop. I deny it; for Irish boycotters did not take the best offer. I deny that the big shop is the best shop; and I especially deny that people go there because it is the best shop. And if I be asked why, I answer at the end with the unanswerable fact with which I began at the beginning. I know it is not merely a matter of business, for the simple reason that the business men themselves tell me it is merely a matter of bluff. It is *they* who say that nothing succeeds like a mere appearance of success. It is *they* who say that publicity influences us without our will or knowledge. It is they who say that "It Pays to Advertise"; that is, to tell people in a bullying way that they must "Do It Now," when they need not do it at all.

On Architecture

Generally Speaking, 1928

We have all of us been hearing for some time about the proposal to pull down the City churches. Some of us have a certain sympathy with the view that it would be much better to pull down the City. In the long reaches of history the irony of the contrast disappears. There must be a good many Greek or Egyptian temples still standing when the towns or villages that clustered about them have dissolved into dust. In looking at those temples we still have, if we are at all imaginative, a sort of mystical sympathy. We have a sense that, after all, the temple did not really exist to serve the city, but to serve the god. But it is a sort of sympathy we seem only able to feel in the case of a heathen god. Any number of neo-pagan poems have been written describing such gods as still hovering like ghosts over such temples. Any number of modern poets have written about ancient ruins still haunted by dog-headed Anubis or great green-eyed Pasht. They seldom expressed much sympathy for the human inhabitants of those vanished cities. But, in the case of the vanished cities, at least the inhabitants did inhabit. They worked, wedded, dined, and slept in their own town, and were often attached to it by a high religion of patriotism. So did the inhabitants of our City, in the days when people built churches there. Now that the City has become a vast warehouse, there is much less cause for a poetic lament over its destruction. The reader will be relieved to hear, however, that I have no immediate intention of setting fire to London, or of attempting to repeat the great conflagration which was recorded (entirely wrong) on the Monument. I merely say, in a general historical sense, that the mysterious description of a man as being Something in the City might have been extended in ancient times even to so humble a calling as being a Priest in the City. And I do say that, when we see humanity in retrospect and perspective, we generally find their religion more interesting than their commerce. Even the most commercial cities of antiquity, like Tyre and Carthage, were not so lively and entertaining when they were making out bills-of-lading or recording the fluctuation of the shekel as compared with the drachma, as when the more poetic side of their nature led them to throw babies into the furnace of Moloch.

But the comparison of commercial and religious centres is connected with another question that is perhaps more immediately modern than the worship of Moloch. We have not got quite so far as reviving that sort of Eastern mysticism as yet, though there is no saying what we may come to eventually, with a judicious combination of neo-pagan nature-worship and our efforts to restrict the population. But, anyhow, it is more and more plain that commerce is cosmopolitan, while religion is generally to some extent national, even if it is also international. Being an expression of the whole life of a people, it gives some expression to the local and traditional life; whereas mere commercialism of its nature becomes more and more a shuffling and interchange of different products. The London churches do preserve a certain historic character of London; they do remind us of a typical passage in the history of England. But the merely commercial life of England becomes less and less English; and the material machinery of London is looking more and more like New York. It seems likely that, as has so often happened, things native and domestic will have to retire into sanctuary. It will be a long time at least before the last monument of Wren vanishes with the fall of St. Paul's Cathedral, as the last monument of the Regent has vanished with the fall of Regent Street.

In that sense it is not so much a question of the preservation of London churches as of the preservation of London. London has a soul of its own; it therefore has a soul to be saved; but nobody seems to bother very much about saving it. And it seems possible that the quaint old Wren churches might still do something towards saving the soul of London, even if we have given up all hope of any churches saving the souls of Londoners. For those seventeenth-century buildings had a character and expressed a spirit, even if it be not what I myself should regard as the highest spirit. I am (as my enemies have discovered with diabolical, but slightly monotonous, glee) a mediævalist; and it is my instinct to seek the highest spirit in what was once the highest spire. For the old Gothic St. Paul's, that stood on Ludgate Hill before the Great Fire, was said to be the loftiest building in Christendom. It must have looked very magnificent, rising to such a height upon such a hill. Old St. Paul's might even have been spared by the American invader as being quite a respectable sky-scraper.

Nevertheless, I do not desire the present Renaissance dome of St. Paul's to be immediately replaced by a Woolworth tower. However it may stand in relation to Christendom, it stands in a very important position in relation to Europe. It does to that extent represent the spirit of Europe; and in this particular conflict I sympathise with the spirit of Europe as against the spirit of America. Something of the same part is played in a smaller way by the other Renaissance churches; in so far as they do testify to the idea that culture is a thing rather of quality than quantity. They do suggest that quaint things in quiet places may reveal the secret of our deep human past often better than buildings that take up much more room in the streets, and also much more room in the newspapers. They do stand, in some fashion, for the moment, for the fact that it is not the sky-scraper that is nearest to the sky. A man must have some little sense of craftsmanship and history to know how good is some of the seventeenth-century carving, even of the florid and lightly classical sort. He does not need anything but a neck to crane and eyes to goggle with in order to appreciate a sky-scraper. The taste for mere size is not merely more vulgar; it is also more backward and barbaric. It is all the difference between Rembrandt or Velasquez studying the subtleties of an ordinary face and the yokels in a village staring at the giant in a show. And, in so far as it is a war between barbarism and civilisation, I hope I am on the side of civilisation not for the first time.

But even where the larger thing is all right in its place, it is here out of place. Even when it is good as a sky-scraper, it is not suited to the sky. The first rule of all good scene-painting is to remember the back-scene. It is an error to paint even Aladdin's Palace without knowing whether its domes and minarets are to be outlined against the back-scene of the Blasted Heath or of the Nile with the barge of Cleopatra. The more inappropriate is the background, the more it will fall forward into the foreground. And our scenery, in several senses, has rather a way of falling down on the actors. Our scenery is of the sort that keeps the scene-shifter very busy shifting. Our back-scene is always a transformation scene. To some it may seem a rather dismal sort of dissolving view. To others (including myself) its cold clouds and gradations of grey seem to be the very vision of real romance. But, anyhow, English weather is emphatically weather; as is implied when we talk of having to weather it. There is no such thing as the English climate. Now the best American architecture is very fine architecture, as, for example, the Pennsylvania Railway Station in New York. But the best American architecture is classical architecture, of the same kind as the best Greek and Roman architecture. At least, it is partly of the same kind, and partly for the same reason. It was built for a climate; it was built to stand up clear and clean-cut against a sky that looks as solid and steady as the stone; a pure pattern of white upon blue. It is suitable to the hard light and the cloudless spaces about the towers of Manhattan; and there, like anything else that is in its place, it is a splendid thing to see. But even the invaders who have brought over American buildings have not yet imported any large blue fragments of American sky.

On Shakespeare

Generally Speaking, 1928

I have recently read with very great interest a book on what is not perhaps entirely a new subject. I refer to the subject of Shakespeare; not without reference to the subject of Shakespeare's Sonnets, of the Dark Lady and the poet's relation to Southampton and Essex and Bacon and various eminent men of his time. The book is by the Comtesse de Chambrun and is published by Appleton; and it seems to me both fascinating and convincing. I hasten to say that the lady is very learned and I am very ignorant. I do not profess to know much about Shakespeare, outside such superfluous trifling as the reading of his literary works. Madame de Chambrun's book is called *Shakespeare, Actor-Poet*; and I must humbly confess that I have known him only in his humbler capacity as a poet, and have never devoted myself to the more exhausting occupation of studying all the green-room gossip about him as an actor. But it is very right that more scholarly people should study the biographical problem; and even a poor literary critic may be allowed to judge their studies as literature. And this study seems to me to be one very valuable to literature; and not, like so many of the Baconian penny-dreadfuls, a mere insult to literature. Indeed some Baconian books are quite as much of an insult to Bacon as to Shakespeare. I have no authority to decide the controversies of fact raised here, about the relation of Southampton to the Sonnets or the discovery of the Dark Lady in the family of Davenant. I can only say that to a plain man the arguments seem at least to be of a plain sort. Thus, I have never had any reason to quarrel with Mr. Frank

Harris or Mr. Bernard Shaw about the claims of Miss Mary Fitton, or to break a lance for or against that questionable queen of beauty. I have lances enough to break with them about more important things. But to my simplicity it does seem rather notable that next to nothing is known about the Dark Lady except that she was dark; and that precious little seems to be known about Mary Fitton except that she was fair. Or again, I profess myself utterly incompetent to consider the question of what "T. T." meant by "W. H."; and I do not think the difficulty will interfere very much with my joy in saying to myself, "But thine immortal beauty shall not fade," or, "Give not a windy night a rainy morrow." But if it be true, as it is here stated, that some of these sonnets were already written when William Herbert, Lord Pembroke, was only eleven years old, he certainly must have been a precocious child if what Shakespeare says about him is at all appropriate. There may be ingenious answers to these things that I do not know. But to guileless ignorance like my own the point seems rather a practical one. As a matter of fact, I have generally found in these cases that the ingenious explanations were a little too ingenious. But, as I have said, I have no intention of dogmatizing on these problems. Madame de Chambrun's theory is that the young man for whom Shakespeare had such a hero-worship was his own patron and protector, the Earl of Southampton; for whom indeed she has some little hero-worship herself. But she gives very good and convincing grounds for regarding him as something of a hero. I am pretty sure she is quite right in saying that the rebellion of Essex and Southampton was essentially just and public-spirited. She says that if it had succeeded they would have been handed down to all history as patriots and reformers. I am also quite sure she is right in saying that it was rather a rebellion against Cecil than against Elizabeth; that alone would make it creditable. It is curious to note that, in this account,

Bacon and Shakespeare, so far from being conspirators and collaborators, were two antagonistic figures in two opposite factions; one on each side of a serious civil war. Bacon was the bitter accuser of Essex; indeed, Bacon had probably become a sort of hack and servant of Cecil. Shakespeare was of course a friend and follower of Southampton, who was a friend and follower of Essex. According to this account, Shakespeare was presenting plays like "Richard II" as deliberate political demonstrations, designed to warn weak sovereigns of the need of greater wisdom, at the very time when Bacon was drawing up the heads of his detailed and virulent denunciation of the rebel. However this may be, it is practically certain that there was the chasm between the two great men, whom some have blended into one great man (we might say into one great monster). This theory would make an even stranger monster of the Baconian version of Bacon. Not only was he capable of leading two separate public lives, but even of figuring in two opposite political parties. He must have been plotting against himself all night and condemning himself to be hanged on the following day.

If I say that this fancy would turn Bacon and Shakespeare into Jekyll and Hyde, the partisans of the two parties will probably dispute rather eagerly about which was which. But I for one have very little doubt on that point. And I am glad to find that Madame de Chambrun thinks very much the same and knows very much more. If ever there was a base business in human history, it was the method of government which Burleigh and his son conducted in England in the name of Elizabeth; and, I am sorry to say, to some extent with the assistance of Bacon. The people whom Robert Cecil destroyed were all more honest than himself (not that that was saying much) and some of them were sufficiently honourable and spirited to dwarf his little hunchbacked figure even by their dignity in the hour of death. Whether it were Essex or Mary

Stuart or even poor Guy Fawkes, they might have stood on the scaffold only in order to make him look small. And I am heartily glad to hear it, if it be true, that this nest of nasty plutocrats, with Cecil in the midst of it, counted among its enemies the greatest of Englishmen. It gives me great pleasure to think that it was of those Tudor politicians that he was thinking, when he talked of strength by limping away disabled, and art made tongue-tied by authority and captive good attending captain ill. The last line must have described a good many scenes on the scaffold in the sixteenth century. It may be difficult to imagine Shakespeare greater than Shakespeare. But it is possible that if his friends had triumphed and his cause and faith revived, he might in some unthinkable transfiguration have been greater than himself.

I know much less of the other problem involved, which is entirely one of private life and not of public policy. I mean the question of that mysterious and sinister woman towards whom the sonneteer revives the ancient rage of inconsistencies; the *odi et amo* ["I hated and I love"] of Catullus. But even I, as a mere casual reader of things in general, had certainly heard of the joke or scandal which is said to have suggested Sir William Davenant was a natural son of William Shakespeare. Whether this was so or not, Shakespeare certainly knew the Davenants, who kept an inn where he visited and where (as the writer of this book explains) Southampton himself appeared on the scene at a later stage. Her theory is that Mrs. Davenant was what we should now call a vamp; that she had at one time vamped the poet and went on later to vamp the peer. But the poet, though his feelings were mixed, could already see through the lady, and was furious at the duping of his friend; and out of this triple tangle of passions came the great tragic sequence of the Sonnets. Upon this I cannot pronounce, beyond repeating that it is set out in this book with great cogency, comprehension, and grip; and without a trace of that indefinable disproportion and lack of balance, which makes many learned and ingenious works on such subjects smell faintly of the madhouse. The writer keeps control of the subject; we feel that, though her conclusions are definite, she would not be seriously upset if they were definitely disproved. She appeals to facts and fairness throughout; and nobody can do more. The documentation and system of references seems to be very thorough; and, in a matter which I am better able to judge, there is nowhere that sense of strain in the argument, or of something altogether farfetched in the explanation, which continually jars us in most reconstructions of this kind, especially in the dangerous era of Elizabeth. Perhaps after all, that era really was the great spiritual battle; and Shakespeare and Bacon really were the spirits that met in conflict. But anyhow, it is a queer paradox that Shakespeare was an obscure and almost unhistorical figure; according to some nameless or worthless, according to others impersonal and self-effacing; but anyhow somewhat elusive and secret; and from him came a cataract of clear song and natural eloquence; while Bacon was a public man of wide renown and national scientific philosophy; and out of him have come riddles and oracles and fantastic cryptograms and a lifelong hobby for lunatics.

The Slavery of Free Verse

Fancies vs. Fads, 1923

The truth most needed to-day is that the end is never the right end. The beginning is the right end at which to begin. The modern man has to read everything backwards; as when he reads journalism first and history afterwards—if at all. He is like a blind man exploring an elephant, and condemned to begin at the very tip of its tail. But he is still more unlucky; for when he has a first principle, it is generally the very last principle that he ought to have. He starts, as it were, with one infallible dogma about the elephant; that its tail is its trunk. He works the wrong way round on principle; and tries to fit all the practical facts to his principle. Because the elephant has no eyes in its tail-end, he calls it a blind elephant; and expatiates on its ignorance, superstition, and need of compulsory education. Because it has no tusks at its tail-end, he says that tusks are a fantastic flourish attributed to a fabulous creature, an ivory chimera that must have come through the ivory gate. Because it does not as a rule pick up things with its tail, he dismisses the magical story that it can pick up things with its trunk. He probably says it is plainly a piece of anthropomorphism to suppose that an elephant can pack its trunk. The result is that he becomes as pallid and worried as a pessimist; the world to him is not only an elephant, but a white elephant. He does not know what to do with it, and cannot be persuaded of the perfectly simple explanation; which is that he has not made the smallest real attempt to make head or tail of the animal. He will not begin at the right end; because he happens to have come first on the wrong end.

But in nothing do I feel this modern trick, of trusting to a fag-end rather than a first principle, more than in the modern treatment of poetry. With this or that particular metrical form, or unmetrical form, or unmetrical formlessness, I might be content or not, as it achieved same particular effect or not. But the whole general tendency, regarded as an emancipation, seems to me more or less of an enslavement. It seems founded on one subconscious idea; that talk is freer than verse; and that verse, therefore, should claim the freedom of talk. But talk, especially in our time, is not free at all. It is tripped up by trivialities, tamed by conventions, loaded with dead words, thwarted by a thousand meaningless things. It does not liberate the soul so much, when a man can say, "You always look so nice," as when he can say, "But your eternal summer shall not fade." The first is an awkward and constrained sentence ending with the weakest word ever used, or rather misused, by man. The second is like the gesture of a giant or the sweeping flight of an archangel; it has the very rush of liberty. I do not despise the man who says the first, because he *means* the second; and what he means is more important than what he says. I have always done my best to emphasize the inner dignity of these daily things, in spite of their dull externals; but I do not think it an improvement that the inner spirit itself should grow more external and more dull. It is thought right to discourage numbers of prosaic people trying to be poetical; but I think it much more of a bore to watch numbers of poetical people trying to be prosaic. In short, it is another case of tail-foremost philosophy; instead of watering the laurel hedge of the cockney villa, we bribe the cockney to brick in the plant of Apollo.

I have always had the fancy that if a man were really free, he would talk in rhythm and even in rhyme. His most hurried post-card would be a sonnet; and his most hasty wires like harp-strings. He would breathe a song into the telephone; a song which would be a lyric or an epic, according to the time involved in awaiting the call; or in his inevitable altercation with the telephone girl, the duel would be also a duet. He would express his preference among the dishes at dinner in short impromptu poems, combining the more mystical gratitude of grace with a certain epigrammatic terseness, more convenient for domestic good feeling. If Mr. Yeats can say, in exquisite verse, the exact number of bean-rows he would like on his plantation, why not the number of beans he would like on his plate? If he can issue a rhymed request to procure the honey-bee, why not to pass the honey? Misunderstandings might arise at first with the richer and more fantastic poets; and Francis Thompson might have asked several times for "the gold skins of undelirious wine" before anybody understood that he wanted the grapes. Nevertheless, I will maintain that his magnificent phrase would be a far more real expression of God's most glorious gift of the vine, than if he had simply said in a peremptory manner "grapes"; especially if the culture of compulsory education had carefully taught him to pronounce it as if it were "gripes." And if a man could ask for a potato in the form of a poem, the poem would not be merely a more romantic but a much more realistic rendering of a potato. For a potato is a poem; it is even an ascending scale of poems; beginning at the root, in subterranean grotesques in the Gothic manner, with humps like the deformities of a goblin and eyes like a beast of Revelation, and rising up through the green shades of the earth to a crown that has the shape of stars and the hue of heaven.

But the truth behind all this is that expressed in that very ancient mystical notion, the music of the spheres. It is the idea that, at the back of everything, existence begins with a harmony and not a chaos; and, therefore, when we really spread our wings and find a wider freedom, we find it in something more continuous and recurrent, and not in something more fragmentary and crude. Freedom is fullness, especially fullness of life; and a full vessel is more rounded and complete than an empty one, and not less so. To vary Browning's phrase, we find in prose the broken arcs, in poetry the perfect round. Prose is not the freedom of poetry; rather prose is the fragments of poetry. Prose, at least in the prosaic sense, is poetry interrupted, held up and cut off from its course; the chariot of Phœbus stopped by a block in the Strand. But when it begins to move again at all, I think we shall find certain old-fashioned things move with it, such as repetition and even measure, rhythm and even rhyme. We shall discover with horror that the wheels of the chariot go round and round; and even that the horses of the chariot have the usual number of feet.

Anyhow, the right way to encourage the cortège is not to put the cart before the horse. It is not to make poetry more poetical by ignoring what distinguishes it from prose. There may be many new ways of making the chariot move again; but I confess that most of the modern theorists seem to me to be lecturing on a new theory of its mechanics, while it is standing still. If a wizard before my very eyes works a miracle with a rope, a boy and a mango plant, I am only theoretically interested in the question of a sceptic, who asks why it should not be done with a garden hose, a maiden aunt and a monkey-tree. Why not, indeed, if he can do it? If a saint performs a miracle to-morrow, by turning a stone into a fish, I shall be the less concerned at being asked, in the abstract, why a man should not also turn a camp-stool into a cockatoo; but let him do it, and not merely explain how it can be done. It is certain that words such as "birds" and "bare," which are as plain as "fish" or "stone," can be combined in such a miracle as "Bare ruined quires where late the sweet birds sang." So far as I can follow my own feelings, the metre and fall of the feet, even the rhyme and place in the sonnet, have a great deal to do with producing such an effect. I do not say there is no other way of producing such an effect. I only ask, not without longing, where else in this wide and weary time is it produced? I know I cannot produce it; and I do not in fact feel it when I hear *vers libres*. I know not where is that Promethean heat; and, even to express my ignorance, I am glad to find better words than my own.

Turning Inside Out

Fancies vs. Fads, 1923

When the author of "If Winter Comes" brought out another book about the life of the family, it was almost as much criticised as the first book was praised. I do not say that there was nothing to criticise, but I do say that I was not convinced by the abstract logic of the criticism. Probably the critics would have accepted it as a true story if the author had not been so incautious as to give it a true moral. And the moral is not fashionable in the press at the moment; for it is to the effect that a woman may gain a professional success at the price of a domestic failure. And it is the convention of journalism at this moment to support what is feminist against what is feminine. Anyhow, while the story might be criticised, the criticisms can certainly be criticised. It is not really conclusive to say that a woman may be ambitious in business without her children going to the bad. It is just as easy to say that a woman may be ambitious in politics without helping to murder an old gentleman in his bed. But that does not make "Macbeth" either inartistic or untrue. It is just as easy to say that a woman may be ambitious in society without tricking her husband into a debtor's prison, so that she may spend the time with a bald-headed nobleman with red whiskers. But that does not make the great scene in "Vanity Fair" unconvincing either in detail or design. The question in fiction is not whether that thing must occur, but whether that sort of thing may occur, and whether it is significant of larger things. Now this business of the woman at work and the woman at home is a very large thing, and this story about it is highly significant.

For in this matter the modern mind is inconsistent with itself. It has managed to get one of its rather crude ideals in flat contradiction to the other. People of the progressive sort are perpetually telling us that the hope of the world is in education. Education is everything. Nothing is so important as training the rising generation. Nothing is really important except the rising generation. They tell us this over and over again, with slight variations of the same formula, and never seem to see what it involves. For if there be any word of truth in all this talk about the education of the child, then there is certainly nothing but nonsense in nine-tenths of the talk about the emancipation of the woman. If education is the highest function in the State, why should anybody want to be emancipated from the highest function in the State? It is as if we talked of commuting the sentence that condemned a man to be President of the United States; or a reprieve coming in time to save him from being Pope. If education is the largest thing in the world, what is the sense of talking about a woman being liberated from the largest thing in the world? It is as if we were to rescue her from the cruel doom of being a poet like Shakespeare; or to pity the limitations of an all-round artist like Leonardo da Vinci. Nor can there be any doubt that there is truth in this claim for education. Only precisely the sort of which it is particularly true is the sort called domestic education. Private education really is universal. Public education can be comparatively narrow. It would really be an exaggeration to say that the schoolmaster who takes his pupils in freehand drawing is training them in all the uses of freedom. It really would be fantastic to say that the harmless foreigner who instructs a class in French or German is talking with all the tongues of men and angels. But the mother dealing with her own daughters in her own home does literally have to deal with all forms of freedom, because she has to deal with all sides of a single human soul. She is obliged, if not to talk with the tongues of men and angels, at least to decide how much she shall talk about angels and how much about men.

In short, if education is really the larger matter, then certainly domestic life is the larger matter; and official or commercial life the lesser matter. It is a mere matter of arithmetic that anything taken from the larger matter will leave it less. It is a mere matter of simple subtraction that the mother must have less time for the family if she has more time for the factory. If education, ethical and cultural, really were a trivial and mechanical matter, the mother might possibly rattle through it as a rapid routine, before going about her more serious business of serving a capitalist for hire. If education were merely instruction, she might briefly instruct her babies in the multiplication tables, before she mounted to higher and nobler spheres as the servant of a Milk Trust or the secretary of a Drug Combine. But the moderns are perpetually assuring us that education is not instruction; they are perpetually insisting that it is not a mechanical exercise, and must on no account be an abbreviated exercise. It must go on at every hour. It must cover every subject. But if it must go on at all hours, it must not be neglected in business hours. And if the child is to be free to cover every subject, the parent must be free to cover every subject too.

For the idea of a non-parental substitute is simply an illusion of wealth. The advanced advocate of this inconsistent and infinite education for the child is generally thinking of the rich child; and all this particular sort of liberty should rather be called luxury. It is natural enough for a fashionable lady to leave her little daughter with the French governess or the Czecho-Slovakian governess or the Ancient Sanskrit governess, and know that one or other of these sides of the infant's intelligence is being developed; while she, the mother, figures in public as a money-lender or some other modern position of dignity. But among poorer people there cannot be five teachers to one pupil.

Generally there are about fifty pupils to one teacher. There it is impossible to cut up the soul of a single child and distribute it among specialists. It is all we can do to tear in pieces the soul of a single schoolmaster, and distribute it in rags and scraps to a whole mob of boys. And even in the case of the wealthy child it is by no means clear that specialists are a substitute for spiritual authority. Even a millionaire can never be certain that he has not left out one governess, in the long procession of governesses perpetually passing under his marble portico; and the omission may be as fatal as that of the king who forgot to ask the bad fairy to the christening. The daughter, after a life of ruin and despair, may look back and say, "Had I but also had a Lithuanian governess, my fate as a diplomatist's wife in Eastern Europe would have been very different." But it seems rather more probable, on the whole, that what she would miss would not be one or other of these special accomplishments, but some commonsense code of morals or general view of life. The millionaire could, no doubt, hire a mahatma or mystical prophet to give his child a general philosophy. But I doubt if the philosophy would be very successful even for the rich child, and it would be quite impossible for the poor child. In the case of comparative poverty, which is the common lot of mankind, we come back to a general parental responsibility, which is the common sense of mankind. We come back to the parent as the person in charge of education. If you exalt the education, you must exalt the parental power with it. If you exaggerate the education, you must exaggerate the parental power with it. If you depreciate the parental power, you most depreciate education with it. If the young are always right and can do as they like, well and good; let us all be jolly, old and young, and free from every kind of responsibility. But in that case do not come pestering us with the importance of education, when nobody has any authority to educate anybody. Make up your mind whether you want unlimited education or unlimited emancipation, but do not be such a fool as to suppose you can have both at once.

There is evidence, as I have noted, that the more hard-headed people, even of the most progressive sort, are beginning to come back to realities in this respect. The new work of Mr. Hutchinson's is only one of many indications among the really independent intelligences, working on modern fiction, that the cruder culture of merely commercial emancipation is beginning to smell a little stale. The work of Miss Clemence Dane and even of Miss Sheila Kaye-Smith contains more than one suggestion of what I mean. People are no longer quite so certain that a woman's liberty consists of having a latch-key without a house. They are no longer wholly convinced that every housekeeper is dull and prosaic, while every bookkeeper is wild and poetical. And among the intelligent the reaction is actually strengthened by all the most modern excitements about psychology and hygiene. We cannot insist that every trick of nerves or train of thought is important enough to be searched for in libraries and laboratories, and not important enough for anybody to watch by simply staying at home. We cannot insist that the first years of infancy are of supreme importance, and that mothers are not of supreme importance; or that motherhood is a topic of sufficient interest for men, but not of sufficient interest for mothers. Every word that is said about the tremendous importance of trivial nursery habits goes to prove that being a nurse is not trivial. All tends to the return of the simple truth that the private work is the great one and the public work the small. The human house is a paradox, for it is larger inside than out.

But in the problem of private versus public life there is another neglected truth. It is true of many masculine problems as well as of this feminine problem. Indeed, feminism falls here into exactly the same mistake as militarism and imperialism. I mean that anything on a grand scale gives the illusion of a grand success. Curiously enough, multiplication acts as a concealment. Repetition actually disguises failure. Take a particular man, and tell him to put on a particular kind of hat and coat and trousers, and to stand in particular attitudes in the back garden; and you will have great difficulty in persuading yourself (or him) that he has passed through a triumph and transfiguration. Order four hundred such hats, and eight hundred such trousers, and you will have turned the fancy costume into a uniform. Make all the four hundred men stand in the special attitudes on Salisbury Plain, and there will rise up before you the spirit of a regiment. Let the regiment march past, and, if you have any life in you above the brutes that perish, you will have an overwhelming sense that something splendid has just happened, or is just going to begin. I sympathise with this moral emotion in militarism; I think it does symbolise something great in the soul, which has given us the image of St. Michael. But I also realise that in practical relations that emotion can get mixed up with an illusion. It is not really possible to know the characters of all the four hundred men in the marching column as well as one might know the character of the one man attitudinizing in the back garden. If all the four hundred men were individual failures, we could still vaguely feel that the whole thing was a success. If we know the one man to be a failure, we cannot think him a success.

That is why a footman has become rather a foolish figure, while a foot-soldier remains rather a sublime one. Or rather, that is one of the reasons; for there are others much more worthy. Anyhow, footmen were only formidable or dignified when they could come in large numbers like foot-soldiers—when they were in fact the feudal army of some great local family, having some of the loyalty of local patriotism. Then a livery was as dignified as a uniform, because it really was a uniform. A man who said he served the Nevilles or rode with the Douglases could once feel much like a man fighting for France or England. But military feeling is mob feeling, noble as mob feeling may be. Parading one footman is like lunching on one pea, or curing baldness by the growth of one hair. There ought not to be anything but a plural for flunkeys, any more than for measles or vermin or animalculæ or the sweets called hundreds and thousands. Strictly speaking, I suppose that a logical Latinist could say, "I have seen an animalcula"; but I never heard of a child having the moderation to remark, "I have eaten a hundred and thousand." Similarly, any one of us can feel that to have hundreds and thousands of slaves, let alone soldiers, might give a certain imaginative pleasure in magnificence. To have one slave reveals all the meanness of slavery. For the solitary flunkey really is the man in fancy dress, the man standing in the back-garden in the strange and the fantastic coat and breeches. His isolation reveals our illusion. We find our failure in the back-garden, when we have been dreaming a dream of success in the market-place. When you ride through the streets amid a great mob of vassals (you may have noticed) you have a genial and not ungenerous sense of being at one with them all. You cannot remember their names or count their numbers, but their very immensity seems a substitute for intimacy. That is what great men have felt at the head of great armies; and the reason why Napoleon or Foch would call his soldiers "*mes enfants*" ["my babies"]. He feels at that moment that they are a part of him, as if he had a million arms and legs. But it is very different if you disband your army of lackeys; or if (as is, after all, possible) you have not got an army of lackeys. It is very different if you look at one lackey; one solitary solemn footman standing in your front hall. You never have the sense of being caught up into a rapture of unity with *him*. All your sense of social solidarity with your social inferiors has dropped from you. It is only in public that people can be so intimate as that. When you look into the eyes of the lonely footman, you see that his soul is far away.

In other words, you find yourself at the foot of a steep and staggering mountain crag, that is the real character and conscience of a man. To be really at one with that man, you would have to solve real problems and believe that your own solutions were real. In dealing with the one man you would really have a far huger and harder job than in dealing with your throng of thousands. And *that* is the job that people run away from when they wish to escape from domesticity to public work, especially educational work. They wish to escape from a sense of failure which is simply a sense of fact. They wish to recapture the illusion of the market-place. It is an illusion that departs in the dark interiors of domesticity, where the realities dwell. As I have said, I am very far from condemning it altogether; it is a lawful pleasure, and a part of life, in its proper proportion, like any other. But I am concerned to point out to the feminists and the faddists that it is not an approach to truth, but rather the opposite. Publicity is rather of the nature of a harmless romance. Public life at its very best will contain a great deal of harmless romancing, and much more often of very harmful romancing. In other words, I am concerned with pointing out that the passage from private life to public life, while it may be right or wrong, or necessary or unnecessary, or desirable or undesirable, is always of necessity a passage from a greater work to a smaller one, and from a harder work to an easier one. And that is why most of the moderns do wish to pass from the great domestic task to the smaller and easier commercial one. They would rather provide the liveries of a hundred footmen than be bothered with the love-affairs of one. They would rather take the salutes of a hundred soldiers than try to save the soul of one. They would rather serve out income-tax papers or telegraph forms to a hundred men than meals, conversation, and moral support to one. They would rather arrange the educational course in history or geography, or correct the examination papers in algebra or trigonometry, for a hundred children, than struggle with the whole human character of one. For anyone who makes himself responsible for one small baby, as a whole, will soon find that he is wrestling with gigantic angels and demons.

In another way there is something of illusion, or of irresponsibility, about the purely public function, especially in the case of public education. The educationist generally deals with only one section of the pupil's mind. But he always deals with only one section of the pupil's life. The parent has to deal, not only with the whole of the child's character, but also with the whole of the child's career. The teacher sows the seed, but the parent reaps as well as sows. The schoolmaster sees more children, but it is not clear that he sees more childhood; certainly he sees less youth and no maturity. The number of little girls who take prussic acid is necessarily small. The boys who hang themselves on bed-posts, after a life of crime, are generally the minority. But the parent has to envisage the whole life of the individual, and not merely the school life of the scholar. It is not probable that the parent will exactly anticipate crime and prussic acid as the crown of the infant's career. But he will anticipate hearing of the crime if it is committed; he will probably be told of the suicide if it takes place. It is quite doubtful whether the schoolmaster or schoolmistress will ever hear of it at all. Everybody knows that teachers have a harassing and often heroic task, but it is not unfair to them to remember that in this sense they have an exceptionally happy task. The cynic would say that the teacher is happy in never seeing the results of his own teaching. I prefer to confine myself to saying that he has not the extra worry of having to estimate it from the other end. The teacher is seldom in at the death. To take a milder theatrical metaphor, he is seldom there on the night. But this is only one of many instances of the same truth: that what is called public life is not larger than private life, but smaller. What we call public life is a fragmentary affair of sections and seasons and impressions; it is only in private life that dwells the fullness of our life bodily.

On Turnpikes and Mediævalism

All I Survey, 1933

Opening my newspaper the other day, I saw a short but emphatic leaderette entitled "A Relic of Mediævalism". It expressed a profound indignation upon the fact that somewhere or other, in some fairly remote corner of this country, there is a turnpike-gate, with a toll. It insisted that this antiquated tyranny is insupportable, because it is supremely important that our road traffic should go very fast; presumably a little faster than it does. So it described the momentary delay in this place as a relic of mediævalism. I fear the future will look at that sentence, somewhat sadly and a little contemptuously, as a very typical relic of modernism. I mean it will be a melancholy relic of the only period in all human history when people were proud of being modern. For though to-day is always to-day and the moment is always modern, we are the only men in all history who fell back upon bragging about the mere fact that to-day is not yesterday. I fear that some in the future will explain it by saying that we had precious little else to brag about. For, whatever the mediæval faults, they went with one merit. Mediæval people never worried about being mediæval; and modern people do worry horribly about being modern. But however that may be, this particular example may give us food for thought, like many other instances of thoughtlessness.

To begin with, note the queer, automatic assumption that it must always mean throwing mud at a thing to call it a relic of mediævalism. The modern world contains a good many relics of mediævalism, and most of us would be surprised if the argument were logically enforced even against the things that are commonly called mediæval. We should express some regret if somebody blew up Westminster Abbey, because it is a relic of mediævalism. Doubts would trouble us if the Government burned all existing copies of Dante's *Divine Comedy* and Chaucer's *Canterbury Tales*, because they are quite certainly relics of mediævalism. We could not throw ourselves into unreserved and enthusiastic rejoicing even if the Tower of Giotto were destroyed as a relic of mediævalism. And only just recently, in Oxford and Paris (themselves, alas! relics of mediævalism), there has been a perverse and pedantic revival of the Thomist Philosophy and the logical method of the mediæval Schoolmen. Similarly, curious and restless minds, among the very youngest artists and art critics, have unaccountably gone back even further into the barbaric period than the limit of the Tower of Giotto, and are even now telling us to look back to the austerity of Cimabue and the Byzantine diagrams of the Dark Ages. These relics must be more mediæval even than mediævalism.

But, in fact, this queer phrase would not cover only what is commonly called mediævalism. If a relic of mediævalism only means something that has come down to us from mediæval times, such writers would probably be surprised at the size and solidity of the relics. If I told these honest pressmen that the Press is a relic of mediævalism, they would probably prove their love of a cliché by accusing me of a paradox. But it is at least certain that the Printing Press is a relic of mediævalism. It was discovered and established by entirely mediæval men, steeped in mediæval ideas, stuffed with the religion and social spirit of the Middle Ages. There are no more typically mediæval words than those noble words of the eulogy that was pronounced by the great English printer on the great English poet; the words of Caxton upon Chaucer. If I were to say that Parliament is a relic of mediævalism, I should be on even stronger ground; for, while the Press did at least come at the end of the Middle Ages, the Parliaments came much more nearly at the beginning of the Middle Ages. They began, I think, in Spain and the provinces of the Pyrenees; but our own traditional date, connecting them with the revolt of Simon de Montfort, if not strictly accurate, does roughly represent the time. I need not say that half the great educational foundations, not only Oxford and Cambridge, but Glasgow and Paris, are relics of mediævalism. It would seem rather hard on the poor journalistic reformer if he is not allowed to pull down a little turnpike-gate till he has proved his right to pull down all these relics of mediævalism.

Next we have, of course, the very considerable historic doubt about whether the turnpike-gate is a relic of mediævalism. I do not know what was the date of this particular turnpike; but turnpikes and tolls of that description were perhaps most widely present, most practically enforced, or, at least, most generally noted, in the eighteenth century. When Pitt and Dundas, both of them roaring drunk, jumped over a turnpike-gate and were fired at with a blunderbuss, I hope nobody will suggest that those two great politicians were relics of mediævalism. Nobody surely could be more modern than Pitt and Dundas, for one of them was a great financial statesman, depending entirely on the bankers, and the other was a swindler. It is possible, of course, that some such local toll was really mediæval, but I rather doubt whether the journalist even enquired whether it was mediæval. He probably regards everything that happened before the time of Jazz and the Yellow Press as mediæval. For him mediæval only means old, and old only means bad; so that we come to the last question, which ought to have been the first question, of whether a turnpike really is necessarily bad.

If we were really relics of mediævalism—that is, if we had really been taught to think—we should have put that question first, and discussed whether a thing is bad or good before discussing whether it is modern or mediæval. There is no space to discuss it here at length, but a very simple test in the matter may be made. The aim and effect of tolls is simply this: that those who use the roads shall pay for the roads. As it is, the poor people of a district, including those who never stir from their villages, and hardly from their firesides, pay to maintain roads which are ploughed up and torn to pieces by the cars and lorries of rich men and big businesses, coming from London and the distant cities. It is not self-evident that this is a more just arrangement than that by which wayfarers pay to keep up the way, even if that arrangement were a relic of mediævalism.

Lastly, we might well ask, is it indeed so certain that our roads suffer from the slowness of petrol traffic; and that, if we can only make every sort of motor go faster and faster, we shall all be saved at last? That motors are more important than men is doubtless an admitted principle of a truly modern philosophy; nevertheless, it might be well to keep some sort of reasonable ration between them, and decide exactly how many human beings should be killed by each car in the course of each year. And I fear that a mere policy of the acceleration of traffic may take us beyond the normal modern recognition of murder into something resembling a recognition of massacre. And about this, I for one still have a scruple; which is probably a relic of mediævalism.

The Drift From Domesticity

The Thing, 1929

In the matter of reforming things, as distinct from deforming them, there is one plain and simple principle; a principle which will probably be called a paradox. There exists in such a case a certain institution or law; let us say, for the sake of simplicity, a fence or gate erected across a road. The more modern type of reformer goes gaily up to it and says, "I don't see the use of this; let us clear it away." To which the more intelligent type of reformer will do well to answer: "If you don't see the use of it, I certainly won't let you clear it away. Go away and think. Then, when you can come back and tell me that you *do* see the use of it, I may allow you to destroy it."

This paradox rests on the most elementary common sense. The gate or fence did not grow there. It was not set up by somnambulists who built it in their sleep. It is highly improbable that it was put there by escaped lunatics who were for some reason loose in the street. Some person had some reason for thinking it would be a good thing for somebody. And until we know what the reason was, we really cannot judge whether the reason was reasonable. It is extremely probable that we have overlooked some whole aspect of the question, if something set up by human beings like ourselves seems to be entirely meaningless and mysterious. There are reformers who get over this difficulty by assuming that all their fathers were fools; but if that be so, we can only say that folly appears to be a hereditary disease. But the truth is that nobody has any business to destroy a social institution until he has really seen it as an historical institution. If he knows how it arose, and what purposes it was supposed to serve, he may really be able to say that they were bad purposes, or that they have since become bad purposes, or that they are purposes which are no longer served. But if he simply stares at the thing as a senseless monstrosity that has somehow sprung up in his path, it is he and not the traditionalist who is suffering from an illusion. We might even say that he is seeing things in a nightmare. This principle applies to a thousand things, to trifles as well as true institutions, to convention as well as to conviction. It was exactly the sort of person, like Joan of Arc, who did know why women wore skirts, who was most justified in not wearing one; it was exactly the sort of person, like St. Francis, who did sympathise with the feast and the fireside, who was most entitled to become a beggar on the open road. And when, in the general emancipation of modern society, the Duchess says she does not see why she shouldn't play leapfrog, or the Dean declares that he sees no valid canonical reason why he should not stand on his head, we may say to these persons with patient benevolence: "Defer, therefore, the operation you contemplate until you have realised by ripe reflection what principle or prejudice you are violating. Then play leapfrog and stand on your head and the Lord be with you."

Among the traditions that are being thus attacked, not intelligently but most unintelligently, is the fundamental human creation called the Household or the Home. That is a typical thing which men attack, not because they can see through it, but because they cannot see it at all. They beat at it blindly, in a fashion entirely haphazard and opportunist; and many of them would pull it down without even pausing to ask why it was ever put up. It is true that only a few of them would have avowed this object in so many words. That only proves how very blind and blundering they are. But they have fallen into a habit of mere drift and gradual detachment from family life; something that is often merely accidental and devoid of any definite theory at all. But though it is accidental it is none the less anarchical. And it is all the more anarchical for not being anarchist. It seems to be largely founded on individual irritation; an irritation which varies with the individual. We are merely told that in this or that case a particular temperament was tormented by a particular environment; but nobody even explained how the evil arose, let alone whether the evil is really escaped. We are told that in this or that family Grandmamma talked a great deal of nonsense, which God knows is true; or that it is very difficult to have intimate intellectual relations with Uncle Gregory without telling him he is a fool, which is indeed the case. But nobody seriously considers the remedy, or even the malady; or whether the existing individualistic dissolution is a remedy at all. Much of this business began with the influence of Ibsen, a very powerful dramatist and an exceedingly feeble philosopher. I suppose that Nora of The Doll's House was intended to be an inconsequent person; but certainly her most inconsequent action was her last. She complained that she was not yet fit to look after children, and then proceeded to get as far as possible from the children, that she might study them more closely.

There is one simple test and type of this neglect of scientific thinking and the sense of a social rule; the neglect which has now left us with nothing but a welter of exceptions. I have read hundreds and thousands of times, in all the novels and newspapers of our epoch, certain phrases about the just right of the young to liberty, about the unjust claim of the elders to control, about the conception that all souls must be free or all citizens equal, about the absurdity of authority or the degradation of obedience. I am not arguing those matters directly at the moment. But what strikes me as astounding, in a logical sense, is that not one of these myriad novelists and newspaper-men ever seems to think of asking the next and most obvious question. It never seems to occur to them to inquire what becomes of the opposite obligation. If the child is free from the first to disregard the parent, why is not the parent free from the first to disregard the child? If Mr. Jones, Senior, and Mr. Jones, Junior, are only two free and equal citizens, why should one citizen sponge on another citizen for the first fifteen years of his life? Why should the elder Mr. Jones be expected to feed, clothe, and shelter out of his own pocket another person who is entirely free of any obligations to him? If the bright young thing cannot be asked to tolerate her grandmother, who has become something of a bore, why should the grandmother or the mother have tolerated the bright young thing at a period of her life when she was by no means bright? Why did they laboriously look after her at a time when her contributions to the conversation were seldom epigrammatic and not often intelligible? Why should Jones Senior stand drinks and free meals to anybody so unpleasant as Jones Junior, especially in the immature phases of his existence? Why should he not throw the baby out of the window; or at any rate, kick the boy out of doors? It is obvious that we are dealing with a real relation, which may be equality, but is certainly not similarity.

Some social reformers try to evade this difficulty, I know, by some vague notions about the State or an abstraction called Education eliminating the parental function. But this, like many notions of solid scientific persons, is a wild illusion of the nature of mere moonshine. It is based on that strange new superstition, the idea of infinite resources of organisation. It is as if officials grew like grass or bred like rabbits. There is supposed to be an endless supply of salaried persons, and of salaries for them; and they are to undertake all that human beings naturally do for themselves; including the care of children. But men cannot live by taking in each other's baby-linen. They cannot provide a tutor for each citizen; who is to tutor the tutors? Men cannot be educated by machinery; and though there might be a Robot bricklayer or scavenger, there will never be a Robot schoolmaster or governess. The actual effect of this theory is that one harassed person has to look after a hundred children, instead of one normal person looking after a normal number of them. Normally that normal person is urged by a natural force, which costs nothing and does not require a salary; the force of natural affection for his young, which exists even among the animals. If you cut off that natural force, and substitute a paid bureaucracy, you are like a fool who should pay men to turn the wheel of his mill, because he refused to use wind or water which he could get for nothing. You are like a lunatic who should carefully water his garden with a watering-can, while holding up an umbrella to keep off the rain.

It is now necessary to recite these truisms; for only by doing so can we begin to get a glimpse of that *reason* for the existence of the family, which I began this essay by demanding. They were all familiar to our fathers, who believed in the links of kinship and also in the links of logic. To-day our logic consists mostly of missing links; and our family largely of absent members. But, anyhow, this is the right end at which to begin any such inquiry; and *not* at the tail-end or the fag-end of some private muddle, by which Dick has become discontented or Susan has gone off on her own. If Dick or Susan wish to destroy the family because they do not see the use of it, I say as I said in the beginning; if they do not see the use of it, they had much better preserve it. They have no business even to think of destroying it until they have seen the use of it.

But it has other uses, besides the obvious fact that it means a necessary social work being done for love when it cannot be done for money; and (one might almost dare to hint) presumably to be repaid with love since it is never repaid in money. On that simple side of the matter the general situation is easy to record. The existing and general system of society, subject in our own age and industrial culture to very gross abuses and painful problems, is nevertheless a normal one. It is the idea that the commonwealth is made up of a number of small kingdoms, of which a man and a woman become the king and queen and in which they exercise a reasonable authority, subject to the common sense of the commonwealth, until those under their care grow up to found similar kingdoms and exercise similar authority. This is the social structure of mankind, far older than all its records and more universal than any of its religions; and all attempts to alter it are mere talk and tomfoolery.

But the other advantage of the small group is now not so much neglected as simply not realised. Here again we have some extraordinary delusions spread all over the literature and journalism of our time. Those delusions now exist in such a degree that we may say, for all practical purposes, that when a thing has been stated about a thousand times as obviously true, it is almost certain to be obviously false. One such statement may be specially noted here. There is undoubtedly something to be said against domesticity and in favour of the general drift towards life in hotels, clubs, colleges, communal settlements, and the rest; or for a social life organised on the plan of the great commercial system of our time. But the truly extraordinary suggestion is often made that this escape from the home is an escape into greater freedom. The change is actually offered as favourable to liberty.

To anybody who can think, of course, it is exactly the opposite. The domestic division of human society is not perfect, being human. It does not achieve complete liberty; a thing somewhat difficult to do or even to define. But it is a mere matter of arithmetic that it puts a larger number of people in supreme control of something, and able to shape it to their personal liking, than do the vast organisations that rule society outside; whether those systems are legal or commercial or even merely social. Even if we were only considering the parents, it is plain that there are more parents than there are policemen or politicians or heads of big businesses or proprietors of hotels. As I shall suggest in a moment, the argument actually applies indirectly to the children as well as directly to the parents. But the main point is that the world *outside* the home is now under a rigid discipline and routine and it is only inside the home that there is really a place for individuality and liberty. Anyone stepping out of the front-door is obliged to step into a procession, all going the same way and to a great extent even obliged to wear the same uniform. Business, especially big business, is now organised like an army. It is, as some would say, a sort of mild militarism without bloodshed; as I should say, a militarism without the military virtues. But anyhow, it is obvious that a hundred clerks in a bank or a hundred waitresses in a teashop are more regimented and under rule than the same individuals when each has gone back to his or her own dwelling or lodging, hung with his or her favourite pictures or fragrant with his or her favourite cheap cigarettes. But this, which is so obvious in the commercial case, is no less true even in the social case. In practise, the pursuit of pleasure is merely the pursuit of fashion. The pursuit of fashion is merely the pursuit of convention; only that it happens to be a new convention. The jazz dances, the joy rides, the big pleasure parties, and hotel entertainments, do not make any more provision for a *really* independent taste than did any of the fashions of the past. If a wealthy young lady wants to do what all the other wealthy young ladies are doing, she will find it great fun, simply because youth is fun and society is fun. She will enjoy being modern exactly as her Victorian grandmother enjoyed being Victorian. And quite right too; but it is the enjoyment of convention, not the enjoyment of liberty. It is perfectly healthy for all young people of all historic periods to herd together, to a reasonable extent, and enthusiastically copy each other. But in that there is nothing particularly fresh and certainly nothing particularly free. The girl who likes shaving her head and powdering her nose and wearing short skirts will find the world organised for her and will march happily with the procession. But a girl who happened to like having her hair down to her heels or loading herself with barbaric gauds and trailing garments or (most awful of all) leaving her nose in its natural state—she will still be well advised to do these things on her own premises. If the Duchess does want to play leapfrog, she must not start suddenly leaping in the manner of a frog across the ballroom of the Babylon Hotel, when it is crowded with the fifty best couples professionally practising the very latest dance, for the instruction of society. The Duchess will find it easier to practise leapfrog to the admiration of her intimate friends in the old oak-panelled hall of Fitzdragon Castle. If the Dean must stand on his head, he will do it with more ease and grace in the calm atmosphere of the Deanery than by attempting to interrupt the programme of some social entertainment already organised for philanthropic purposes.

If there is this impersonal routine in commercial and even in social things, it goes without saying that it exists and always must exist in political and legal things. For instance, the punishments of the State must be sweeping generalizations. It is only the punishments of the home that can possibly be adapted to the individual case; because it is only there that the judge can know anything of the individual. If Tommy takes a silver thimble out of a work-basket, his mother may act very differently according as she knows that he did it for fun or for spite or to sell to somebody, or to get somebody into trouble. But if Tomkins takes a silver thimble out of a shop, the law not only can but must punish him according to the rule made for all shoplifters or stealers of silver. It is only the domestic discipline that can show any sympathy or especially any humour.

I do not say that the family always does do this; but I say that the state never ought to attempt it. So that even if we consider the parents alone as independent princes, and the children merely as subjects, the relative freedom of the family can and often does work to the advantage of those subjects. But so long as the children are children, they will always be the subjects of somebody. The question is whether they are to be distributed naturally under their natural princes, as the old phrase went, who normally feel for them what nobody else will feel, a natural affection. It seems to me clear that this normal distribution gives the largest amount of liberty to the largest number of people.

My complaint of the anti-domestic drift is that it is unintelligent. People do not know what they are doing; because they do not know what they are undoing. There are a multitude of modern manifestations, from the largest to the smallest, ranging from a divorce to a picnic party. But each is a separate escape or evasion; and especially an evasion of the point at issue. People ought to decide in a philosophical fashion whether they desire the traditional social order or not; or if there is any particular alternative to be desired. As it is they treat the public question merely as a mess or medley of private questions. Even in being anti-domestic they are much too domestic in their test of domesticity. Each family considers only its own case and the result is merely narrow and negative. Each case is an exception to a rule that does not exist. The family, especially in the modern state, stands in need of considerable correction and reconstruction; most things do in the modern state. But the family mansion should be preserved or destroyed or rebuilt; it should not be allowed to fall to pieces brick by brick because nobody has any historic sense of the object of bricklaying. For instance, the architects of the restoration should rebuild the house with wide and easily opened doors, for the practise of the ancient virtue of hospitality. In other words, private property should be distributed with sufficiently decent equality to allow of a margin for festive intercourse. But the hospitality of a house will always be different from the hospitality of a hotel. And it will be different in being more individual, more independent, more interesting than the hospitality of a hotel. It is perfectly right that the young Browns and the young Robinsons should meet and mix and dance and make asses of themselves, according to the design of their Creator. But there will always be some difference between the Browns entertaining the Robinsons and the Robinsons entertaining the Browns. And it will be a difference to the advantage of variety, of personality, of the potentialities of the mind of man; or, in other words, of life, liberty and the pursuit of happiness.

On Vulgarity

Come to Think of It, 1930

Most of us must have wondered if we could find a real definition of Vulgarity. For it is generally difficult to destroy, or even to defy, a thing that we cannot define. I suspect, to begin with, that we should discover, in the case of this word, a difficulty that exists with regard to a great many modern words. They were invented after the age of doctrine and definition. They are at best artistic and atmospheric. They have come to stand for strong impressions which are real enough, but to stand for them merely as symbols, sometimes poetical, sometimes arbitrary and accidental. And I rather fancy that, in the case of Vulgarity and other verbal symbols, we should find that the inquiry ended in an odd way. When we had really managed to put into other words the thing we meant by this particular word, we should probably find that it was a very incorrect word for it.

Thus Vulgarity, as a vice which we can all feel rather vividly (I should imagine) in the affairs and fashions around us, is not really connected with the ancient *vulgus*; not even with the *profanum vulgus* [the common crowd]. The mob has its own vices, but it is not necessarily vulgar. The mass of mankind has its own weaknesses, but we do not necessarily feel those weaknesses as vulgarizing. The particular thing we mean, or at any rate the thing I mean, when I use this word, is something much more subtle and certainly much more poisonous. But I really do not know any other word for it. I could easily give examples of it from the press, but this would be a rather cheap and unfair way of filling the pages in this book. So, with a full sense of the rashness of the experiment, I will make an attempt to state the real nature of the thing I call Vulgarity; and I wish I knew a worse name for it.

What I mean by Vulgarity is this. When six men stand up and we suddenly see that one of them is a dwarf, we are startled to find him so stunted. We only realise that he is stunted because he is standing up; because he is stretching himself to his full height. When the mind of man stretches itself, in order to show off, and is still stunted, that is the revelation that I mean. It is by the showing off that we see how little there is to show. When somebody tries to impress us, either with his wit or assurance, or knowledge of the world, or power, or grace, or even poetry and ideality, and in the very act of doing so shows he has low ideas of all these things—that is Vulgarity. In other words, a thing is only vulgar when its best is base.

That is why many things commonly called vulgar do not seem to me vulgar at all. The red-nosed comedian, the man who sits on his hat, the joke about the drunken man, these are not the sort of thing of which I am thinking; indeed, they are the very reverse. For the man who sits on his hat is not standing up. The drunkard is not stretching himself; he is (as he will explain) enjoying relaxation. The red-nosed comedian is not pretending to be at his best. These things may have dangers or weaknesses of their own, but they do not indicate that a man is base even at his best. The man who sits on his hat on the stage may be perfectly dignified when he sits on his chair at home, or takes off his hat in church. The red-nosed comedian, when he has hung up his red nose along with his little hat, may be in private life a blend of Bayard and Socrates. We can appeal from Philip drunk to Philip sober. But we can appeal no further, if we find that even Philip sober is a boor and a brute. If he is base at his best, and baser in his attempt to impress us with his best, then we have a certain sensation for which I know no other name. It appears when the man does pretend to be Bayard, and can only manage to be Barnum. It appears when the man does go to church and take off his hat, and seems to care more about the hat than the church. It appears, in short, when there is something about him that seems to debase and flatten everything he touches; and most of all when he touches worthy and exalted things. Thus there is the man who wishes first to prove that he is a gentleman, and only proves two things; first, that he is vulgar enough to prefer being a gentleman to being a man; and second, that he has a hideously stunted and half-witted notion even of being a gentleman. There is the man who wishes to show that he has lived in the best society; and shows even in showing it that he does not know the best society from the worst.

There are any number of lesser and often more excusable examples, but this is the touch that makes the difference. There is the man who is always being tactful without tact. There is the man who jokes loudly and laughs heartily, and so proves that he has no sense of humour. There is the man who talks a great deal about understanding women, and with every word helps us with a ghastly clarity to understand him. There is the man who tells stories of the wonderful affability and friendliness of very rich men he has known, and thereby reveals his secret religion—that rich men are gods and that he is a fortunate favourite of the gods. All these men have the mark that I call for convenience vulgar; the mark that they give us their own moral and spiritual measure by stretching themselves to their full stature. If they had been a little lax and casual and humble, we might never have found them out. If they had not been so clever, we might never have known that they were fools. If they had not been so gentlemanly, we should not have seen that they were cads.

If I have in any faint degree described this indescribable thing, I would ask the reader to run his eye down a large number of current columns, and see whether there is not something hurting our heritage of culture, something all the more vulgar because it is subtle. It is seldom or never indecent, at any rate in England. It would perhaps be less dangerous if it were less decent. It keeps on one side of one line, but its very posture in balancing on that line is offensive. As I have said, in my sense, the notion of going on the spree is not vulgar, but the perpetual implication that everybody is going nowhere except to the best restaurants is vulgar. For Vulgarity is a thing of visions and even ideals; and men are judged by their dreams.

On a Humiliating Heresy

Come to Think of It, 1930

I cannot understand why so many modern people like to be regarded as slaves. I mean the most dismal and degraded sort of slaves; moral and spiritual slaves. Popular preachers and fashionable novelists can safely repeat that men are only what their destiny makes them; and that there is no choice or challenge in the lot of man. Dean Inge declares, with a sort of gloomy glee, that some absurd American statistics or experiments show that heredity is an incurable disease and that education is no cure for it. Mr. Arnold Bennett says that many of his friends drink too much; but that it cannot be helped, because they cannot help it. I am not Puritanic about drink; I have drunk all sorts of things; and in my youth, often more than was good for me. But in any conceivable condition, drunk or sober, I should be furious at the suggestion that I could not help it. I should have wanted to punch the head of the consoling fatalist who told me so. Yet nobody seems to punch the heads of consoling fatalists. This, which seems to me the most elementary form of self-respect, seems to be the one thing about which even the sensitive are insensible. These modern persons are very sensitive about some things. They would be furious if somebody said they were not gentlemen; though there is really no more historical reason for pretending that every man is a gentleman than that every man is a marquis, or a man-at-arms. They are frightfully indignant if we say they are not Christians; though they hold themselves free to deny or doubt every conceivable idea of Christianity, even the historical existence of Christ. In the current cant of journalism and politics, they would almost prosecute us for slander if we said they were not Democrats; though any number of them actually prefer aristocracy or autocracy; and the real Democrats in English society are rather a select few. We might almost say that the true believers in democracy are themselves an aristocracy. About all these words men can be morbidly excitable and touchy. They must not be called pagans or plebeians or plain men or reactionaries or oligarchs. But they may be called slaves; they may be called monkeys; and, above all, they may be called machines. One would imagine that the really intolerable insult to human dignity would be to say that human life is not determined by human will. But so long as we do not say they are heathen, we may say they are not human. We may say that they develop as blindly as a plant or turn as automatically as a wheel.

There are all sorts of ways in which this humiliating heresy expresses itself. One is the perpetual itch to describe all crime as lunacy. Now, quite apart from virtue, I would much rather be thought a criminal than a criminal lunatic. As a point not of virtue but of vanity, I should be less insulted by the title of a murderer than by the title of a homicidal maniac. The murderer might be said, not unfairly, to have lost the first fragrance of his innocence, and all that keeps the child near to the cherubim. But the maniac has lost more than innocence; he has lost essence; the complete personality that makes him a man. Yet everybody is talking as if it would be quite natural, and even nice, to be excused for immorality on the ground of idiocy. The principle is applied, with every flourish of liberality and charity, to personalities whom one would imagine quite proud of being personal. It is applied not only to the trivial and transient villains of real life, but to the far more solid and convincing villains of romance.

A distinguished doctor has written a book about the madmen of Shakespeare. By which he did not mean those few fantastic and manifest madmen, whom we might almost call professional madmen, who merely witnessed to the late Elizabethan craze for lurid and horrible grotesques. Ford or Webster, or some of their fellows, would hardly have hesitated to have a ballet or chorus of maniacs, like a chorus of fairies or fashionable beauties. But the medical gentleman seems to have said that any number of the serious characters were mad. Macbeth was mad; Hamlet was mad; Ophelia was congenitally mad; and so on. If Hamlet was really mad, there does not seem much point in his pretending to be mad. If Ophelia was always mad there does not seem much point in her going mad. But anyhow I think a saner criticism will always maintain that Hamlet was sane. He must be sane even in order to be sad; for when we get into a world of complete unreality, even tragedy is unreal. No lunatic ever had so good a sense of humour as Hamlet. A homicidal maniac does not say: "Your wisdom would show itself more richer to signify that to his doctor"; he is a little too sensitive on the subject of doctors. The whole point of Hamlet is that he is really saner than anybody else in the play; though I admit that being sane is not identical with what some call being sensible. Being outside the world, he sees all round it; where everybody else sees his own side of the world, his own worldly ambition, or hatred or love. But, after all, Hamlet pretended to be mad in order to deceive fools. We cannot complain if he has succeeded.

But, whatever we may say about Hamlet, we must not say this about Macbeth. Hamlet was only a mild sort of murderer; a more or less accidental and parenthetical murderer; an amateur. But Macbeth was a good, solid, serious, self-respecting murderer; and we must not have any nonsense about him. For the play of *Macbeth* is, in the supreme and special sense, the Christian Tragedy; to be set against the pagan Tragedy of Oedipus. It is the whole point about Oedipus that he does not know what he is doing. And it is the whole point about Macbeth that he does know what he is doing. It is not a tragedy of Fate but a tragedy of Freewill. He is tempted of a devil, but he is not driven by a destiny. If the actor pronounces the words properly, the whole audience ought to feel that the story may yet have an entirely new ending, when Macbeth says suddenly, "We will proceed no further in this business." The incredible confusion of modern thought is always suggesting that any indication that men have been influenced is an indication that they have been forced. All men are always being influenced; for every incident is an influence. The question is, which incident shall we allow to be most influential. Macbeth was influenced; but he consented to be influenced. He was not, like a blind tragic pagan, obeying something he thought he ought to obey. He does not worship the Three Witches like the Three Fates. He is a good enlightened Christian, and sins against the light.

The fancy for reading fatalism into this play, where it is most absent, is probably due to the fallacy of a series; or three things in a row. It misleads Macbeth's critics just as it misleads Macbeth. Almost all our pseudo-science proceeds on the principle of saying that one thing follows on another thing, and then dogmatizing about the third thing that is to follow. The whole argument about the Superman, for instance, as developed by Nietzsche and other sophists, depends entirely on this trick of the incomplete triad. First the scientist or sophist asserts that when there was a monkey, there was bound to be a man. Then he simply prophesies that something will follow the man, as the man followed the monkey. This is exactly the trick used by the Witches in Macbeth. They give him first a fact he knows already, that he is Thane of Glamis; then one fact really confirmed in the future, that he is Thane of Cawdor; and then something that is not a fact at all, and need never be a fact at all, unless he chooses to make it one out of his own murderous fancy. This false series, seeming to point at something, though the first term is trivial and the last untrue, does certainly mislead many with a fallacious sense of fate. It has been used by materialists in many ways to destroy the sense of moral liberty; and it has murdered many things besides Duncan.

On Original Sin

Come to Think of It, 1930

Once upon a time when Mr. H. G. Wells was setting forth on his varied and splendid voyage from Utopia to Utopia, he announced as a sort of watchword or war-cry that the new world would have nothing to do with the idea of Original Sin. He did not specially speak, and, indeed, there was no reason for him to speak, about his other beliefs or unbeliefs. He had not then compared the Trinity to a dance; but neither had he called adoring multitudes to the shrine of the Invisible King. But, standing at the end of the great scientific nineteenth century, he thought it time to announce that the one doctrine he did not believe in was Original Sin. Standing at the beginning of the still more scientific twentieth century, Mr. Aldous Huxley calmly announces that the one doctrine he *does* believe in is Original Sin. He may be a sceptic or a heretic about many things, but on that point he is quite orthodox. He may not hold many theological dogmas, but about this dogma he is quite dogmatic. There is one fragment of the ancient creed which he not only clings to, but declares to be necessary to all clear minds of the new generation. And that is the very fragment which Mr. Wells threw away thirty years ago, as something that would never be needed anymore. The stone that the builder of Utopia rejected ...

It is not a mere verbal coincidence that original thinkers believe in Original Sin. For really original thinkers like to think about origins. That should be obvious even to the negative thinkers of the nineteenth-century tradition, who for two or three generations claimed all originality, all novelty, all revolutionary change of thought for a book called *The Origin of Species*. But it is even more true of moral discovery than of material discovery; and it is even more true of the twentieth-century reaction than of the nineteenth-century revolution. Men who wish to get down to fundamentals perceive that there is a fundamental problem of evil. Men content to be more superficial are also content with a superficial fuss and bustle of improvement. The man in the mere routine of modern life is content to say that a modern gallows is a relatively humane instrument or that a modern cat-o'-nine tails is milder than an ancient Roman *flagellum*. But the original thinker will ask why any scourge or gibbet was ever needed, or ever even alleged to be needed? And that brings the original thinker back to original sin. For that is not affected as a universal thing by whether we approve or disapprove of the particular things. Whether we call it infamous tyranny or inevitable restraint, there is some sort of sin either in the scourger or the scourged.

Nevertheless, I often feel that the original thinker is not quite original enough. I mean that he does not get quite so near to the truth as the old tradition could take him. I say it without arrogance, for many of us owe the truth as much to tradition as to originality. But I am often struck by the fact that original thinkers originate trains of thought, but do not finish them. It is the great trouble with the advanced that they will not advance any further. Now Mr. Aldous Huxley sees very clearly that mediæval religion was more realistic than modern idealism and optimism. He says that the latest scientific view is more like the old Catholic view than was the intervening illusion of the Romantic Movement. But he adds that the scientific view of man necessitates a sort of original sin, if it be only the residuum of his animal ancestry.

Now, that is exactly where I should like him to advance a step further; and he does not. For sin, whatever else it is, is not *merely* the dregs of a bestial existence. It is something more subtle and spiritual, and is in some way connected with the very supremacy of the human spirit. Mr. Huxley must know well enough that this is so with the most execrable sins, such as often figure in his own admirable satires. It is not merely a matter of letting the ape and tiger die, for apes are not Pharisees, nor are tigers prigs. The elephant does not turn up his long nose at everything with any superior intention; and the totally unjust charge of hypocrisy might well be resented by any really sensitive and thin-skinned crocodile. The giraffe might be called a highbrow, but he is not really supercilious about his powers of Uplift. Man has scattered his own vices as well as virtues very arbitrarily among the animals, and there may be no more reason to accuse the peacock of pride than to accuse the pelican of charity.

The worst things in man are only possible to man. At least we must confine their existence to men, unless we are prepared to admit the existence of demons. There is thus another truth in the original conception of original sin, since even in sinning man originated something. His body may have come from animals, and his soul may be torn in pieces by all sorts of doctrinal disputes and quarrels among men. But, roughly speaking, it is quite clear that he did manufacture out of the old mud or blood of material origins, with whatever mixture of more mysterious elements, a special and a mortal poison. That poison is his own recipe; it is not merely decaying animal matter. That poison is most poisonous where there are fine scientific intellects or artistic imaginations to mix it. It is just as likely to be at its best—that is, at its worst—at the end of a civilisation as at the beginning. Of this sort are all the hideous corruptions of culture; the pride, the perversions, the intellectual cruelties, the horrors of emotional exhaustion. You cannot explain that monstrous fruit by saying that our ancestors were arboreal; save, indeed, as an allegory of the Tree of Knowledge. The poison can take the form of every sort of culture—as, for instance, bacteria-culture. But the poison itself has always been there. Indeed it is as old as any memory of man. Wherefore, we have to posit of it that it also was of the human source and fountainhead, that it was in the beginning, or, as the old theology affirms, original.

I suggest, therefore, with great respect, that it is not even now a case of having to admit that the old religion had come very near to the truths of the most modern science. It is rather a case of the most modern science having come very near to the truths of the old religion—but not quite near enough.

On Jane Austen in the General Election

Come to Think of It, 1930

I saw recently a remark about Jane Austen in connection with the General Election. We have most of us seen a good many remarks about Jane Austen in connection with the Flapper or the New Woman or the Modern View of Marriage, or some of those funny things. And those happy few of us who happen to have read Jane Austen have generally come to the conclusion that those who refer to her have not read her. Feminists are, as their name implies, opposed to anything feminine. But sometimes they disparaged the earlier forms of the feminine, even when they showed qualities commonly called masculine. They talk of *Sense and Sensibility* without knowing that the moral is on the side of Sense. They talk about fainting. I do not remember any woman fainting in any novel of Jane Austen. There may be an exception that I have forgotten; there is indeed a lady who falls with a great whack off the Cobb at Lyme Regis. But few ladies would do that as a mere affected pose of sentiment. But rarely does a lady dash herself from Shakespeare's Cliff or the Monument solely to assume a graceful attitude below. Jane Austen herself was certainly not of the fainting sort. Nor were her favourite heroines, like Emma Woodhouse or Elizabeth Bennett. The real case against Jane Austen (if anybody is so base and thankless as to want to make a case against her) is not that she is sentimental, but that she is rather cynical. Allowing for the different conventions of subject-matter in the two periods, she was rather like Miss Rose Macaulay. But Miss Rose Macaulay finds herself in a world where fainting-fits would be a very mild form of excitement.

There is something very amusing about this appeal to a comparison between the novels of the two periods. The heroine of many a modern novel writhes and reels her way through the story, chews and flings away fifty half-smoked cigarettes, is perpetually stifling a scream or else not stifling it, howling for solitude or howling for society, goading every mood to the verge of madness, seeing red mists before her eyes, seeing green flames dance in her brain, dashing to the druggist and then collapsing on the doorstep of the psycho-analyst; and all the time congratulating herself on her rational superiority to the weak sensibility of Jane Austen.

I do not say the new woman is like the new neurotic heroine; any more than I think the older woman was like the artificial fainting heroine. But if the critics have a right to argue from the old novels, we have a right to argue from the new. And what I say is true of the novels of some new novelists; and what they say is not true of the novels of Jane Austen. But, as I have said, we are already familiar with this sort of journalistic comment on Jane Austen's novels. It was always sufficiently shallow and trivial, being based on a vague association, connected with ladies who wore drooping ringlets and were therefore supposed to droop. But the particular example that I observed the other day was more unique and interesting, because it has a special point of application to-day. A writer in a leading daily paper, in the course of a highly optimistic account of the new attitude of women to men, as it would appear in the General Election, made the remark that a modern girl would see through the insincerity of Mr. Wickham, in *Pride and Prejudice*, in five minutes.

Now this is a highly interesting instance of the sort of injustice done to Jane Austen. The crowd (I fear the considerable crowd) of those who read that newspaper and do not read that author will certainly go away with the idea that Mr. Wickham was some sort of florid and vulgar impostor—like

Mr. Mantalini. But Jane Austen was a much more shrewd and solid psychologist than that. She did not make Elizabeth Bennett to be a person easily deceived, and she did not make her deceiver a vulgar impostor. Mr. Wickham was one of those very formidable people who tell lies by telling the truth. He did not merely swagger or sentimentalize or strike attitudes; he simply told the girl, as if reluctantly, that he had been promised a living in the Church by old Mr. Darcy, and that young Mr. Darcy had not carried out the scheme. This was true as far as it went; anybody might have believed it; most people would have believed it, if it were told with modesty and restraint. Mr. Wickham could be trusted to tell it with modesty and restraint. What Mr. Wickham could not be trusted to do was to tell the rest of the story; which made it a very different story. He did not think it necessary to mention that he had misbehaved himself in so flagrant a fashion that no responsible squire could possibly make him a parson; so that the squire had compensated him and he had become an officer in a fashionable regiment instead. Now that is a very quiet, commonplace, everyday sort of incident, and the sort of incident that does really occur. It is a perfectly sound and realistic example of the way in which quite sensible people can be deceived by quite unreliable people. And the novelist knew her business much too well to make the unreliable person obviously unreliable. That sort of quiet and plausible liar does exist; I certainly see no reason to think he has ceased to exist. I think Jane Austen was right in supposing that Elizabeth Bennett might have believed him. I think Jane Austen herself might have believed him. And I am quite certain that the Modern Girl might believe him any day.

But the rather queer application of all this to the case of the General Election is not without a moral, after all. The optimistic journalist, who gloried in the infallible intuition of the Flappers' Vote, chose a very unlucky example for his own purpose when he chose the ingenious Mr. Wickham. For Mr. Wickham was, or is, exactly the sort of man who does make a success of political elections. Sometimes he is just a little too successful to succeed. Sometimes he is actually found out, by some accident, doing very dexterous things in the art of finance; and he disappears suddenly, but even then silently. But in the main he is made for Parliamentary life. And he owes his success to two qualities, both exhibited in the novel in which he figures. First, the talent for telling a lie by telling half of the truth. And second, the art of telling a lie not loudly and offensively, but with an appearance of gentlemanly and graceful regret. It was a very fortunate day for professional politicians when some reactionaries began to accuse them of being demagogues. The truth is that they seldom dare to be demagogues; and their greatest success is when they talk with delicacy and reserve like diplomatists. A dictator has to be a demagogue; a man like Mussolini cannot be ashamed to shout. He cannot afford to be a mere gentleman. His whole power depends on convincing the populace that he knows what he wants, and wants it badly. But a politician will be much wiser if he disguises himself as a gentleman. His power consists very largely in getting people to take things lightly. It is in getting them to be content with his sketchy and superficial version of the real state of things. Nothing tends more happily to this result than the shining qualities of Mr. Wickham; good manners and good nature and a light touch. All sorts of answers are given by Ministers to questions asked in Parliament, which could only be delivered in this way. If such palpable nonsense were thundered by an orator, or shouted by a demagogue, or in any way made striking and decisive, even the House of Commons would rise in riot or roar with laughter. Nonsense so nonsensical as that can only be uttered in the tones of a sensible man.

So vividly do I see Mr. Wickham as a politician that I feel inclined to rewrite the whole of *Pride and Prejudice* to suit the politics of to-day. It would be amusing to send the Bennett girls rushing round to canvass: Elizabeth with amusement, and Jane with dignified reluctance. As for Lydia, she would be a great success in modern politics. But her husband would be the greatest success of all; and he might become a Cabinet Minister while poor old Darcy was sulking in the provinces, a decent, truthful, honourable Diehard, cursing the taxes and swearing the country was going to the dogs—and especially to the puppies.

On Essays

Come to Think of It, 1930

There are dark and morbid moods in which I am tempted to feel that Evil re-entered the world in the form of Essays. The Essay is like the Serpent, smooth and graceful and easy of movement, also wavering or wandering. Besides, I suppose that the very word Essay had the original meaning of "trying it on." The serpent was in every sense of the word tentative. The tempter is always feeling his way, and finding out how much other people will stand. That misleading air of irresponsibility about the Essay is very disarming through appearing to be disarmed. But the serpent can strike without claws, as it can run without legs. It is the emblem of all those arts which are elusive, evasive, impressionistic, and shading away from tint to tint. I suppose that the Essay, so far as England at least is concerned, was almost invented by Francis Bacon. I can well believe it. I always thought he was the villain of English history.

It may be well to explain that I do not really regard all Essayists as wicked men. I have myself been an essayist, or tried to be an essayist; or pretended to be an essayist. Nor do I in the least dislike essays. I take perhaps my greatest literary pleasure in reading them; after such really serious necessities of the intellect as detective stories and tracts written by madmen. There is no better reading in the world than some contemporary essays, like those of Mr. E. V. Lucas or Mr. Robert Lynd. And though, unlike Mr. Lucas and Mr. Lynd, I am quite incapable of writing a really good essay, the motive of my dark suggestion is not a diabolic jealousy or envy. It is merely a natural taste for exaggeration, when dealing with a point too subtle to permit of exactitude. If I may myself imitate the timid and tentative tone of the true essayist, I will confine myself to saying that there is something in what I say. There is really an element in modern letters which is at once indefinite and dangerous.

What I mean is this. The distinction between certain old forms and certain relatively recent forms of literature is that the old were limited by a logical purpose. The Drama and the Sonnet were of the old kind; the Essay and the Novel are of the new. If a sonnet breaks out of the sonnet form, it ceases to be a sonnet. It may become a wild and inspiring specimen of free verse; but you do not have to call it a sonnet because you have nothing else to call it. But in the case of the new sort of novel, you do very often have to call it a novel because you have nothing else to call it. It is sometimes called a novel when it is hardly even a narrative. There is nothing to test or define it, except that it is not spaced like an epic poem, and often has even less of a story. The same applies to the apparently attractive leisure and liberty of the essay. By its very nature it does not exactly explain what it is trying to do, and thus escapes a decisive judgment about whether it has really done it. But in the case of the essay there is a practical peril; precisely because it deals so often with theoretical matters. It is always dealing with theoretical matters without the responsibility of being theoretical, or of propounding a theory.

For instance, there is any amount of sense and nonsense talked both for and against what is called mediævalism. There is also any amount of sense and nonsense talked for and against what is called modernism. I have occasionally tried to talk a little of the sense, with the result that I have been generally credited with all the nonsense. But if a man wanted one real and rational test, which really does distinguish the mediæval from the modern mood, it might be stated thus. The mediæval man thought in terms of the Thesis, where the modern man thinks in terms of the Essay. It would be unfair, perhaps, to say that the modern man only essays to think—or, in other words, makes a desperate attempt to think. But it would be true to say that the modern man often only essays, or attempts, to come to a conclusion. Whereas the mediæval man hardly thought it worth while to think at all, unless he could come to a conclusion. That is why he took a definite thing called a Thesis, and proposed to prove it. That is why Martin Luther, a very mediæval man in most ways, nailed up on the door the theses he proposed to prove. Many people suppose that he was doing something revolutionary, and even modernist, in doing this. In fact, he was doing exactly what all the other mediæval students and doctors had done ever since the twilight of the Dark Ages. If the really modern Modernist attempted to do it, he would probably find that he had never arranged his thoughts in the forms of theses at all. Well, it is quite an error to suppose, so far as I am concerned, that it is any question of restoring the rigid apparatus of the mediæval system. But I do think that the Essay has wandered too far away from the Thesis.

There is a sort of irrational and indefensible quality in many of the most brilliant phrases of the most beautiful essays. There is no essayist I enjoy more than Stevenson; there is probably no man now alive who admires Stevenson more than I. But if we take some favourite and frequently quoted sentence, such as, "To travel hopefully is better than to arrive," we shall see that it gives a loophole for every sort of sophistry and unreason. If it could be stated as a thesis, it could not be defended as a thought. A man would not travel hopefully at all, if he thought that the goal would be disappointing as compared with the travels. It is tenable that travel is the more enjoyable; but in that case it cannot be called hopeful. For the traveller is here presumed to hope for the end of travel, not merely for its continuance.

Now, of course, I do not mean that pleasant paradoxes of this sort have not a place in literature; and because of them the essay has a place in literature. There is room for the merely idle and wandering essayist, as for the merely idle and wandering traveller. The trouble is that the essayists have become the only ethical philosophers. The wandering thinkers have become the wandering preachers, and our only substitute for preaching friars. And whether our system is to be materialist or moralist, or sceptical or transcendental, we need more of a system than that. After a certain amount of wandering the mind wants either to get there or to go home. It is one thing to travel hopefully, and say half in jest that it is better than to arrive. It is another thing to travel hopelessly, because you know you will never arrive.

I was struck by the same tendency in re-reading some of the best essays ever written, which were especially enjoyed by Stevenson—the essays of Hazlitt. "You can live like a gentleman on Hazlitt's ideas," as Mr. Augustine Birrell truly remarked; but even in these we see the beginning of this inconsistent and irresponsible temper. For instance, Hazlitt was a Radical and constantly railed at Tories for not trusting men or mobs. I think it was he who lectured Walter Scott for so small a matter as making the mediæval mob in *Ivanhoe* jeer ungenerously at the retreat of the Templars. Anyhow, from any number of passages, one would infer that Hazlitt offered himself as a friend of the people. But he offered himself most furiously as an enemy of the Public. When he began to write about the Public, he described exactly the same many-headed monster of ignorance and cowardice and cruelty which the worst Tories called the Mob.

Now, if Hazlitt has been obliged to set forth his thoughts on Democracy in the theses of a mediæval schoolman, he would have had to think much more clearly and make up his mind much more decisively. I will leave the last word with the essayist; and admit that I am not sure whether he would have written such good essays.

On Evil Euphemisms

Come to Think of It, 1932

Somebody has just sent me a book on Companionate Marriage; so called because the people involved are not married and will very rapidly cease to be companions. I have no intention of discussing here that somewhat crude colonial project. I will merely say that it is here accompanied with sub-titles and other statements about the rising generation and the revolt of youth. And it seems to me exceedingly funny that, just when the rising generation boasts of not being sentimental, when it talks of being very scientific and sociological—at that very moment everybody seems to have forgotten altogether what was the social use of marriage and to be thinking wholly and solely of the sentimental. The practical purposes mentioned as the first two reasons for marriage, in the Anglican marriage service, seem to have gone completely out of sight for some people, who talk as if there were nothing but a rather wild version of the third, which may relatively be called romantic. And this, if you please, is supposed to be an emancipation from Victorian sentiment and romance.

But I only mention this matter as one of many, and one which illustrates a still more curious contradiction in this modern claim. We are perpetually being told that this rising generation is very frank and free, and that its whole social idea is frankness and freedom. Now I am not at all afraid of frankness. What I am afraid of is fickleness. And there is a truth in the old proverbial connection between what is fickle and what is false. There is in the very titles and terminology of all this sort of thing a pervading element of falsehood. Everything is to be called something that it is not; as in the characteristic example of Companionate Marriage. Everything is to be recommended to the public by some sort of synonym which is really a pseudonym. It is a talent that goes with the time of electioneering and advertisement and newspaper headlines; but whatever else such a time may be, it certainly is not specially a time of truth.

In short, these friends of frankness depend almost entirely on Euphemism. They introduce their horrible heresies under new and carefully complimentary names; as the Furies were called the Eumenides. The names are always flattery; the names are also nonsense. The name of Birth-Control, for instance, is sheer nonsense. Everybody has always exercised birth-control; even when they were so paradoxical as to permit the process to end in a birth. Everybody has always known about birth-control, even if it took the wild and unthinkable form of self-control. The question at issue concerns different forms of birth-prevention; and I am not going to debate it here. But if I did debate it, I would call it by its name. The same is true of an older piece of sentiment indulged in by the frank and free: the expression "Free Love." That also is a euphemism; that is, it is a refusal of people to say what they mean. In that sense, it is impossible to prevent *love* being free, but the moral problem challenged concerns not the passions, but the will. There are a great many other examples of this sort of polite fiction; these respectable disguises adopted by those who are always railing against respectability. In the immediate future there will probably be more still. There really seems no necessary limit to the process; and however far the anarchy of ethics may go, it may always be accompanied with this curious and pompous ceremonial. The sensitive youth of the future will never be called upon to accept Forgery as Forgery. It will be easy enough to call it Homoeography or Script-Assimilation, or something else that would suggest, to the simple or the superficial, that nothing was involved but a sort of socializing or unification of individual handwriting. We should not, like the more honest Mr. Fagin, teach little boys to pick pockets; for Mr. Fagin becomes far less honest when he becomes Professor Faginski, the great sociologist, of the University of Jena. But we should call it by some name implying the transference of something; I cannot at the moment remember the Greek either for pocket or pocket-handkerchief. As for the social justification of murder, that has already begun; and earnest thinkers had better begin at once to think about a nice inoffensive name for it. The case for murder, on modern relative and evolutionary ethics, is quite overwhelming. There is hardly one of us who does not, in looking round his or her social circle, recognize some chatty person or energetic social character whose disappearance, without undue fuss or farewell, would be a bright event for us all. Nor is it true that such a person is dangerous only because he wields unjust legal or social powers. The problem is often purely psychological, and not in the least legal; and no legal emancipations would solve it. Nothing would solve it but the introduction of that new form of liberty which we may agree to call, perhaps, the practise of Social Subtraction. Or, if we like, we can model the new name on the other names I have mentioned. We may call it Life-Control or Free Death; or anything else that has as little to do with the point of it as Companionate Marriage has to do with either marriage or companionship.

Anyhow, I respectfully refuse to be impressed by the claim to candour and realism put forward just now for men, women, and movements. It seems to me obvious that this is not really the age of audacity, but merely of advertisement; which may rather be described as caution kicking up a fuss. Much of the mistake arises from the double sense of the word publicity. For publicity also is a thoroughly typical euphemism or evasive term.

Publicity does not mean revealing public life in the interests of public spirit. It means merely flattering private enterprises in the interests of private persons. It means paying compliments in public; but not offering criticisms in public. We should all be very much surprised if we walked out of our front door one morning and saw a hoarding on one side of the road saying, "Use Miggle's Milk; It is All Cream," and a hoarding on the other side of the road inscribed: "Don't Use Miggle's Milk; It's Nearly All Water." The modern world would be much upset if I were allowed to set up a flaming sky-sign proclaiming my precise opinion of the Colonial Port Wine praised in the flaming sign opposite. All this advertisement may have something to do with the freedom of trade; but it has nothing to do with the freedom of truth. Publicity must be praise and praise must to some extent be euphemism. It must put the matter in a milder and more inoffensive form than it might be put, however much that mildness may seem to shout through megaphones or flare in headlines. And just as this sort of loud evasion is used in favour of bad wine and bad milk, so it is used in favour of bad morals. When somebody wishes to wage a social war against what all normal people have regarded as a social decency, the very first thing he does is to find some artificial term that shall sound relatively decent. He has no more of the real courage that would pit vice against virtue than the ordinary advertiser has the courage to advertise ale as arsenic. His intelligence, such as it is, is entirely a commercial intelligence and to that extent entirely conventional. He is a shopkeeper who dresses the shop-window; he is certainly the very reverse of a rebel or a rioter who breaks the shop-window. If only for this reason, I remain cold and decline the due reverence to Companionate Marriage and the book which speaks so reverentially about the Revolt of Youth. For this sort of revolt strikes me as nothing except revolting; and certainly not particularly realistic. With the passions which are natural to youth we all sympathise; with the pain that often arises from loyalty and duty we all sympathise still more; but nobody need sympathise with publicity experts picking pleasant expressions for unpleasant things; and I for one prefer the coarse language of our fathers.

A Plea for Prohibition

Sidelights, 1932

After a careful study of the operations of Prohibition in America, I have come to the conclusion that one of the best things that the Government could do would be to prohibit everything.

That the story of Mephistopheles, the fiend who tempted Faust, is in reality an allegory of the story of Prohibition in America, is admitted by all serious scholars whose authority carries weight in the modern world. Critics admiring the sarcasm of Mephistopheles have repeatedly referred to his humour as "dry"—a term now impossible to separate from its political content. The promise of the devil to produce a new and youthful Faust, in place of the old one, is obviously an allusion to the promise of the Prohibitionist to produce a new and fresh generation of American youth, unspoiled by the taste of alcohol. The allegory is not only clear about the sort of things that Prohibition promised, but is especially clear about the sort of things that Prohibition really performed. One of the things, for instance, which Mephistopheles really performed (if I remember rightly) was to make holes in a tavern table and draw out of the dead timber some magic hell-brew of his own, saying something like,

> *Wine is sap and grapes are wood;*
> *This wooden board yields wine as good.*

Could there possibly be a more self-evident and convincing reference to the abuse arising from wood alcohol? Any critic who would evade so crushing a conclusion, as if it were a coincidence, must be indeed lacking in the logic that has lent stability and consistency to the Higher Criticism. When the fiend describes himself as "the spirit who denies," it is plain enough that we are to read it in the sense of one who denies people the use of spirits. But the conclusive argument to my mind, in the light of all the circumstances both in literature and life, is the fact that Mephistopheles distinctly says of himself, "I am he who always wills the bad and always works the good."

That Prohibition and Prohibitionists willed the bad no righteous or Christian person will doubt for a moment. That Prohibition and Prohibitionists eventually work the good may appear for the moment more doubtful. And yet there is one sense in which Prohibition has already worked some good; and may yet work very much more good. Wood alcohol is not in itself a happy example; and no judicious wine-taster will expect to find the best vintages in a liquid drawn by a devil out of a dinner-table. But there really is already in America a large number of people who are producing drinks in an equally domestic fashion; and drinks for their own dinner-tables if not out of them. It is not by any means true that all this home-made drink is poison. The presence of the devil is plain enough in the pleasing scheme of the American Government to poison all the alcohol under its control, so that anybody drinking it may be duly murdered; but murder has become almost the ordinary official method of the enforcement of a teetotal taste in beverages.

But the private brews differ very widely; multitudes are quite harmless and some are quite excellent. I know an American university where practically every one of the professors brews his own beer; some of them experimenting in two or three different kinds. But what is especially delightful is this: that with this widespread revival of the old human habit of home-brewing, much of that old human atmosphere that went with it has really reappeared. The professor of the higher metaphysics will be proud of his strong ale; the professor of the lower mathematics (otherwise known as high finance) will allege something more subtle in his milder ale; the professor of moral theology (whose ale I am sure is the strongest of all) will offer to drink all the other dons under the table without any ill effect on the health. Prohibition has to that extent actually worked the good, in spite of so malignantly and murderously willing the evil. And the good is this: the restoration of legitimate praise and pride for the creative crafts of the home.

This being the case, it seems that some of our more ardent supporters might well favour a strong, simple, and sweeping policy. Let Congress or Parliament pass a law not only prohibiting fermented liquor, but practically prohibiting everything else. Let the Government forbid bread, beef, boots, hats, and coats; let there be a law against anybody indulging in chalk, cheese, leather, linen, tools, toys, tales, pictures, or newspapers. Then, it would seem by serious sociological analogy, all human families will begin vigorously to produce all these things for themselves; and the youth of the world will really return.

The American Ideal

Sidelights, 1932

There is nothing the matter with Americans except their ideals. The real American is all right; it is the ideal American who is all wrong. It is the code and conception of life imposed from above, much more than the merely human faults and weaknesses working up from below.

In so far as the citizens of the Western democracy have really gone wrong, they have not inherently or quite naturally gone wrong. They have been taught wrong; instructed wrong; educated wrong; exalted and uplifted wrong. A huge heresy, rather peculiar to modern times, yet singularly uncriticised by modern critics, has actually perverted them in a way which is not really very consonant to their personalities. The real, natural Americans are candid, generous, capable of a beautiful wonder and gratitude; enthusiastic about things external to themselves; easily contented and not particularly conceited. They have been deliberately and dogmatically taught to be conceited. They have been systematically educated in a theory of enthusiasm, which degrades it into mere egotism. The American has received as a sort of religion the notion that blowing his own trumpet is as important as the trump of doom.

It is, I am almost certain, in the main an example of the hardening effect of a heresy, and even of a hostile heresy. There are more examples of it than those admit who ignore the peril of heresy. The Scots are an example; they were never naturally Calvinists; and when they break free, it is to become very romantic figures like Stevenson or Cunninghame Graham. The Americans were never naturally boomsters or business bullies. They would have been much happier and more themselves as a race of simple and warm-hearted country people eager for country sports or gazing at the wonders in country fairs. An egotistic heresy, produced by the modern heathenry, has taught them against all their Christian instincts that boasting is better than courtesy and pride better than humility.

It is queer to note how raw and recent is the heresy; and how little it has been spotted by any heresy-hunt. We have heard much of modern polygamy or promiscuity reversing the Christian idea of purity. We have heard something, and we ought to hear more, of modern capitalism and commercialism reversing the Christian idea of charity to the poor. But we have not heard much about Advertisement, with its push, publicity, and self-assertion, reversing the idea of Christian humility. Yet we can at once test the ethics of publicity by removing it from public life; by merely applying it to private life. What should we think, in a private party, if an old gentleman had written on his shirtfront in large fine flowing hand: "I am the only well-bred person in this company." What should we think of any person of taste and humour who went about wearing a placard inscribed "Please note quiet charm of my personality." What should we say if people gravely engraved on their visiting card the claim to be the handsomest or the wittiest or the most subtly, strangely attractive people about town. We should not only think, with great accuracy, that they were behaving like asses, and certainly destroying beforehand any social advantages they might really have. We should also think they were wantonly reversing and destroying a principle of social amenity and moral delicacy, recognized in all civilised states and ages, but especially emphasized in the ethics of Christianity. Yet modern business, especially in America, does really enforce this sort of publicity in public life; and has begun to press it even in private life. But the point to be emphasized here is that it is really pressed upon most of the Americans;

they are goaded and driven into this sort of public life; large numbers of them would have been perfectly contented with private life. They would have endured it even if it had retained all the old decency and dignity of private life. For this is where the critic must deal most delicately with the subtlety of their simplicity.

The Americans are always excused as a new nation; though it is no longer exactly a new excuse. But in truth these terms are very misleading; and in some ways they have rather the atmosphere of an old nation. Over whole tracts of that vast country, they are certainly what we should call an old-fashioned nation. In no nation in the world are so many people attached to a certain sort of old texts, familiar quotations, or the pieces of sentiment that were written on the pink pages of Victorian albums. A popular book was published, while I was in America, bearing the somewhat alarming name of *Heart Throbs*, from which compilation one might learn that some great and grim judge of High Court had for his favourite poem "Grandmother's Blessing," or that some colossus of commerce, a Steel-King or an Oil-King, preferred the simple lines entitled, "Daddy's Hat." It is only fair to say that some of these hard-headed and ruthless rulers had never forgotten the real classical claims of "Love's Young Dream," or "The Seven Ages of Man." Some may sneer at these extracts, but surely not at their novelty or crudity. I do not mention them for the purpose of sneering at them, but, on the contrary, for the purpose of showing that there must be a great block of solid and normal sentiment, even of traditional sentiment. And people having that sentiment, people inheriting that tradition, would not necessarily, on their own account, have become believers in selfish, sensational self-advertisement. I suspect, as a matter of fact, that there is rather less of such callous and contemptuous egoism in America than anywhere else. The older civilisations, some of which I will venture to call the more civilised civilisations, have a great many advantages in variety of culture and a conspectus of criticism; but I should guess that their wickedness is more wicked. A Frenchman can be much more cynical and sceptical than an American; a German much more morbid and perverted than an American; an Englishman much more frozen and sophisticated with pride. What has happened to America is that a number of people who were meant to be heroic and fighting farmers, at once peasants and pioneers, have been swept by the pestilence of a particular fad or false doctrine; the ideal which has and deserves the detestable title of Making Good. The very words are a hypocrisy, that would have been utterly unintelligible to any man of any other age or creed; as meaningless to a Greek sophist as to a Buddhist monk. For they manage, by one mean twist of words, to combine the notion of making money with the entirely opposite notion of being good. But the abnormality of this notion can best be seen, as I have said, in its heathen and barbaric appeal to a brazen self-praise. Selling the goods meant incidentally, of course, lying about the goods; but it was almost worse that it meant bragging about the goods.

There is a very real sense in which certain crudities in the Americans are not so much a part of American crudity as actually a part of American culture. They are not mere outbreaks of human nature; they are something systematically impressed upon human nature. It is not for nothing that some of the most prominent features of their actual academic training are things like schools of commerce or schools of journalism. There is a vital distinction between these things and all that the world has generally meant by a school; especially the most scholastic sort of school. Even those who think little of learning Greek and Latin will agree that it carried with it a vague suggestion of admiring Greeks and Latins. The schoolboy was supposed in some sense to feel inferior. But even in a commercial academy the boy is not occupied in gazing at some great millionaire doing a straddle in wheat, with the feelings of the simplest pagan of antiquity gazing at the Colossus of Rhodes. It would not do him much good if he did; but in general practise he does not. If he learns anything, he learns to do a straddle in wheat himself, or to hope that he will do it as acrobatically as any other acrobat. He does not even learn to venerate Mr. Rockefeller, but only to imitate Mr. Rockefeller.

Nor does the practical study of journalism lead to any particular veneration for literature. The qualities inculcated and encouraged are the same as those which commerce inculcates and encourages. I say it with no particular hostility or bitterness, but it is a fact that the school of commerce or the school of journalism might almost as well be called a school of impudence or a school of swagger or a school of grab and greed.

But the point is that people are taught to be impudent or greedy, not that they are naturally impudent and greedy. As a matter of fact, they are not. And that is the whole paradox of the position, which I have already suggested and should like here to expand. I have seen in the United States young people, coming out of this course of culture, who actually pulled themselves together to be rude, as normal young people have always pulled themselves together to be polite. They were shy in fact and shameless on principle. They would ask rude questions, but they were as timid about asking a rude question as an ordinary youth about paying a compliment. They would use the most brazen methods to induce somebody to see them, and anybody who did see them would pity them for their bashfulness. They were always storming the stage in a state of stage fright.

The very simple explanation of this puzzling contradiction is that they were perfectly nice and normal people in themselves, but they had never been left to themselves by those who were always telling them to assert themselves. They had been bounced into bouncing and bullied into being bullies. And the explanation is the existence of this modern heresy, or false ideal, that has been preached to everybody by every organ of publicity and plutocracy: the theory that self-praise is the only real recommendation.

I have suggested that the American character might have developed in an infinitely more healthy and human fashion if it had not been for this heresy. Of course the American character would in any case have been very much more alert and lively and impetuous than the English character. But that has nothing to do with the particular features and fashions of commercial advertisement and ambition. There are many other races that are more vivacious or vehement than the English and who yet live the normal life of contented country folk, and practise the traditional ideas of modesty and courtesy.

The trouble with the false commercial ideal is that it has made these men struggle against modesty as if it were morbidity; and actually try to coarsen their natural courtesy, as other men stifle a natural crudity. I do not think that bragging and go-getting are American faults. I hate them as American virtues; I think the quarrel is not so much with the men as with the gods: the false gods they have been taught to worship and still only worship with half their hearts. And these gods of the heathen are stone and brass, but especially brass; and there is an eternal struggle in that half-hearted idolatry; for often, while the gods are of brass, the hearts are of gold.

Marriage and the Modern Mind

Sidelights, 1932

I have been requested to write something about Marriage and the Modern Mind. It would perhaps be more appropriate to write about Marriage and the Modern Absence of Mind. In much of their current conduct, those who call themselves "modern" seem to have abandoned the use of reason; they have sunk back into their own subconsciousness, perhaps under the influence of the psychology now most fashionable in the drawing-room; and it is an understatement to say that they act more automatically than the animals. Wives and husbands seem to leave home more in the manner of somnambulists.

If anybody thinks I exaggerate the mindlessness of modern comment on this matter, I am content to refer him to the inscription under a large photograph of a languishing lady, in the newspaper now before me. It states that the lady has covered herself with glory as the inventor of "Companionate Divorce." It goes on to state, in her own words, that she will marry her husband again if he asks her again; and that she has been living with him ever since she was divorced from him. If mortal muddle-headedness can go deeper than that, in this vale of tears, I should like to see it. The newspaper picture and paragraph I can actually see; and stupidity so stupendous as that has never been known in human history before. The first thing to say about marriage and the modern mind, therefore, is that it is natural enough that people with no mind should want to have no marriage.

But there is another simple yet curious illustration of modern stupidity in the matter. And that is that, while I have known thousands of people arguing about marriage, sometimes furiously against it, sometimes rather feebly in favour of it, I have never known any one of the disputants begin by asking what marriage is. They nibble at it with negative criticism; they chip pieces off it and exhibit them as specimens, called "hard cases"; they treat every example of the rule as an exception to the rule; but they never look at the rule. They never ask, even in the name of history or human curiosity, what the thing is, or why it is, or why the overwhelming mass of mankind believes that it must be. Let us begin with the alphabet, as one does with infants.

Marriage, humanly considered, rests upon a fact of human nature, which we may call a fact of natural history. All the higher animals require much longer parental protection than do the lower; the baby elephant is a baby much longer than the baby jellyfish. But even beyond this natural tutelage, man needs something quite unique in nature. Man alone needs education. I know that animals train their young in particular tricks; as cats teach kittens to catch mice. But this is a very limited and rudimentary education. It is what the hustling millionaires call Business Education; that is, it is not education at all. Even at that, I doubt whether any pupil presenting himself for Matriculation or entrance into Standard VI, would now be accepted if flaunting the stubborn boast of a capacity to catch mice. Education is a complex and many-sided culture to meet a complex and many-sided world; and the animals, especially the lower animals, do not require it. It is said that the herring lays thousands of eggs in a day. But, though evidently untouched by the stunt of Birth-Control, in other ways the herring is highly modern. The mother herring has no need to remember her own children, and certainly therefore, no need to remember her own mate. But then the duties of a young herring, just entering upon life, are very simple and largely instinctive; they come, like a modern religion, from within. A herring does not have to be taught to take a bath; for he never takes anything else. He does not have to be trained to take off a hat to a lady herring, for he never puts on a hat, or any other Puritanical disguise to hamper the Greek grace of his movements. Consequently his father and mother have no common task or responsibility; and they can safely model their union upon the boldest and most advanced of the new novels and plays. Doubtless the female herring does say to the male herring, "True marriage must be free from the dogmas of priests; it must be a thing of one exquisite moment." Doubtless the male herring does say to the female herring, "When Love has died in the heart, Marriage is a mockery in the home."

This philosophy, common among the lower forms of life, is obviously of no use among the higher. This way of talking, however suitable for herrings, or even for rats and rabbits, who are said to be so prolific, does not meet the case of the creature endowed with reason. The young of the human species, if they are to reach the full possibilities of the human culture, so various, so laborious, so elaborate, must be under the protection of responsible persons through very long periods of mental and moral growth. I know there are some who grow merely impatient and irrational at this point; and say they could do just as well without education. But they lie; for they could not even express that opinion, if they had not laboriously learnt one particular language in which to talk nonsense. The moment we have realised this, we understand why the relations of the sexes normally remain static; and in most cases, permanent. For though, taking this argument alone, there would be a case for the father and mother parting when the children were mature, the number of people who at the age of fifty really wish to bolt with the typist or be abducted by the chauffeur is less than is now frequently supposed.

Well, even if the family held together as long as that, it would be better than nothing; but in fact even such belated divorce is based on bad psychology. All the modern licence is based on bad psychology; because it is based on the latest psychology. And that is like knowing the last proposition in Euclid without knowing the first. It is the first elements of psychology that the people called "modern" do not know. One of the things they cannot comprehend is the thing called "atmosphere"; as they show by shrieking with derision when anybody demands "a religious atmosphere" in the schools. The atmosphere of something safe and settled can only exist where people see it in the future as well as in the past. Children know exactly what is meant by having really come home; and the happier of them keep something of the feeling as they grow up. But they cannot keep the feeling for ten minutes, if there is an assumption that Papa is only waiting for Tommy's twenty-first birthday to carry the typist off to Trouville; or that the chauffeur actually has the car at the door, that Mrs. Brown may go off the moment Miss Brown has "come out."

That is, in practical experience, the basic idea of marriage; that the founding of a family must be on a firm foundation; that the rearing of the immature must be protected by something patient and enduring. It is the common conclusion of all mankind; and all common sense is on its side. A small minority of what may be called the idle Intelligentsia, have, just recently and in our corner of the world, criticised this idea of Marriage in the name of what they call the Modern Mind. The first obvious or apparent question is how they deal with the practical problem of children. The first apparent answer is that they do not deal with it at all.

At best, they propose to get rid of babies, or the problem of babies, in one of three typically modern ways. One is to say that there shall be no babies. This suggestion may be addressed to the individual; but it is addressed to every individual. Another is that the father should instantly send the babies, especially if they are boys, to a distant and inaccessible school, with bounds like a prison, that the babies may become men, in a manner that is considered impossible in the society of their own father. But this is rapidly ceasing to be a Modern method; and even the Moderns have found that it is rather behind the times. The third way, which is unimpeachably Modern, is to imitate Rousseau, who left his baby on the door-step of the Foundling Hospital. It is true that, among the Moderns, it is generally nothing so human or traditional as the Foundling Hospital. The baby is to be left on the door-step of the State Department for Education and Universal Social Adjustment. In short, these people mean, with various degrees of vagueness, that the place of the Family can now be taken by the State.

The difficulty of the first method, and so far, of the second and third, is that they may be carried out. The suggestion is made to everybody in the hope that it will not be accepted by everybody; it is offered to all in the hope that it may not be accepted by all. If *nobody* has any children, everybody can still be satisfied by Birth-Control methods and justified by Birth-Control arguments. Even the reformers do not want this; but they cannot offer any objection to any individual—or every individual. In somewhat the same way, Rousseau may act as an individual and not as a social philosopher, but he could not prevent all the other individuals acting as individuals. And if all the babies born in the world were left on the door-step of the Foundling Hospital, the Hospital, and the door-step, would have to be considerably enlarged. Now something like this is what has really happened, in the vague and drifting centralization of our time. The Hospital has been enlarged into the School and then into the State; not the guardian of some abnormal children, but the guardian of all normal children. Modern mothers and fathers, of the emancipated sort, could not do their quick-change acts of bewildering divorce and scattered polygamy, if they did not believe in a big benevolent Grandmother, who could ultimately take over ten million children by very grandmotherly legislation.

This modern notion about the State is a delusion. It is not founded on the history of real States, but entirely on reading about unreal or ideal States, like the Utopias of Mr. Wells. The real State, though a necessary human combination, always has been and always will be, far too large, loose, clumsy, indirect and even insecure, to be the "home" of the human young who are to be trained in the human tradition. If mankind had not been organised into families, it would never have had the organic power to be organised into commonwealths. Human culture is handed down in the customs of countless households; it is the only way in which human culture can remain human. The households are right to confess a common loyalty or federation under some king or republic. But the king cannot be the nurse in every nursery; or even the government become the governess in every schoolroom. Look at the real story of States, modern as well as ancient, and you will see a dissolving view of distant and uncontrollable things, making up most of the politics of the earth. Take the most populous centre. China is now called a Republic. In consequence it is ruled by five contending armies and is much less settled than when it was an Empire. What has preserved China has been its domestic religion. South America, like all Latin lands, is full of domestic graces and gaieties; but it is governed by a series of revolutions. We ourselves may be governed by a Dictator; or by a General Strike; or by a banker living in New York. Government grows more elusive every day. But the traditions of humanity support humanity; and the central one is this tradition of Marriage. And the essential of it is that a free man and a free woman choose to found on earth the only voluntary state; the only state which creates and which loves its citizens. So long as these real responsible beings stand together, they can survive all the vast changes, deadlocks, and disappointments which make up mere political history. But if they fail each other, it is as certain as death that "the State" will fail them.

Magic and Fantasy in Fiction

Sidelights, 1932

It may seem but a mild form of dalliance to trifle with the word Magic as a term of criticism, when it has recently been so useful to the clergy as a term of abuse. We know that Dr. Barnes of Birmingham has shown all the ancient activity of a witch-smeller, in pursuing those suspected of believing it, as the witch-smellers pursued those suspected of practising it. He does this, I understand, to show that he is a Liberal Churchman. I have no intention of discussing such matters here; but it does happen that this use of the term, considered as a text, throws some light on the first facts of its relation to literature, and especially to legend. The ecclesiastic in question always uses it as covering all the rather wide field of religious doctrines in which he does not happen to believe. But in this we have at the start the neglect of an important and rather interesting distinction. The word Magic was widely used as a term of abuse, because it was really a question of abuse in more senses than one. Magic was the abuse of preternatural powers, by lower agents whose work was preternatural but not supernatural. It was founded on that profound maxim of *diabolus simius Dei*; the devil is the ape of God. Magic was a monkey trick of imitation of the divine functions; and there was therefore nothing stranger in either the similarity or the dissimilarity. But to talk of the higher mysteries or miracles as forms of magic, or as coming forth from magic, is to reverse the whole story. It is as if we were to say that the Black Mass gradually evolved into the Mass. It is like saying that an Abbot establishing the rule of St. Benedict was a parody of the Abbot of Misrule. It is like saying that the disciples who said the Lord's Prayer had borrowed it from the witches who said it backwards.

But in all that mythology and popular poetry, out of which our written literature sprang, this distinction is dimly felt long before it was clarified by Christianity. There is always the sense of one sort of magic which is an enemy and an enslaver. We all know that there are jokes of philology, or examples in which a word has been turned upside down and come to mean the contrary of itself. The learned will readily grow gay over the history of the word "buxom," or the word "nervous." There is almost as comic a contradiction in our use of the word "enchantment" when we say "I was enchanted to meet Mr. Miggs," or "The view of Brixton from the station is simply enchanting." But in the vast unwritten literature of mankind enchantment was almost always regarded as a curse. There is in enchantment almost always an idea of captivity. Sometimes the stricken victim is literally struck motionless, as when men are turned to stone by Gorgon, or the prince of the Arabian Tale is clamped to the earth in marble. Quite as often the victim of enchantment wanders through the woods as a white hind, or flies with apparent freedom as a parrot or a wild swan. But he always talks of his very freedom as a wandering imprisonment. And the reason is that there is always in such witchcraft the note of travesty; the man is disguised and in a double sense "guyed"; as when the youth in Apuleius feels literally that the witches have made an ass of him. In contrast with this, it will be noted that the good miracles, the acts of the saints and heroes, are always acts of restoration. They give the victim back his personality; and it is a normal and not a super-normal personality. The miracle gives back his legs to the lame man; but it does not turn him into a large centipede. It gives eyes to the blind; but only a regular and respectable number of eyes. The paralytic is told to stretch forth his hands, which is the gesture of liberation from fetters; but not to spread himself as a sort of Briarean octopus radiating in all directions and losing the human form. There runs through the whole tradition the idea that black magic is that which blots out or disguises the true form of a thing; while white magic, in the good sense, restores it to its own form and not another. St. Nicholas brings two children alive out of a pot when they have already been boiled down into soup; which may be said to mark the extreme assertion of form against formlessness. But Medea, being a witch, puts an old man into a pot and promises to bring out a young man; that is, another man. Also Medea, being a witch, does not keep her word.

This division, even in the deep roots of legend and primitive literature, would help critics very much in judging the real principles of uncanny or fantastic fiction. There is no reason within reason, why literature should not describe the demonic as well as the divine aspect of mystery or myth. What is really remarkable is that in modern fiction, in an age accused of frivolity, in an age perhaps only too headlong in its pursuit of happiness, or at least of hedonism, the only popular sort of fantasy is the unhappy fantasy. There is a certain amount of fantasy that is avowedly fantastic, in the sense of unreal; mostly in the form of fairy-tales ostensibly written for children. But, on the whole, when the serious modern novel has dealt with the serious preternatural agency, it has not only been serious but sad. This contrast appears first and most vividly in the comfortable and even convivial Victorian novelists. They often thought it enough to make their human characters comfortable; but if they did suggest any superhuman characters, they were generally uncomfortable as well as uncanny. These humanitarians of the nineteenth century were haunted by no spirits, except a few thin ghosts; but these were the lost spirits of Calvinists of the seventeenth century. In their philosophies, the humanitarians believed in heaven but not in hell. In their novels, they believed in hell but not in heaven. Dickens did indeed attempt in the *Christmas Carol* to make a positive polytheism of three versions of Father Christmas; a curious temporal Trinity. But the warmest Dickensian (and I hope I am one of the warmest) will admit that these solid guides are far less convincing than the visions that they reveal. They have not that purely poetic reality that does belong to the hints of horror and the glimpses of nightmare in the novels of Dickens. The man with the waxen face, in one of his short stories, is by every definition a ghost; but he is a ghost in whom we can believe, as compared with these gods in whom we cannot believe. It was even more marked in Wilkie Collins, who had less sense of the serious need of spiritual things. He could indulge himself in dubious superstition; he would have thought it superstitious to indulge in the symbols of positive religion. The whole point of *Armadale* is a family curse as frankly psychic as a family ghost. But we should be much disconcerted, in wandering through a Wilkie Collins story, to meet an angel with wings and a halo when we were looking for a gentleman with whiskers and a high hat.

In short, in so far as humanity became once more heathen, it believed more and more in the old dehumanizing spell, the freezing of the will by trance or terror, and less in the other legend of the hero or the helper who can break the spell. There has lately been a return to the more heartening heroic legend; but that is exactly in so far as there has been a reaction against the merely heathen spirit. A story like *The Bridge of San Luis Rey* is strictly supernatural and not merely preternatural. But even here the habit of the nineteenth century persists into the twentieth, especially in the instinctive selection of form. No man has done more to bring back a breath of happiness into fantasy than Mr. Walter de la Mare. He has testified that even when we do look through magic casements, it is not absolutely necessary that the faerie lands should be forlorn. But, by something almost like a sense of delicacy, he has generally brought his good news in the form of rhymes; and in a sense merely of nursery rhymes. It gives a note, not exactly of irresponsibility, but of a certain shyness and appeal to innocence. But when it is a matter of more massive treatment, even he inherits something of the now established "modern" spirit, which can deal most decisively with the darker experience. And few things that he, or indeed anybody else, has written have so much of what can really be called realism as the diabolism of "Seaton's Aunt."

It is perhaps a symbol that Henry James called one of his books "The Two Magics"; but entirely forgot to mention any magic except one. For in the other case the word is a mere metaphor, used of some trick or tact; and the only tale that is really about magic is about black magic. It was a horrible and powerful story about two children practically possessed of devils. I wish somebody with the genius of James could really write a book on "The Two Magics"; and say something in the other of the gesture that can cast out devils. As it is, even the most sensitive and spiritual modern fiction leaves us rather with the Swinburnian impression that "even He who cast seven devils out of Magdalene" could scarcely do the same for Seaton's aunt. I am well aware that there has been an interlude of a rather different sort of magic, which professed for a time to be neither black nor white. If I call it colourless magic, I do not mean it in contempt; but rather as crystals are colourless, or diamonds or clear water. It came with what was called the Celtic School when Victorian ethics, always rather exhausting, were rather exhausted. In that reaction it was rational enough for Mr. W.B. Yeats to bid us "Come clear of the nets of wrong and of right"; and so ignore even the two kinds of positive magic, the net of St. Peter and the snare of Satan. But I, who have an inexhaustible admiration for everything that Mr. Yeats says and writes, may be allowed to testify that any attempt to live entirely in the crystal of colourless magic ends in the very convincing exclamation of the elf in his own play, "I am tired of winds and waters and pale lights." So were we; and so eventually was Mr. Yeats; for his powerful mind seems to have turned more and more of late to structural visions of the whole course of history and humanity; social and rather sweeping statements like intellectual cyclones, which must nevertheless in their nature be not only mystical but moral. And though I do not care very much myself for the cabalistic games and cryptograms that seem to amuse him at present, they have a certain mathematical solidity like Babylonian bricks. It is a good thing in that sense to be a Cubist, when winds and water have tempted you too much to be a Curvist. But in any case I am convinced that every deep or delicate treatment of the magical theme, from the lightest jingle of Peacock Pie, which may seem as nonsensical as Lear, to the most profound shaking of the phenomenal world, as in some of the best stories of Algernon Blackwood, will always be found to imply an indirect relation to the ancient blessing and cursing; and it is almost as vital that it should be moral as that it should not be moralizing. Magic for magic's sake, like art for art's sake, is found in fact to be too shallow, and to be unable to live without drawing upon things deeper than itself. To say that all real art is in black and white is but another way of saying that it is in light and darkness; and there is no fantasy so irresponsible as really to escape from the alternative.

After all, it is perhaps no matter of surprise that Bishop Barnes of Birmingham should see a link between the Magician and the Mass. There is a sort of logical link between them; the logical link that connects Yes and No. In other words, they are exact contraries; like light and darkness, which are often classed together because they are often mentioned at once. They cross each other with the complete collision and contradiction that belongs to "The Two Magics." The Magician is the Man when he seeks to become a God, and, being a usurper, can hardly fail to be a tyrant. Not being the maker, but only the distorter, he twists all things out of their intended shape, and imprisons natural things in unnatural forms. But the Mass is exactly the opposite of a Man seeking to be a God. It is a God seeking to be a Man; it is God giving His creative life to mankind as such, and restoring the original pattern of their manhood; making not gods, nor beasts, nor angels; but, by the original blast and miracle that makes all things new, turning men into men.

On the New Prudery

Avowals and Denials, 1934

I have discovered that the New Prudery is much narrower and more prudish than the Old Prudery; even of the most dingy and dismal latter days of Puritanism. The discovery interests me not a little, for I always thought I had a pure and perfect and spotless hatred of the ordinary sort of Puritanism. But the pure Puritan is not so grim and negative and repressive as the pure Progressive. The New Prudery does not come out of stale sects or old shabby chapels: it comes out of all the new clubs, new leagues, new guilds of art and culture, new summer schools of science and philanthropy. It is altogether a thing of the Future; or at least of the Futurists, who think they will dominate the future. It is even notably a thing of the young, and, what is far more extraordinary, of the young who call themselves the free. And the Ten Commandments of the Christian, or even the Ten Hundred Commandments of the Puritan, are themselves like perfect freedom compared with the terrorism and rigidity of its new Taboos.

I will give a practical case to prove the sober truth of what I say. A certain lady, who happened to be looking after the child of a younger lady, discovered the infant to be showing a dark and morbid interest in the story of Joan of Arc. The younger lady belonged to this school which prides itself upon being young; not at all in the sense in which the poet speaks of drinking ale in the country of the young, but rather in that curious country of the young where nobody is allowed to drink ale, but either cold water or cocktails—sometimes winding up with arsenic. In short, she had all the most progressive ideas, and she, the lady who was the mother, informed the other lady, who was acting *in loco parentis*, that the following rules must be strictly observed in the teaching, or for that matter, the playtime, of her child. (1) The child must never read fairy-tales or be allowed to hear about fairies. (2) The child must never hear of the very existence of fighting in any form. (3) The child must be strictly guarded from the shameful rumour that there is such a thing as religion or religious beliefs. I will leave the lady confronted with the problem of narrating, under these limitations, the historical story of St. Joan of Arc. The child must not hear of the childhood of St. Joan, when she played round the tree of the fairies; the child must not hear of the life of St. Joan, which I fear was largely occupied with fighting; the child must not hear of the death of St. Joan, which was a result of the fighting and raises the very indelicate question of faith; or what St. Joan was fighting about and what she was dying for. I should like to see the expurgated or bowdlerized life of the fifteenth-century heroine.

Now it is nonsense to say that this sort of thing is liberal or emancipated; it is nonsense to pretend that it is not much more narrow and obscurantist than the blackest pessimism of the worst days of Puritanism. I am not comparing it with my own religion: I am comparing it with the religion I dislike most; and I say it is quite certain that the Puritanism I dislike most was a wild burst of freedom, and a paradise of pleasures and liberties, compared with this sort of thing. I do not like the Scottish Sabbath, or the old dark shuttered houses, or the long days passed in reading dull divinity or in doing nothing. But they were better fun than this; they were a great deal more free than this. For instance, it is not a plea for Puritanism, it is a part of the proverbial protest against Puritanism, to say that people were only allowed to read the Bible, especially on Sundays. But the Bible is an Arabian Nights of romantic and passionate stories compared with the limitations laid down by this enlightened person. The Bible is an *Encyclopaedia Britannica* of varied topics and multitudinous human interests compared with the amount of knowledge that can be conveyed under those new conditions. Nobody could read the Bible without gaining a glorious mass of information about fighting, about faith, about religions true and false, about mystical or magical or mysterious beings such as hover round man in all the legends and literature of the world. The little boys who grew up in the dark Calvinistic houses of our great-grandfathers did, in actual fact, grow up with their heads full of a noble noise of conflict and crisis; valiant and vigorous action described in the grandest English that our national history has known; the noise of the captains and the shouting; the chariots of Israel and the horses thereof; and he that drew a bow at a venture and smote the king between the joints of the harness; and he whose driving was known from afar off, for he drove furiously. That, under all its other disadvantages, is what I call being educated; certainly it is being much better educated than a miserable little prig who must not be told that Joan of Arc carried a battle-banner, but must be assured that she only carried an umbrella.

So far to limit war literature is simply to limit literature, and the Bible alone would be a better training than a silly scrupulosity that should remain ignorant of the war-horse whose neck was clothed with thunder, or that wild quarry that laughed at the shaking of the spear. It is odd, however, to remember that in those dark Puritan homes of which I have spoken, another exception was proverbially made, and children, even on Sundays, were allowed to read *The Pilgrim's Progress*. That is, they were allowed to read what may be a fairy-tale: what is certainly a fighting tale and what has actually, according to countless testimonies, been no bad substitute for other nursery novels or romances. Anyhow, a child with a free soul might find something in it of a fighting spirit; and never forget the instant when Apollyon straddled over the whole breadth of the way; or the dying Great-heart gave up his sword and all the trumpets sounded for him on the other side. I would rather be a dingy, dusty, bewildered seventeenth-century Calvinistic tinker than never have heard in this vale of tears any distant note of that trumpet.

The intellectual interest of this bit of bigotry lies in this: that the new philosophies and new religions and new social systems cannot draw up their own plans for emancipating mankind without still further enslaving mankind. They cannot carry out even what they regard as the most ordinary reforms without instantly imposing the most extraordinary restrictions. We are to live under a sort of martial law lest we should hear of anything martial. All our children are to be watched by governesses lest they should be told, even by accident, of a fairy or a fight with robbers. Everybody is to be drilled with an anti-militarist discipline which is quite as stiff and strict as a militarist discipline. All the nursery stories are to be subject to a Censor, who shall object if they are too pretty, as the very dullest sort of Victorian or philistine Censor would object if they were too ugly. A new Mrs. Grundy shall arise, who will blush not at natural facts, but only at preternatural fancies. A new Paul Pry will be sent to sneak about our houses, or look through our keyholes, to find out whether (in some den of infamy) a child is being taught to admire courage. Whatever we may think of the relative claims of the two religions, one fact is now logically self-evident: that the new religion, every bit as much as the old religion, will be a persecuting religion. It will be, by its very nature, a thing fighting for its life against the normal forces of human nature; every bit as much as has been alleged of any system of asceticism or self-denial in the past. It is indeed a case in which extremes meet; though, in truth, extremes often meet because they are much less extreme than people suppose. The modern Pacifist is really very like the ancient Puritan; the man who now has a horror of all theology is very like the man who then had a horror of all things except theology. And the proof is in the practical case. The old Calvinist, like the new Communist, really did forbid children to read stories about fairies. The old Puritan, like the new peace-man, really would forbid boys to read a penny dreadful about pirates. The new idealist is not even new, in the manner of the babe unborn. He is our own Puritan great-grandfather dreadfully risen from the dead.

On the Return of the Barbarian

Avowals and Denials, 1934

The common or garden German may be described as the beer-garden German. As such, I love and embrace him. Just lately, and at historic intervals, he becomes the bear-garden German. As such I regard him with a love more mystical and distant, and would prefer to avoid his embrace. For the embraces of bears, even in the most festive and gorgeously illuminated bear-gardens, are apt to show that over-emphasis, or excess of pressure, which is the fault of the German temperament.

Now, ever since Herr Hitler began to turn the beer-garden into a bear-garden, there has been an increasing impression on sensitive and intelligent minds that something very dangerous has occurred. A particular sort of civilisation has turned back towards barbarism. When I say this, I do not mean what half a hundred intellectuals of the enlightened and emancipated Press mean, or imagine that they mean. I do not mean that fighting, or fierce anger, or the unmasking of the respectable, or even the despoliation of the rich, is necessarily barbarism. It is not; even if it is wrong, it is not. It might arise from a perfectly rational, and indeed from a perfectly traditional, inheritance of human protest. Nor do I mean (God forbid) that modern banks, or modern books, or remarkable realistic studies of this or that, or the perpetually shifting fog that they call physical science, or the cranks who run naked because they have never thought about clothes, or the louts who go Communist because they have never thought about private property, or the wasters who sponge on six wives and call it Free Love—I do not mean that any of that sort of liberty or laxity or liberal-mindedness has ever had anything to do with civilisation. The very word civilisation is from a city. The very nature of a city is something that has to be built according to a plan; and with some sacrifice from the citizens in fitting in with that plan. There are many modern things called Culture which one would be glad to see destroyed by Goths and Vandals, let alone by mild modern Germans, who do whatever they are told. There are many modern books, advertised as masterpieces of literary art, which I should be glad to see destroyed by rats and worms, let alone Hitlerites. There are many idiotic experiments in nakedness, in the northern climate of Europe, which might well be exterminated by germs, let alone by Germans.

No; the essential point does not concern any of those questions, such as arose also in the fall of Roman civilisation; questions in which the barbarians might happen to be right, and the decayed citizens of civilisation might happen to be wrong. It is none the less true that civilised men must defend civilisation against any sort of barbarians. And the reason is, that civilisation retains the power of curing its own diseases, whereas it is only by an accident that the barbarians may be free from the disease. If England is prostrate with influenza, it may conceivably (of course) be invaded by Eskimos, who may conceivably (of course) be generically immune from influenza. But that does not mean that Eskimo culture is really superior to English culture. It does not even mean that Eskimos could guard against influenza so promptly or practically as Englishmen could guard against a return of influenza. The advantage is with our culture—even germ-culture. The bother with the barbarian is that he is right by accident, and sometimes does not even know why he is right. The case for the civilised man is that he is wrong by his own fault, and knows it is his own fault; and, knowing that he is wrong, may have some reason to put himself right. Never be merely on the side of barbarism, for it always means the destruction of all that men have ever understood, by men who do not understand it.

That is the sense in which a detached and dispassionate person, watching that strange turn of the tide in the centre of tribal Germany, will be disposed to suspect a tragedy. The Germans have done many things that many of us may think right, but there is nothing to hold them back from doing anything that all of us think wrong. There have been many such ethical eddies in history, and the trouble with the German ones is that they have always been more ethnical than ethical. That is, they have perpetually turned back, by a sort of introspective or centripetal movement, from the judgment of Christendom to the judgment of Germany. The debate always turned from considering whether the German was really right to considering how really right the real German had always been. It is quite true that the word German is used to cover a vast variety of tribes and trends, about which historians may debate as they please. But it is a manifest modern fact that this racial mass has been, even if only recently, solidified by a staggering sense of triumph, and a hypnotic faith, that it is all one people. Oddly enough, indeed, its really staggering triumph was followed very rapidly by a much more staggering defeat. But that is the advantage of hypnotism. That is the charm of illusion and the compelling power of unreality. The Germans, not being realistic, have already forgotten that they were defeated ten years ago; but they still remember vividly that they were victorious fifty years ago. That is the advantage of being a sentimentalist. You only remember what you like to remember. It is also the advantage of being a barbarian.

When we say that something must have its head, we generally say it of some animal with a rather inferior head. A horse may occasionally have its head, but a horseman who had his head, in that blind and instinctive sense, would probably have his head punched by other and more judicious horsemen. The danger of the emergence of anything really barbaric in the world is that we do not know what it will do next, or where it will turn up at last; just as we do not know whether a runaway horse will be stopped by the nearest policeman or will be smashed in a shop-window two miles away. And this, let it be noted, has very little to do with the original cause of the accident, or with whether it was the sort of incident we should call an excuse for the horse, or even a justification for the horse. The horse might have been subjected to a shock that no normal horse could be expected to stand. There would always be, in judging the horse as a horse, a difference between his having shied because a baby threw a ball, or bolted because an anarchist threw a bomb. But we are still judging, justly or unjustly, according to what is called the nature of the beast. Now Barbarism is a beast, and has the nature of the beast. It is not peculiar to any particular movement among Teutons, any more than among Turks or Mongols or Slavs. But in all of these we can mark the moment of history when men turned back towards it, and delayed for centuries the civilisation of mankind. What is really disquieting about this new note of narrow nationalism or tribalism in the north is that there is something shrill and wild about it, that has been heard in those destructive crises of history. There are many marks by which anybody of historical imagination can recognize the recurrence: the monstrous and monotonous omnipresence of one symbol, and that a symbol of which nobody knows the meaning; the relish of the tyrant for exaggerating even his own tyranny, and barking so loud that nobody can even suspect that his bark is worse than his bite; the impatient indifference to all the former friends of Germany, among those who are yet making Germany the only test—all these things have a savour of savage and hasty simplification, which may, in many individuals, correspond to an honest indignation or even idealism, but which, when taken altogether, give an uncomfortable impression of wild men who have merely grown weary of the complexity that we call civilisation.

On Man: Heir of All Ages

Avowals and Denials, 1934

If the modern man is indeed the heir of all the ages, he is often the kind of heir who tells the family solicitor to sell the whole damned estate, lock, stock, and barrel, and give him a little ready money to throw away at the races or the night-clubs. He is certainly not the kind of heir who ever visits his estate: and, if he really owns all the historic lands of ancient and modern history, he is a very absentee landlord. He does not really go down the mines on the historic property, whether they are the Caves of the Cave-Man or the Catacombs of the Christians, but is content with a very hasty and often misleading report from a very superficial and sometimes dishonest mining expert. He allows any wild theories, like wild thickets of thorn and briar, to grow all over the garden and even the graveyard. He will always believe modern testimony in a text-book against contemporary testimony on a tombstone. He sells the family portraits with much more than the carelessness of Charles Surface, and seldom even knows enough about the family even to save a favourite uncle from the wreck. For the adjective "fast," which was a condemnation when applied to profligates, has become a compliment when applied to progressives. I know there are any number of men in the modern world to whom all this does not in the least apply; but the point is that, even where it is obviously applicable, it is not thought particularly culpable. Nevertheless, there are some of us who do hold that the metaphor of inheritance from human history is a true metaphor, and that any man who is cut off from the past, and content with the future, is a man most unjustly disinherited; and all the more unjustly if he is happy in his lot, and is not permitted even to know what he has lost. And I, for one, believe that the mind of man is at its largest, and especially at its broadest, when it feels the brotherhood of humanity linking it up with remote and primitive and even barbaric things.

Mr. Christopher Dawson has written studies of historic and prehistoric problems which have been admired by men distinguished in every way, and especially distinguished from each other. His work has been most warmly praised by critics as different as Dean Inge and Mr. Aldous Huxley and the Rev. C. C. Martindale. But I, for one, value his researches for one particular reason above the rest: that he has given the first tolerably clear and convincing account of the real stages of what his less lucid predecessors loved to call the Evolution of Religion. Whether myths and mystical cults were really evolved along one consistent line, I do not know. But theories about mythology or cults or mysteries were most certainly not evolved along any consistent line. They cut across each other and almost immediately became a tangle of contradictions. First we had the Sun Myth illuminating everything like the sun, and enabling Bishop Whately to prove that Napoleon was a mythical character. Then we had Herbert Spencer and Grant Allen, who said that everything came from ghosts and graves and the worship of ancestors; and then Professor Frazer, who (with all his genius) could not see the sacred tree for the golden bough. Now whatever else be true of these theories of evolution, they are not evolved. The grave does not grow out of the sun; nor even the oak out of the grave; and on no possible theory is Frazer a development of Spencer. They are contrary guesses; and if there is evidence for all of them (as no doubt there is), the evidence only increases the confusion. Mr. Dawson has ordered the confusion without contradicting the evidence; and his conclusion is that there were, broadly, four stages in the spiritual story of humanity.

The first notion, with which the lowest and most primitive savages seem to have begun, was very like the notion with which many of our Higher Thinkers hope that all humanity will end. It was a broad belief in what is now called "the spiritual element in life"; in a spirit almost impersonal but still superior to our material minds; of which we may gain encouraging glimpses and visions. This is the stage of the Shaman, or medicine-man, who, as an independent individual mystic, can tap the vast and vague supernatural power that pervades the world. By special magic rites, with special material objects, herbs, or stones or what not, he could release the mysterious force. For note that this is not pantheism; the sacred tree is hidden in the wood or the dryad is imprisoned in the tree. Now I could not be content with this magic, whether or no it would suit the Higher Thinkers. But I have no sympathy with a man who has no sympathy with this magic; I count no man large-minded or imaginative who has not sometimes felt like a medicine-man. It is quite natural to me, walking in the woods, to wonder fancifully whether whistling back the note of a certain bird, or tasting the juice of a certain berry, would release a glamour or give back a fairyland. I call that being the heir of all the ages.

The second stage is that of the static archaic culture, in which a whole people live a ritual life, generally founded on the seasons of seed or harvest, in which there is no distinction between sacred and profane, because ploughing or fishing are religious forms; and no distinction between king and priest, because the Sacred Emperor rules the whole round of ritual life like a god. China and Egypt and other cultures were of that sort. Here again, I should be dissatisfied with a religion that was a pageant of nature; for I feel the soul, in Sir Thomas Browne's noble phrase, as something other than the elements, that owes no homage unto the sun. But I am much more dissatisfied with a man, pretending to be a man of culture, who merely despises that ritual. I can never see the pageant of harvest without feeling that it is religious, and it gratifies me to think that I am feeling like the first Emperor of China. I call that being the heir of all the ages.

The third phase described is the rise of the world religions, the moral and universal religions; for Buddha and Confucius and the Hebrew Prophets and the first Greek philosophers appeared roughly about the same time. And with them appeared the idea expressed in Sir Thomas Browne's phrase: that the soul is greater than the sun. Henceforth the conscience is more than the cosmos. Either it condemns the cosmos, or ignores the cosmos, as in Buddhism; or it gives it a mystical meaning, as in Platonism; or it sees it as an instrument for producing a grander good, as in Judaism and Christianity. Now I do not myself care about the Buddhist extreme, which almost unmakes the world to make the soul. I do not like Nirvana, which seems indistinguishable from death. But I would not be seen dead in a field, not in the field of any paradise, negative or positive, with the man who has no admiration for the superb renunciation of Buddha, or for the Western equivalent, the star-defying despair of the Stoics. No man has really been alive who has not some time felt that the skies might fall, so that the justice within his conscience should be done; and in the richer tapestry of the Christian there is also a dark thread of the Stoic. I call that being the heir of all the ages.

I will not complete the four phases here, because the last deals with the more controversial question of the Christian system. I merely use them as a convenient classification to illustrate a neglected truth: that a complete human being ought to have all these things stratified in him, so long as they are in the right order of importance, and that man should be a prince looking from the pinnacle of a tower built by his fathers, and not a contemptuous cad, perpetually kicking down the ladders by which he climbed.

On the Instability of the State

Avowals and Denials, 1934

The foreign news which comes to us by the newest and most scientific methods of communication is much more confusing than it was when it was mere gossip. Good communications corrupt good manners. At any rate, they corrupt good methods; and certainly they corrupt good messages. The different statements, for instance, that have been made about the policy of Hitler might almost lead the superstitious to suppose that there are two Hitlers; as some legend once suggested that there were two Neros. Without deciding between the contrasted conceptions, or going at the moment into the question of the value of either of them, it may be worth remarking that one contradiction of this kind has been concerned with this pivotal problem of The Family. On the one side, it would really seem that the German Dictator is concerned to restore the sane and solid status of The Family. He has insisted, though sometimes in rather florid and foolish language, that a woman may fulfil herself rightly in the personal relation; and that she does not find her only freedom in the financial or official relation. He has said a word for large families; and for the resumption of the patriarchal dignity that has figured from the beginning of history. At the same time, we see statements in the newspapers about schemes for supporting all the fads that have recently attacked the family. We read of all the stale theories of Eugenics; the talk of compulsory action to keep the breed in a certain state of bestial excellence; of nosing out every secret of sex or origin, so that nobody may survive who is not Nordic; of setting a hundred quack doctors to preserve an imaginary race in its imaginary purity. Now Eugenics of that sort is, always has been, and always must be, merely a violent assault on The Family. It is, by definition, the taking away from The Family of the decisions that ought to belong to The Family. When those decisions are made in the domestic and individual way, in which they should be made, nobody in his senses ever dreams of describing the decision as Eugenics. The private persons involved do not call the issue of their own private affairs Eugenics; they call it love, or childbirth, or childlessness, or whatever they choose. The whole point of these pseudo-scientific theories always was that they were to be applied wholesale, by some more sweeping and generalizing power than the individual husband or wife or household. The way in which the newspaper reports refer to them, in the case of the New Germany, is not reassuring. But then, on the other hand, the newspaper reports may be lies. Or again, the other and contrary newspaper reports may be lies. I shall here go no further than recording that they cannot both of them be true.

But there is one point about this particular problem of The Family which connects itself, in another way, with the present revolutions and counter-revolutions of Europe. There are certain sayings which for the last hundred years or so have not been considered quite respectable, because they were religious; or perhaps connected with the sort of religion that was not quite respectable. One of those statements is this: "The Family comes first; it comes before the State; its authority and necessity are anterior to those of the State." This always sounded perfectly horrid to rows and rows of earnest young people, learning statistics for Fabian Socialism at the London School of Economics. To that type, to that generation, the State was everything; that great official machine, which managed the traffic and took over the telephone system, was the very cosmos in which these people lived. For them, The Family was a stuffy thing somewhere in the suburbs which only existed to be the subject of Problem Plays and Problem Novels. The only question about it was whether its gloom should be brightened up by suicide; or its selfishness exalted by self-indulgence. But the whole of this view, though it is a view very nearly universal in the big modern towns, only exists because the big modern town is an entirely artificial society. Those inside it know no more about the normal life of humanity than the equally select society inside Colney Hatch or inside Portland Gaol. In some ways a lunatic asylum or a convict settlement are much better organised, are certainly much more elaborately organised, than the hugger-mugger of human beings doing as they like outside. But it is the human beings outside who are human; and it is their life that is the life of humanity.

Now the sweeping social revolutions that have swept backwards and forwards across Europe of late, the stroke of the Bolshevists, the counter-stroke of the Fascists, the imitation of it in Hitlerite Germany, the recovery of the secret societies in Spain, the new creation in Ireland, all these great governmental changes may serve to bring men's minds back to that big fundamental fact which the big cities have fancied to be a paradox. The big cities had this notion for a perfectly simple reason: that in the modern moment in which they lived, and, especially in an industrial country like ours, the framework of the State did really look stronger than the framework of The Family. The modern industrial mob was accustomed to the endless and tragic trail of broken families; of tenants failing to pay their rents; of slums being condemned and their inhabitants scattered; of husband or wife wandering in search of work or swept apart by separation or divorce. In those conditions, The Family seemed the frailest thing in the world; and the State the strongest thing in the world. But it is not really so. It is not so, when we take the life of man over large areas of time or space. It is not so, when we pass from the static nineteenth century to the staggering twentieth century. It is not so when we pass out of peaceful England to riotous Germany or gun-governed America. Over all the world tremendous transformations are passing over the State, so that a man may go to bed in one State and get up in another. The very name of his nation, the very nature of his common law, the very definition of his citizenship, the uniform and meaning of the policeman at the corner of his street, may be totally transformed to-morrow, as in a fairy-tale. He cannot really refer the daily domestic problems of his life to a State that may be turned upside-down every twenty-four hours. He must, in fact, fall back on that primal and prehistoric institution; the fact that he has a mate and they have a child; and the three must get on together somehow, under whatever law or lawlessness they are supposed to be living.

Take a very influential and creative culture in which the family has always been fundamental; take China. Is there any earthly sense, at this moment, in telling a Chinaman that he must cease to belong to The Family, and be content to belong to the State? He may not unnaturally ask, "What State?" The Japanese armies may advance to-day, over the land occupied by one of five rival Chinese generals yesterday. To-morrow, both of them may have disappeared from practical politics; a national reaction may have restored the Son of Heaven to his sacred palace in Pekin; or the Russian Communists may have swept across China and plotted it out under Commissars, that "the State" may start another Five-Year Plan. It is simply not possible for men to regard these vast tempestuous changes, in what the Chinese might call the Upper Air, as having the same real relation to themselves as the mother that bore them, or the child that is born to them. In the break-up of the modern world, The Family will stand out stark and strong as it did before the beginning of history; the only thing that can really remain a loyalty, because it is also a liberty.

The Romance of Childhood

All is Grist, 1931

I am just old enough to remember the world before telephones. And I remember that my father and my uncle fitted up with their own metal and chemicals the first telephone I ever saw: a miniature telephone reaching from the top bedroom under the roof to the remote end of the garden. I was really impressed imaginatively by this; and I do not think I have ever been so much impressed since by any extension of it. The point is rather important in the whole theory of imagination. It did startle me that a voice should sound in the room when it was really as distant as the next street. It would hardly have startled me more if it had been as distant as the next town. It does not startle me any more if it is as distant as the next continent. The miracle is over. Thus I admired even the large scientific things most on a small scale. So I always found that I was much more attracted by the microscope than the telescope. I was not overwhelmed in childhood by being told of remote stars which the sun never reached, any more than in manhood by being told of the empire on which the sun never set. I had no use for an empire that had no sunsets. But I was inspired and thrilled by looking through a little hole at a crystal like a pin's head, and seeing it change pattern and colour like a pygmy sunset.

I have already picked two quarrels with better men than myself, who were enthusiasts for childish romance, upon the reality of the romance of childhood. First, I disagree with them when they treat the infantile imagination as a sort of dream; whereas I remember it rather as a man dreaming might remember the world where he was awake. And second, I deny that children have suffered under a tyranny of moral tales. For I remember the time when it would have seemed the most hideous tyranny to take my moral tales away from me. And, in order to make this clear, I must contradict yet another common assumption in the romantic description of the dawn of life. The point is not very easy to explain; indeed, I have spent the greater part of my life in an unsuccessful attempt to explain it. Upon the cartloads of ill-constructed books in which I have completely failed to do so I have no desire to dwell. But perhaps, as a general definition, this might be useful; or, if not as a definition, at least a suggestion. From the first vaguely, and of late more and more clearly, I have felt that the world is conceiving liberty as something that merely works outwards. And I have always conceived it as something that works inwards.

The ordinary poetic description of the first dreams of life is a description of mere longing for larger and larger horizons. The imagination is supposed to work towards the infinite; though in that sense the infinite is the opposite of the imagination. For the imagination deals with an image, and an image is in its nature a thing that has an outline, and therefore a limit. Now I will maintain, paradoxical as it may seem, that the child does not desire merely to fall out of the window, or even to fly through the air or to be drowned in the sea. When he wishes to go to other places, they are still places, even if nobody has ever been there. But, in truth, the case is much stronger than that. It is plain on the face of the facts that the child is positively in love with limits. He uses his imagination to invent imaginary limits. The nurse and the governess have never told him that it is his moral duty to step on alternate paving-stones. He deliberately deprives this world of half its paving-stones, in order to exult in a challenge that he has offered to himself. I played that kind of game with myself all over the mats and boards and carpets of the house; and, at the risk of being detained during His Majesty's pleasure, I will admit that I often play it still. In that sense I have constantly tried to cut down the actual space at my disposal; to divide and subdivide, into these happy prisons, the house in which I was quite free to run wild. I believe that there is in this psychological freak a truth without which the whole modern world is missing its main opportunity. If we look at the favourite nursery romances, or at least if we have the patience to look at them twice, we shall find that they all really support this view, even when they have largely been accepted as supporting the opposite view. The charm of Robinson Crusoe is not in the fact that he could find his way to a remote island, but in the fact that he could not find any way of getting away from it. It is that fact which gives an intensive interest and excitement to all the things that he had with him on the island; the axe and the parrot and the guns and the little hoard of grain. The tale of *Treasure Island* is not the record of a vague desire to go on a sea voyage for one's health. It ends where it began; and it began with Stevenson drawing a map of the island, with all its bays and capes cut out as clearly as fretwork. The eternal interest of the Noah's Ark, considered as a toy, consists in its complete suggestion of compactness and isolation; of creatures so comically remote and fantastic being all locked up in one box; as if Noah had been told to pack up the sun and moon with his luggage. In other words, it is exactly the same game that I have played myself, by piling all the things I wanted on a sofa, and imagining that the carpet around me was the surrounding sea.

This game of self-limitation is one of the secret pleasures of life. As it says in the little manuals about such sports, the game is played in several forms. One very good way of playing it is to look at the nearest bookcase and wonder whether you would find sufficient entertainment in that chance collection, even if you had no other books. But always it is dominated by this principle of division and restriction, which begins with the game played by the child with the paving-stones. But I dwell upon it here because it must be understood as something real and rooted, so far as I am concerned, in order that the other views I have offered about these things may make any sort of sense. If anybody chooses to say that I have founded all my social philosophy on the antics of a baby, I am quite satisfied to bow and smile.

I have no great hopes that my own private Utopia, the Utopia of subdivision and self-limitation, is likely to be rapidly established in the real world. I do not immediately expect that the landlord with five hundred acres will instantly cut it down to fifty acres, and stand in startled admiration of the fresh and pleasing shape, the entirely new and attractive map or outline of his domains. I hardly suppose that he will be romantically enraptured, all at once, at the discovery of the enchanted island that I have cut out for him, out of the dull and dreary sea of his solid landed estate. I doubt whether the simple kindly act of stealing half his books will drive him to reading the other half; I am not sure that the traditional childish present, of a little garden marked out in the middle of his large garden, will instantly change him to a little child. But I do know that great historic changes always begin at exactly the opposite end to the end the world is pursuing, and that the human search, so long turned outwards, will turn inwards very soon.

The Surrender upon Sex

The Well and the Shallows, 1935

I have explained that these are sketches of six separate occasions, on which I should have become a Catholic, if I had not been the one and only kind of human being who cannot become a Catholic. The excitement of conversion is still open to the atheist and the diabolist; and everybody can be converted except the convert. In my first outline, I mentioned that one of the crises, which would in any case have driven me the way I had gone already, was the shilly-shallying and sham liberality of the famous Lambeth Report on what is quaintly called Birth Control. It is in fact, of course, a scheme for preventing birth in order to escape control. But this particular case was only the culmination of a long process of compromise and cowardice about the problem of sex; the final surrender after a continuous retreat.

There is one historical human fact which now seems to me so plain and solid, that I think that even if I were to lose the Faith, I could not lose sight of the fact. It has rather the character of a fact of chemistry or geology; though from another side it is mysterious enough, like many other manifest and unmistakable facts. It is this: that at the moment when Religion lost touch with Rome, it changed instantly and internally, from top to bottom, in its very substance and the stuff of which it was made. It changed in substance; it did not necessarily change in form or features or externals. It might do the same things; but it could not be the same thing. It might go on saying the same things; but it was not the same thing that was saying them. At the very beginning, indeed, the situation was almost exactly like that. Henry VIII was a Catholic in everything except that he was not a Catholic. He observed everything down to the last bead and candle; he accepted everything down to the last deduction from a definition; he accepted everything except Rome. And in that instant of refusal, his religion became a different religion; a different sort of religion; a different sort of thing. In that instant it began to change; and it has not stopped changing yet. We are all somewhat wearily aware that some Modern Churchmen call such continuous change progress; as when we remark that a corpse crawling with worms has an increased vitality; or that a snow-man, slowly turning into a puddle, is purifying itself of its accretions. But I am not concerned with this argument here. The point is that a dead man may look like a sleeping man a moment after he is dead; but decomposition has actually begun. The point is that the snow-man may in theory be made in the real image of man. Michelangelo made a statue in snow; and it might quite easily have been an exact replica of one of his statues in marble; but it was not in marble. Most probably the snow-man has begun to melt almost as soon as it is made. But even if the frost holds, it is still a stuff capable of melting when the frost goes. It seemed to many that Protestantism would long continue to be, in the popular phrase, a perfect frost. But that does not alter the difference between ice and marble; and marble does not melt.

The same sort of Progressives are always telling us to have a trust in the Future. As a fact, the one thing that a progressive cannot possibly have is a trust in the Future. He cannot have a trust in his own Future; let alone in his own Futurism. If he sets no limit to change, it may change all his own progressive views as much as his conservative views. It was so with the Church first founded by Henry VIII; who was, in almost everything commonly cursed as Popery, rather more Popish than the Pope. He thought he might trust it to go on being orthodox; to go on being sacramentalist; to go on being sacerdotalist; to go on being ritualist, and the rest. There was only one little weakness. It could not trust itself to go on being itself. Nothing else, except the Faith, can trust itself to go on being itself.

Now touching this truth in relation to Sex, I may be permitted to introduce a trivial journalistic anecdote. A few years before the War, some of my fellow-journalists, Socialists as well as Tories, were questioning me about what I really meant by Democracy; and especially if I really thought there was anything in Rousseau's ideal of the General Will. I said I thought (and I think I still think) that there can be such a thing, but it must be much more solid and unanimous than a mere majority, such as rules in party politics. I applied the old phrase of the Man in the Street, by saying that if I looked out of the window at a strange man walking past my house, I could bet heavily on his thinking some things, but not the common controversial things. The Liberals might have a huge majority, but he need not be a Liberal; statistics might prove England to be preponderantly Conservative, but I would not bet a button that he would be Conservative. But (I said) I should bet that he believes in wearing clothes. And my Socialist questioners did not question this; they, too, accepted clothes as so universal an agreement of common sense and civilisation, that we might attribute the tradition to a total stranger, unless he were a lunatic. Such a little while ago! To-day, when I see the stranger walking down the street, I should not bet that he believes even in clothes. The country is dotted with Nudist Colonies; the bookstalls are littered with Nudist magazines; the papers swarm with polite little paragraphs, praising the brownness and braveness of the special sort of anarchical asses here in question. At any given moment, there may be a General Will; but it is an uncommonly weak and wavering sort of will, without the Faith to support it.

As in that one matter of modesty, or the mere externals of sex, so in all the deeper matters of sex, the modern will has been amazingly weak and wavering. And I suppose it is because the Church has known from the first this weakness which we have all discovered at last, that about certain sexual matters. She has been very decisive and dogmatic; as many good people have quite honestly thought, too decisive and dogmatic. Now a Catholic is a person who has plucked up courage to face the incredible and inconceivable idea that something else may be wiser than he is. And the most striking and outstanding illustration is perhaps to be found in the Catholic view of marriage as compared with the modern theory of divorce; not, it must be noted, the *very* modern theory of divorce, which is the mere negation of marriage; but even more the slightly less modern and more moderate theory of divorce, which was generally accepted even when I was a boy. This is the very vital point or test of the question; for it explains the Church's rejection of the moderate as well as the immoderate theory. It illustrates the very fact I am pointing out, that Divorce has already turned into something totally different from what was intended, even by those who first proposed it. Already we must think ourselves back into a different world of thought, in order to understand how anybody ever thought it was compatible with Victorian virtue; and many very virtuous Victorians did. But they only tolerated this social solution as an exception; and many other modern social solutions they would not have tolerated at all. My own parents were not even orthodox Puritans or High Church people; they were Universalists more akin to Unitarians. But they would have regarded Birth-Prevention exactly as they would have regarded Infanticide. Yet about Divorce such liberal Protestants did hold an intermediate view, which was substantially this. They thought the normal necessity and duty of all married people was to remain faithful to their marriage; that this could be demanded of them, like common honesty or any other virtue. But they thought that in some very extreme and extraordinary cases a divorce was allowable. Now, putting aside our own mystical and sacramental doctrine, this was not, on the face of it, an unreasonable position. It certainly was not meant to be an anarchical position. But the Catholic Church, standing almost alone, declared that it would in fact lead to an anarchical position; and the Catholic Church was right.

Any man with eyes in his head, whatever the ideas in his head, who looks at the world as it is to-day, must know that the whole social substance of marriage has changed; just as the whole social substance of Christianity changed with the divorce of Henry VIII. As in the other case, the externals remained for a time and some of them remain still. Some divorced persons, who can be married quite legally by a registrar, go on complaining bitterly that they cannot be married by a priest. They regard a church as a peculiarly suitable place in which to make and break the same vow at the same moment. And the Bishop of London, who was supposed to sympathise with the more sacramental party, recently submitted to such a demand on the ground that it was a special case. As if every human being's case were not a special case. That decision was one of the occasions on which I should have done a bolt, if I had delayed it so long. But the general social atmosphere is much the most important matter. Numbers of normal people are getting married, thinking already that they may be divorced. The instant that idea enters, the whole conception of the old Protestant compromise vanishes. The sincere and innocent Victorian would never have married a woman reflecting that he could divorce her. He would as soon have married a woman reflecting that he could murder her. These things were not supposed to be among the daydreams of the honeymoon. The psychological substance of the whole thing has altered; the marble has turned to ice; and the ice has melted with most amazing rapidity. The Church was right to refuse even the exception. The world has admitted the exception; and the exception has become the rule.

As I have said, the weak and inconclusive pronouncement upon Birth-Prevention was only the culmination of this long intellectual corruption. I need not discuss the particular problem again at this point; beyond saying that the same truth applies as in the case of Divorce. People propose an easy way out of certain human responsibilities and difficulties; including a way out of the responsibility and difficulty of doing economic justice and achieving better payment for the poor. But these people propose this easy method, in the hope that some people will only use it to a moderate extent; whereas it is much more probable that an indefinite number will use it to an indefinite extent. It is odd that they do not see this; because the writers and thinkers among them are no longer by any means optimistic about human nature, like Rousseau; but much more pessimistic about human nature than we are. Considering mankind as described, for instance, by Mr. Aldous Huxley, it is hard to see what answer he could possibly give, except the answer which we give, if the question were put thus: "On the one side, there is an easy way out of the difficulty by avoiding childbirth; on the other side, there is a very difficult way out of the difficulty, by reconstructing the whole social system and toiling and perhaps fighting for the better system. Which way are the men you describe more likely to take?" But my concern is not with open and direct opponents like Mr. Huxley; but with all to whom I might once have looked to defend the country of the Christian altars. They ought surely to know that the foe now on the frontiers offers no terms of compromise; but threatens a complete destruction. And they have sold the pass.

Reflections on a Rotten Apple

The Well and the Shallows, 1935

Our age is obviously the Nonsense Age; the wiser sort of nonsense being provided for the children and the sillier sort of nonsense for the grown-up people. The eighteenth century has been called the Age of Reason; I suppose there is no doubt that the twentieth century is the Age of Unreason. But even that is an understatement. The Age of Reason was nicknamed from a famous rationalist book. But the rationalist was not really so much concerned to urge the rational against the irrational; but rather specially to urge the natural against the supernatural. But there is a degree of the unreasonable that would go even beyond the unnatural. It is not merely an incredible tale, but an inconsistent idea. As I pointed out to somebody long ago, it is one thing to believe that a beanstalk scaled the sky, and quite another to believe that fifty-seven beans make five.

For instance, a man may disbelieve in miracles; normally on some *a priori* principle of determinist thought; in some cases even on examination of the evidence. But on being told of the miracle of the multiplication of the loaves and fishes, he is told something that is logical if it is not natural. He is not told that there were fewer fishes because the fishes had been multiplied. Multiplication is still a mathematical term; and a mob all feeding on miraculous fishes is a less mysterious or monstrous sight than a man saying that multiplication is the same as subtraction. Such a story, for such a sceptic, does not carry conviction; but it does make sense. He can recognise the logical consequence, if he cannot understand the logical cause. But no pope or priest ever asked him to believe that thousands died of starvation in the desert because they were loaded with loaves and fishes. No creed or dogma ever declared that there was too little food because there was too much fish. But that is the precise, practical, and prosaic definition of the present situation in the modern science of economics. And the man of the Nonsense Age must bow his head and repeat his *credo*, the motto of his time, *Credo quia impossibile.* [I believe because it is impossible.]

Or again, the term unreason is sometimes used rather more reasonably; for a sort of loose or elliptical statement, which is at least illogical in form. The most popular case is what was called the Irish Bull; often suspected of resembling the Papal Bull, in being a supernatural monster bred of credulity and superstition. But even this old sort of confusion stopped short of the new sort of contradiction. If any Irishman really does say, "We are not birds, to be in two places at once," at least we know what he means, even if it is not what he says. But suppose he says that one bird has been miraculously multiplied into a million birds, and that in consequence there are fewer birds in the world than there were before. We should then be dealing, not merely with an Irish Bull but with a Mad Bull, and concerned not with the incredible but with the incomprehensible. Or, to apply the parable, the Irish have sometimes been accused of unbalanced emotion or morbid sentiment. But nobody says that they merely imagined the Great Famine, in which multitudes starved because the potatoes were few and small. Only suppose an Irishman had said that they starved because the potatoes were gigantic and innumerable. I think we should not yet have heard the last of the wrong-headed absurdity of that Irishman. Yet that is an exact description of the economic condition to-day as it affects the Englishman. And, to a great extent, the American. We learn that there is a famine because there is not a scarcity; and there is such a good potato-crop that there are no potatoes. The

Irishman, with his bull or his bird, is quite a hard-headed realist and rationalist compared to that. Thus, the old examples of the fantastic fell far short of the modern fact; whether they were mysteries supposed to be above reason or merely muddles supposed to be below it. Their miracles were more normal than our scientific averages; and the Irish blunder was less illogical than the actual logic of events.

For it seems that we live to-day in a world of witchcraft, in which the orchards wither because they prosper, and the multitude of apples on the apple-tree of itself turns them into forbidden fruit, and makes the effort to consume them in every sense fruitless. This is the modern economic paradox, which is called Over-Production, or a glut in the market, and though at first sight it sounds like the wildest fantasy, it is well to realise in what sense it is the most solid of facts. Let it be clearly understood, therefore, that as a description of the objective social situation at this instant in this industrial society, the paradox is perfectly true. But it is not really true that the contradiction in terms is true. If we take it, not as a description but as a definition, if we take it as a matter of abstract argument, then certainly the contradiction is untrue, as every contradiction is untrue. The truth is that a third element has entered into the matter, which is not mentioned in this abstract statement of it. That element might be stated in many ways; perhaps the shortest statement of it is in the fable of the man who sold razors, and afterwards explained to an indignant customer, with simple dignity, that he had never said the razors would shave. When asked if razors were not made to shave, he replied that they were made to sell. That is A Short History of Trade and Industry During the Nineteenth and Early Twentieth Centuries.

God made a world of reason as sure as God made little apples (as the beautiful proverb goes); and God did not make little apples larger than large apples. It is not true that a man whose apple-tree is loaded with apples will suffer from a want of apples; though he may indulge in a waste of apples. But if he never looks upon apples as things to eat, but always looks on them as things to sell, he will really get into another sort of complication; which may end in a sort of contradiction. If, instead of producing as many apples as he wants, he produces as many apples as he imagines the whole world wants, with the hope of capturing the trade of the whole world—then he will be either successful or unsuccessful in competing with the man next door who also wants the whole world's trade to himself. Between them, they will produce so many apples that apples in the market will be about as valuable as pebbles on the beach. Thus each of them will find he has very little money in his pocket, with which to go and buy fresh pears at the fruiterer's shop. If he had never expected to get fruit at the fruiterer's shop, but had put up his hand and pulled them off his own tree, his difficulty would never have arisen. It seems simple; but at the root of all apple-trees and apple-growing, it is really as simple as that.

Of course I do not mean that the practise is at present simple; for no practical problem is simple, least of all at the present time, when everything is confused by the corrupt and evasive muddlers who are called practical politicians. But the principle is simple; and the only way to proceed through a complex situation is to start with the right first principle. How far we can do without, or control, or merely modify the disadvantages of buying and selling is quite another matter. But the disadvantages do arise from buying and selling, and not from producing: not even from over-producing. And it is some satisfaction to realise that we are not living in a nightmare in which No is the same as Yes; that even the modern world has not actually gone mad, with all its ingenious attempts to do so; that two and two do in fact make four; and that the man who has four apples really has more than the man who has three. For some modern metaphysicians and moral philosophers seem disposed to leave us in doubt on these points. It is not the fundamental reason in things that is at fault; it is a particular hitch or falsification, arising from a very recent trick of regarding everything only in relation to trade. Trade is all very well in its way, but Trade has been put in the place of Truth. Trade, which is in its nature a secondary or dependent thing, has been treated as a primary and independent thing; as an absolute. The moderns, mad upon mere multiplication, have even made a plural out of what is eternally singular, in the sense of single. They have taken what all ancient philosophers called the Good, and translated it as the Goods.

I believe that certain mystics, in the American business world, protested against the slump by pinning labels to their coats inscribed, "Trade Is Good," along with other similar proclamations, such as, "Capone Is Dead," or "Cancer Is Pleasant," or "Death Is Abolished," or any other hard realistic truths for which they might find space upon their persons. But what interests me about these magicians is that, having decided to call up ideal conditions by means of spells and incantations to control the elements, they did not (so to speak) understand the elements of the elements. They did not go to the root of the matter, and imagine that their troubles had really come to an end. Rather they worshipped the means instead of the end. While they were about it, they ought to have said, not "Trade Is Good," but "Living Is Good," or "Life Is Good." I suppose it would be too much to expect such thoroughly respectable people to say, "God Is Good"; but it is really true that their conception of what is good lacks the philosophical finality that belonged to the goodness of God. When God looked on created things and saw that they were good, it meant that they were good in themselves and as they stood; but by the modern mercantile idea, God would only have looked at them and seen that they were The Goods. In other words, there would be a label tied to the tree or the hill, as to the hat of the Mad Hatter, with "This Style, 10/6." All the flowers and birds would be ticketed with their reduced prices; all the creation would be for sale or all the creatures seeking employment; with all the morning stars making sky-signs together and all the Sons of God shouting for jobs. In other words, these people are incapable of imagining any good except that which comes from bartering something for something else. The idea of a man enjoying a thing in itself, for himself, is inconceivable to them. The notion of a man eating his own apples off his own apple-tree seems like a fairy-tale. Yet the fall from that first creation that was called good has very largely come from the restless impotence for valuing things in themselves; the madness of the trader who cannot see any good in a good, except as something to get rid of. It was once admitted that with sin and death there entered the world something that we call change. It is none the less true and tragic, because what we called change, we called afterwards exchange. Anyhow, the result of that extravagance of exchange has been that when there are too many apples there are too few apple-eaters. I do not insist on the symbol of Eden, or the parable of the apple-tree, but it is odd to notice that even that accidental image pursues us at every stage of this strange story. The last result of treating a tree as a shop or a store instead of as a store-room, the last effect of treating apples as goods rather than as good, has been in a desperate drive of public charity and in poor men selling apples in the street.

In all normal civilisations the trader existed and must exist. But in all normal civilisations the trader was the exception; certainly he was never the rule; and most certainly he was never the ruler. The predominance which he has gained in the modern world is the cause of all the disasters of the modern world. The universal habit of humanity has been to produce and consume as part of the same process; largely conducted by the same people in the same place. Sometimes goods were produced and consumed on the same great feudal manor; sometimes even on the same small peasant farm. Sometimes there was a tribute from serfs as yet hardly distinguishable from slaves; sometimes there was a co-operation between free-men which the superficial can hardly distinguish from communism. But none of these many historical methods, whatever their vices or limitations, was strangled in the particular tangle of our own time; because most of the people, for most of the time, were thinking about growing food and then eating it; not entirely about growing food and selling it at the stiffest price to somebody who had nothing to eat. And I for one do not believe that there is any way out of the modern tangle, except to increase the proportion of the people who are living according to the ancient simplicity. Nobody in his five wits proposes that there should be no trade and no traders. Nevertheless, it is important to remember, as a matter of mere logic, that there might conceivably be great wealth, even if there were no trade and no traders. It is important for the sort of man whose only hope is that Trade Is Good or whose only secret terror is that Trade Is Bad. In principle, prosperity might be very great, even if trade were very bad. If a village were so fortunately situated that, for some reason, it was easy for every family to keep its own chickens, to grow its own vegetables, to milk its own cow and (I will add) to brew its own beer, the standard of life and property might be very high indeed, even though the long memory of the Oldest Inhabitant only recorded two or three pure transactions of trade; if he could only recall the one far-off event of his neighbour buying a new hat from a gipsy's barrow; or the singular incident of Farmer Billings purchasing an umbrella.

As I have said, I do not imagine, or desire, that things would ever be quite so simple as that. But we must understand things in their simplicity before we can explain or correct their complexity. The complexity of commercial society has become intolerable, because that society is commercial and nothing else. The whole mind of the community is occupied, not with the idea of possessing things, but with the idea of passing them on. When the simple enthusiasts already mentioned say that Trade is Good, they mean that all the people who possess goods are perpetually parting with them. These Optimists presumably invoke the poet, with some slight emendation of the poet's meaning, when he cries aloud, "Our souls are love and a perpetual farewell." In that sense, our individualistic and commercial modern society is actually the very reverse of a society founded on Private Property. I mean that the actual direct and isolated enjoyment of private property, as distinct from the excitement of exchanging it or getting a profit on it, is rather rarer than in many simple communities that seem almost communal in their simplicity. In the case of this sort of private consumption, which is also private production, it is very unlikely that it will run continually into overproduction. There is a limit to the number of apples a man can eat, and there will probably be a limit, drawn by his rich and healthy hatred of work, to the number of apples which he will produce but cannot eat. But there is no limit to the number of apples he may possibly sell; and he soon becomes a pushing, dexterous and successful Salesman and turns the whole world upside-down. For it is he who produces this huge pantomimic paradox with which this rambling reflection began. It is he who makes a wilder revolution than the apple of Adam which was the loosening of death, or the apple of Newton which was the apocalypse of gravitation, by proclaiming the supreme blasphemy and heresy, that the apple was made for the market and not for the mouth. It was he, by starting the wild race of pouring endless apples into a bottomless market, who opened the abyss of irony and contradiction into which we are staring to-day. That trick of treating the trade as the test, and the only test, has left us face to face with a piece of stark staring nonsense written in gigantic letters across the world; more gigantic than all its own absurd advertisements and announcements; the statement that the more we produce the less we possess.

Oscar Wilde would probably have fainted with equal promptitude, if told he was being used in an argument about American salesmanship, or in defence of a thrifty and respectable family life on the farm. But it does so happen that one true epigram, among many of his false epigrams, sums up correctly and compactly a certain truth, not (I am happy to say) about Art, but about all that he desired to separate from Art; ethics and even economics. He said in one of his plays: "A cynic is a man who knows the price of everything and the value of nothing." It is extraordinarily true; and the answer to most other things that he said. But it is yet more extraordinary that the modern men who make that mistake most obviously are not the cynics. On the contrary, they are those who call themselves the Optimists; perhaps even those who would call themselves the Idealists; certainly those who regard themselves as the Regular Guys and the Sons of Service and Uplift. It is too often those very people who have spoilt all their good effect, and weakened their considerable good example in work and social contact, by that very error: that things are to be judged by the price and not by the value. And since Price is a crazy and incalculable thing, while Value is an intrinsic and indestructible thing, they have swept us into a society which is no longer solid but fluid, as unfathomable as a sea and as treacherous as a quicksand. Whether anything more solid can be built again upon a social philosophy of values, there is now no space to discuss at length here; but I am certain that nothing solid can be built on any other philosophy; certainly not upon the utterly unphilosophical philosophy of blind buying and selling; of bullying people into purchasing what they do not want; of making it badly so that they may break it and imagine they want it again; of keeping rubbish in rapid circulation like a dust-storm in a desert; and pretending that you are teaching men to hope, because you do not leave them one intelligent instant in which to despair.

Babies and Distributism

The Well and the Shallows, 1935

I hope it is not a secret arrogance to say that I do not think I am exceptionally arrogant; or if I were, my religion would prevent me from being proud of my pride. Nevertheless, for those of such a philosophy, there is a very terrible temptation to intellectual pride, in the welter of wordy and worthless philosophies that surround us to-day. Yet there are not many things that move me to anything like a personal contempt. I do not feel any contempt for an atheist, who is often a man limited and constrained by his own logic to a very sad simplification. I do not feel any contempt for a Bolshevist, who is a man driven to the same negative simplification by a revolt against very positive wrongs. But there is one type of person for whom I feel what I can only call contempt. And that is the popular propagandist of what he or she absurdly describes as Birth-Control.

I despise Birth-Control first because it is a weak and wobbly and cowardly word. It is also an entirely meaningless word; and is used so as to curry favour even with those who would at first recoil from its real meaning. The proceeding these quack doctors recommend does not *control* any birth. It only makes sure that there shall never be any birth to control. It cannot, for instance, determine sex, or even make any selection in the style of the pseudo-science of Eugenics. Normal people can only act so as to produce birth; and these people can only act so as to prevent birth. But these people know perfectly well that they dare not write the plain word Birth-Prevention, in any one of the hundred places where they write the hypocritical word Birth-Control. They know as well as I do that the very word Birth-Prevention would strike a chill into the public, the instant it was blazoned on headlines, or proclaimed on platforms, or scattered in advertisements like any other quack medicine. They dare not call it by its name, because its name is very bad advertising. Therefore they use a conventional and unmeaning word, which may make the quack medicine sound more innocuous.

Second, I despise Birth-Control because it is a weak and wobbly and cowardly thing. It is not even a step along the muddy road they call Eugenics; it is a flat refusal to take the first and most obvious step along the road of Eugenics. Once grant that their philosophy is right, and their course of action is obvious; and they dare not take it; they dare not even declare it. If there is no authority in things which Christendom has called moral, because their origins were mystical, then they are clearly free to ignore all difference between animals and men; and treat men as we treat animals. They need not palter with the stale and timid compromise and convention called Birth-Control. Nobody applies it to the cat. The obvious course for Eugenists is to act towards babies as they act towards kittens. Let all the babies be born; and then let us drown those we do not like. I cannot see any objection to it; except the moral or mystical sort of objection that we advance against Birth-Prevention. And that would be real and even reasonable Eugenics; for we could then select the best, or at least the healthiest, and sacrifice what are called the unfit. By the weak compromise of Birth-Prevention, we are very probably sacrificing the fit and only producing the unfit. The births we prevent may be the births of the best and most beautiful children; those we allow, the weakest or worst. Indeed, it is probable; for the habit discourages the early parentage of young and vigorous people; and lets them put off the experience to later years, mostly from mercenary motives. Until I see a real pioneer and progressive leader coming out with a good, bold, scientific programme for drowning babies, I will not join the movement.

But there is a third reason for my contempt, much deeper and therefore much more difficult to express; in which is rooted all my reasons for being anything I am or attempt to be; and above all, for being a Distributist. Perhaps the nearest to a description of it is to say this: that my contempt boils over into bad behaviour when I hear the common suggestion that a birth is avoided because people want to be "free" to go to the cinema or buy a gramophone or a loudspeaker. What makes me want to walk over such people like doormats is that they use the word "free." By every act of that sort they chain themselves to the most servile and mechanical system yet tolerated by men. The cinema is a machine for unrolling certain regular patterns called pictures; expressing the most vulgar millionaires' notion of the taste of the most vulgar millions. The gramophone is a machine for recording such tunes as certain shops and other organisations choose to sell. The wireless is better; but even that is marked by the modern mark of all three; the impotence of the receptive party. The amateur cannot challenge the actor; the householder will find it vain to go and shout into the gramophone; the mob cannot pelt the modern speaker, especially when he is a loud-speaker. It is all a central mechanism giving out to men exactly what their masters think they should have.

Now a child is the very sign and sacrament of personal freedom. He is a fresh free will added to the wills of the world; he is something that his parents have freely chosen to produce and which they freely agree to protect. They can feel that any amusement he gives (which is often considerable) really comes from him and from them, and from nobody else. He has been born without the intervention of any master or lord. He is a creation and a contribution; he is their own creative contribution to creation. He is also a much more beautiful, wonderful, amusing, and astonishing thing than any of the stale stories or jingling jazz tunes turned out by the machines. When men no longer feel that he is so, they have lost the appreciation of primary things, and therefore all sense of proportion about the world. People who prefer the mechanical pleasures, to such a miracle, are jaded and enslaved. They are preferring the very dregs of life to the first fountains of life. They are preferring the last, crooked, indirect, borrowed, repeated, and exhausted things of our dying Capitalist civilisation, to the reality which is the only rejuvenation of all civilisation. It is they who are hugging the chains of their old slavery; it is the child who is ready for the new world.

The Rout of Reason

Where Are the Dead? 1928

Many people seem to be wondering what will become of the human soul in another world. I am wondering what has become of the human mind in this world. I am especially wondering what has become of the human power of reason in this age. Hume or Huxley, or any of the rationalists who were really rational, could never have kept a straight face in the presence of the preposterous confusions of thought that are now called arguments by Sir Arthur Keith or the Bishop of Birmingham. It is as if the brain itself had broken down. An inquirer writes to the *Daily News* gravely asking how there can be room in eternity for all the souls enjoying immortality. Apparently he has read the great text about "many mansions"; and supposes they are all limited and numbered like Artillery Mansions or Overstrand Mansions. I do not know how many commodious flats, with kitchen and bathroom, he will permit Omnipotence to erect, before it becomes necessary to announce in the headlines that there is a Housing Problem in Heaven. That is the sort of philosophical doubt which we are apparently called upon to "meet" nowadays. The example is extraordinary enough; but I really think it is every bit as intelligent as Bishop Barnes on the Sacrament or Sir Arthur Keith on the Soul.

In the case of Sir Arthur Keith I can pardon a traditional atmosphere and an almost sentimental sensibility to quaint old-fashioned metaphors, like that of the candle. It seems strange at first sight that a man of Sir Arthur Keith's ability and deserved distinction should be duped by such a clumsy figure of speech; but I take it he was attracted to it because of its antiquity.

Whatever else may be said against Sir Arthur, nobody can accuse him of being unduly modern or offensively up-to-date. He defends the Darwinian tradition because it is a tradition; and a great national tradition. But when Mr. Belloc quoted Vialleton against it, Sir Arthur Keith calmly told him that there was no such remark in Vialleton at all. Whereupon it was discovered, to the wonder of the world, that Sir Arthur had (apparently) never even heard of Vialleton's recent and famous book, and had read nothing later than an old text-book. I do not blame him for that; I never take the trouble to read the latest literature myself; but I do not go out of my way to give somebody else the lie about it. The same romantic taste for lingering in the shades of old libraries, which I share with Sir Arthur, has doubtless kept him loyal to the parable of the soul as a little flame. So he is still measuring eternity, as Alfred the Great measured time, by candles. But even a leading scientist might by this time have heard of electricity. If we must have material parables, in an age that has lost the power of abstract thought, the more modern parable would obviously be much the closer of the two. Of course, such analogies are inadequate anyhow, as any thinker could have seen in the time of Anselm, if not of Alfred.

Asking for them is like asking, as did the Mad Hatter or the March Hare, for a drawing of muchness. But there are metaphors and metaphors; and the candle is a very bad metaphor. The flame is not the principle of life in a candle; it is only some of its elements mixed with air and presenting another form to the senses. But suppose there were something in a candle that made it jump out of the candlestick, dance on the table, run round the room, and hit a muddle-headed materialist over the head. We might then begin to ask what was the principle of activity in the candle. If the candle then tumbled down and remained inert as before, we might well ask where its principle of activity had gone to.

We should not have the remotest reason, if we were rational, for saying that its principle of activity could not be active anywhere else. On the electric parallel, for instance, the same battery might be making a three-legged stool dance in the next room. But of course the parallel is only a parable. We cannot describe mind in terms of matter; if only for the reason that we cannot even perceive matter except by mind. That was why Huxley, in the days when agnostics could think, said that if he had to choose between denying mind or matter, he would deny matter. Huxley would have said, of course, that he did not know whether the soul survived. If you had told him that "a medical man" could certify that it did not survive (as Sir Arthur suggests) he would have enjoyed a very hearty laugh.

What troubles me is not that a very able anthropologist doubts immortality, or even that he denies immortality; thousands of men, wise and foolish, have denied or doubted it from the beginning of time. Generally, though not invariably, it was the wise who doubted and the fools who denied. What troubles me is that the denial is no longer rational; that any rationalist could see that it is not rational. Nobody needs a medical man to tell him that a dead man is materially as dead as mutton. Nobody need believe a medical man, any more than a muffin-man, or any other kind of man, upon the totally different metaphysical point of whether the abstract principle of energy has ceased or been withdrawn. The whole of that question of religious belief begins where all this leaves off; but it begins on a clear ground of agnosticism. Sir Arthur's ground is not clear and it is not agnostic. There was exactly the same muddle about the position of the Bishop of Birmingham when he uttered his celebrated howler on the subject of the sacramental philosophy. I am not here dealing with it considered as an attack on my religion. I am dealing with it as an attack on everybody's reason; or rather, as an example of the weakening of the reason, so that it cannot even attack. When Bishop Barnes suggested that chemical investigation might test Transubstantiation, it was no occasion for the skies to fall, as at a sublime blasphemy. It was simply that the solid earth of reason and common sense, on which we all walk, gave way under us with a faint crash. It was the human mind that had collapsed.

So far as that goes, it is merely a coincidence that the Bishop's argument was urged against a point of faith, which I myself believe to be a fact. The Bishop's argument would be quite as silly, if it were used against something that really is a fable. It would be so, for instance, if it were an ordinary fairy-tale. Somebody says: "The princess is enchanted under the form of a parrot in a golden cage." The proper answer of the sceptic, according to his degree of prudence, is either "Bosh!" or "There is no proof of that," or "You may believe in magic, but I do not," or "I have no reason to think that a princess can turn into a parrot." All these answers are reasonable in their relative degrees. But suppose somebody says, "I will test it; I will count all the feathers and find out if they look like feathers; I will show you that it flies like a parrot, screams like a parrot, claws and clutches like a parrot. . . ." Even in a fairy-tale the other man would have the sense to say: "Well, of course it does, idiot! I said she had turned into a parrot; and you are only repeating what I said. I think it is you that have turned into a parrot."

This is no place in which to explain why some of us hold that even fairy-tales are only false or fantastic shadows thrown by mysterious realities; and that such a mysterious reality can be present, under the appearances of the Sacred Elements. I need only say that anybody who really believes it fully understands how some people do not believe it. But whether or no anybody believes it, it is absurd to talk of anybody disproving it. All that any analysis could possibly prove is that the appearances continue to appear. But it was we who said, from the very beginning, that the appearances do continue to appear. Our doctrine concerns the metaphysical reality inside all appearances; and rational people either ignore such metaphysical things altogether, or reason about them on their own metaphysical plane. It is as if a man were to talk about digging up a cube root with a spade. As I say, the old lucid agnostics would have said it was impossible ultimately to define the mind. But they did not find it impossible to use the mind; and that is rapidly becoming the more pressing peril.

In short, we seem to have fallen to an altogether lower level of scepticism. Men are endlessly repeating (and that repetition is itself a mark of the degeneration) that this or that has shaken the foundations of faith. What I complain of is that it has shaken the foundations of doubt. It has altered, and very much lowered, the grounds even of unbelief. The criticisms sound like the cries of children or savages, compared with the wary and well-poised consistency of some of the old masters of negation. A Hottentot might offer to cut open a wafer and see whether it was a god. A Choctaw might say of a medicine man what is quoted above about a medical man. There must be something very queer and deleterious at work in the world, when this unreason saps, as it does sap, the minds of very acute and brilliant men, as well as those merely receptive. I am not at all disturbed about the future of the Faith; but I am disturbed about the future of the doubters, and the prospect of such very unphilosophic doubt; in which the very blasphemies have grown feeble and even stark nothing cannot remain unclouded or unconfused.

Mary Queen of Scots

Revaluations, 1931

Throughout a long and irregular career I have found that when I have had to give lectures, I almost invariably have to begin with an apology. On this occasion I begin with about six apologies in a sort of stratified form. First of all, I am only just recovering, so far as anybody ever recovers, from a visit to America. I do not wish to plead in *forma pauperis* on that point, but I appeal to your pity. I think it will be sufficient appeal to say I delivered a great many lectures in that country. Miserable as is my condition, what must be the condition of the audiences! If you find my remarks this evening, as you most certainly will, extraordinarily rambling and inadequate, please remember this is about the ninety-first lecture and you are its victims.

Secondly, I have been overwhelmed by accidental adventures in every shape, on which I will not dwell, beyond saying that compared with my hairbreadth escapes in order to reach you, from interviewers, photographers, people who wanted to draw my picture, and so on, the escape of Mary Stuart from Loch Leven and all her other adventures are comparatively prosaic. I have therefore turned up in the most disreputable condition in every sense of the word, and not disguised as a lecturer. But if my external condition is comparatively calamitous, it is nothing to the disreputable state of my mind. I hope you will forgive me on that ground if my remarks are somewhat scrappy and disconnected.

Next, I have to apologize for the amazing impudence of proposing to talk on this subject at all. I cannot think, to tell you the truth, how I ever came to agree to talk about Mary Queen of Scots. She is a problem which historians of the most learned sort regard as profound and inscrutable, and I am not a historian, not learned, barely even educated, as compared with the people who study these things. So that I am in every way, to begin with, at a disadvantage.

Lastly, I should like to explain that I do know enough about the story of Mary Stuart to know that it has about a thousand different aspects, and should be the subject—I will not say of a thousand lectures at this Institute, which perhaps might exhaust it unduly—but at any rate of a very large number of lectures by very much more learned men, who could treat it from all kinds of angles. I propose this evening to treat it only from one angle. It might be called Mary Stuart in Modern Literature; or if one may put it so, the successive estimates of Mary Stuart that have been made by popular writers during the last hundred years or so.

So much is a very thin and insufficient section or selection of my apologies. If I gave all my apologies they would occupy the whole time of the lecture.

I would suggest this evening, in a very tentative fashion, a view of Mary Stuart that seems to me to have received insufficient attention. Of course it has received some attention, but it is a question of proportion. In order to approach it, I think it best to consider how, generally speaking, the literary legend of Mary Stuart has stood in our common culture for some time past. I do not know how to put it better than by taking as a kind of motto, to begin with, those lines Swinburne wrote, I think in a kind of lyrical epilogue to his rather interminable (if a thing can be rather interminable, I am sure the Professor of Logic has his eye upon me when I use that phrase) or somewhat lengthy dramas about Mary Stuart. He put at the end, as if to relieve the gloom, a separate poem which you probably all know very well; if I remember aright (for in the rush of my difficulties I have had no opportunity of consulting any books or authorities before addressing you) I think it ran something like this—

> Princess, for whom my fathers fought,
> My fathers fell,
> Red star of boyhood's fiery thought,
> Farewell!

and later he said—

> Some faults the gods will give to fetter
> Man's highest intent,
> But surely you were something better
> Than innocent.
> No maiden stepping all unwary
> Through snares unseen,
> But one to live and die for, Mary
> The Queen.

I think that Swinburne in those verses stated a very important truth which he did not in the least understand, and which all the rest of his remarks completely contradicted. That (as I say) forms a quite workable text on which to examine the points to which I refer.

Touching the general estimates of Mary Queen of Scots, I suppose we all know (though I always have a feeling in these cases that I am remembering things that happened thousands of years before anybody in this room was born), still I think we most of us know that there did straggle down the centuries from the time of Mary Stuart a controversy, especially a Scottish controversy, between those who were her champions and those who were her enemies. I need not say they were in practise divided in religion; that is part of my other lecture on the religious interpretation of history. There is no other interpretation of history. Anyhow, I only mention that in passing, because I wish to get rid, first of all, of (shall I say?) a somewhat limited legend which many of my own co-religionists fought for enthusiastically and even fanatically for many centuries. I do not propose to hold myself in any sense responsible for that legend. It was romantic, it was melodramatic, it was sentimental, and it was very largely true; but it was not entirely true.

The view which I refer to was generally to the effect that Mary was throughout all her life a sort of Catholic saint, and that in so far as she suffered the violence of Bothwell and the vengeance of Elizabeth, she was simply a Catholic martyr. I do not believe in that simplification. I think it was more nearly true than the opposite version, but I am not going to identify myself with it in any way. I only refer to it in passing as an indication that I do know the various versions of the case. According to that theory, of course, Mary was simply a pure and devout Catholic woman, abandoned as she certainly was to barbarians, forced by a particular barbarian into a Protestant marriage, held in captivity, delivered over to Elizabeth to be murdered. I only mention that version, because while, as I say, I think it is much truer than the opposite version, I do not in the least accept it. I think it entirely underrates the enormous power of the pagan Renaissance, the spirit of almost lawless joy that there was in the princes and princesses of the period, and certainly in her as much as the others. She was not a Grande Dame of the age of Brantôme for nothing.

Secondly, in answer to that theory of the case, there was what I may call the ordinary, Whig-Victorian view, which was, I take it, roughly this. Mary was one of those snakes who, unfortunately, are charmers as well as snakes. She had a sort of power over men as is expressed in the metaphor of the old legend of the vampire, which is now I regret to say abbreviated to "vamp." She was in all positive matters poisonous and barren, she served no purpose except to upset human relations with her fascinations, and over against this typical "movie vamp" there was set the cold, Anglo-Saxon, arrogant but powerful and self-respecting Elizabeth, the "Lion of the North."

Well, that is all bosh, of course. It does not correspond at any point with any single historical fact. The chief fact about Queen Elizabeth is that for the greater part of her life, poor woman, she suffered from abominably bad health. The chief determining fact of the history of Elizabeth on the history of England is the fact that she was a "crock". I should not like, even at the distance of three hundred years, to speak disrespectfully of a woman simply because she was an invalid; but it was the main, dominating fact about Elizabeth that, like most of the Tudors, she was a "crock." And the whole history of that time turns upon the fact that Mary Stuart was living and Elizabeth Tudor was dying.

Elizabeth Tudor was a woman, like most of the great ladies of her time, of very considerable culture and also of a great deal of personal intelligence. She counted for a great deal; as a Princess when by some extraordinary accident she possesses intelligence always counts for a great deal. But it was not she who did any of the things that are attributed to her as a great, powerful mover of her time. Above all, it was not she who killed Mary Queen of Scots; it was Cecil and the great lords. Elizabeth did not have any of those petty, feminine jealousies which for some reason or other have been attributed to her by friends and foes. I think it probable that Elizabeth was very reluctant to execute Mary Stuart at all. Mary Stuart was executed for quite a different reason, as I shall point out in a moment.

At this moment I am only concerned with what I may call the Victorian or nineteenth-century Whig view of Mary Stuart, and that was almost entirely due to that very peculiar quality in the Victorians which has never been properly blamed or praised or criticised or understood by those who are perpetually talking about Victorians, and attributing to them all the qualities they did not possess. The quality which the Victorians did possess was an astonishing power of romantic creation, and secondly, the power of believing in their own romantic creation; so that when they had made a romantic creation they called it realistic; they thought it was true.

The best example, perhaps of all, is the conception which the Victorian English had of England itself. All through the great Victorian literature you will find running the assumption that the Englishman is sensible, sturdy, straightforward, prosaic, ordinary, does not care for art or poetry and so on, is a fine, manly, upstanding fellow. That creature was a myth, of course; he was a creation of pure imagination, of the very great poetic imagination of the English nation. They wanted to imagine a heroic figure for themselves and they imagined John Bull. John Bull never existed; at least the only person I ever heard of who was in the least bit like John Bull was Cobbett, whom the English slanged, prosecuted, sent to prison, and ruined in every possible fashion the moment they saw him. It was a poetical creation, but the power the Victorians had was the power of making these creations and then believing that they were the solid, sensible truth.

If you take a writer like Thackeray, who is a thoroughly typical Victorian in that sense, you will find he got into a great row with the jolly old romantics of Scotland, because he was said to have insulted Mary Queen of Scots; as indeed he did. He used a phrase indicating clearly that he thought Mary Queen of Scots had murdered her husband. It is very interesting to notice, not only Thackeray's remarks, but all the remarks of the contemporary English critics, answering the Scottish scream of protest, or the protest from the old romantic Jacobite, or Catholic Scotsman, against this. The English critics said, "Yes, we admire the romantic legend about

Mary Queen of Scots, and we sympathise with Scotch patriotism and dear Walter Scott and all that. But Mr. Thackeray is talking about the bald unvarnished facts of history. And of course he, like a solid Englishman, has been talking plain truth."

Now as a matter of fact, Thackeray was talking pure romance. He was even talking his own romance. He had made up his mind that Mary Stuart was a person like Becky Sharp. He saw Becky Sharp so vividly that he could easily believe that any historical character was Becky Sharp. Therefore he accepted the tradition that Mary Stuart was, as we should now say, "a vamp," that she was an adventuress, that she slid and sidled into society through the influence she had upon men, and he could very easily believe that a woman of that sort might end up with murdering her husband; just as he could very easily believe that Becky Sharp ended up by poisoning the absurd brother of Amelia; though I for one could never believe it. In other words, Thackeray was acting under a romantic impulse. He wanted to see that dramatic duel between the strong, sensible woman, Elizabeth, and the emotional, morbid, diseased, but deadly and fascinating person, Mary.

That view has held the field (I think) to a very considerable extent in England and, as I say, it is simply a romantic view. It supposes that all the people of Mary's period were all exclusively excited about what we now call "making love" as everybody is in modern novels, magazines, novelettes, and all the rest. But was the story of Mary Stuart mainly a love-story at all? That is a question I should be inclined to ask at the very start. Mary is indeed a very romantic and fascinating person. She is, as Swinburne put it, the "red star of boyhood's fiery thought"; but boyhood's thought is often more fiery than exact. And I think that the key of a great deal of Mary's existence is to be found in totally other considerations and ideas.

Let us take, broadly speaking, the story as it is generally told. I naturally assume that you know all about the actual history of Mary Stuart, as you are all far more learned than I. And I am sure you know all about the legend of Mary Stuart, because it is strewn about everywhere. And had you not known the mere outline of the case, the admirable rapid sketch of Mary's earlier life the Chairman himself gave, would have informed you. At an incredibly early age Mary went through a rapid succession of royal thrones or positions. She was turned out of throne after throne almost as rapidly as somebody playing musical chairs is turned out one chair after another; but she had the strong sixteenth-century feeling of the greatness of a Queen. She also had the very strong intoxication—I do not know what word one can use exactly—of the Renaissance. I think no problem in history is more subtle or more difficult than that of deciding exactly how far the great men and women who drank the new wine of the new learning, who came suddenly into the full current of the old pagan culture, really lost their heads: I will not say lost their souls. On the whole, my own opinion is that a person like Mary Stuart very probably did lose her head and most certainly did not lose her soul. But you have got to allow for that passionate pagan culture; and that is where the ordinary, narrow, pietistic, Scottish Catholic legend is I think untrue. Mary was most certainly not a mere virgin martyr dragged from one prison to another and only longing for martyrdom. She was not a French princess for nothing. She did not live for nothing in the time when the tales of the Princess of Navarre were written: the time when the whole sublime expansion of the imagination and of the senses opened like a sea across Europe. I have no difficulty in believing that Mary may at some time or other have, shall we say, gone over the traces, kicked up her heels, made a fool of herself in some manner or other. Large numbers of princesses of that time did. But I am quite certain that she was occupied all her life with the conception which the historians have hardly even considered: the conception of government. In other words, the conception that she was there to govern and to guard her realm.

It seems to me very extraordinary that nobody, or very few people, have noticed that perfectly simple point about the relations between Mary and Bothwell. You know that it has always been something of a puzzle. Mary certainly did have the most abominable bad luck in men that any woman in this world ever had; and what would have happened if she had been in a position to write modern novels, I cannot think. She first of all was married to a boy who died. She was then married to a boy who was also a booby and ought to have died. Whether she had anything to do with killing him or not, it is quite certain he was the sort of person one would kill, if one killed anybody. Then she appears as suddenly more or less collapsing under the influence of this queer, hulking, border baron, a man with a squint, a man who was notoriously ugly, who was certainly vigorous and virile; but a savage by her own social standard. The common theory has been, either that she was simply his captive led in chains like a Christian martyr; that she had not offered any sort of consent at all, but was simply a victim—that was the old pro-Mary legend—or the other theory which has been much more generally accepted: that she was insanely infatuated with him; that she was passionately in love. Well, they may either of them be true. It is always well to leave a very wide margin of agnosticism in history, because all sorts of new things may be discovered. But I am within my rights in saying that the theory that she was romantically infatuated with Bothwell very largely rested upon the Casket Letters; those documents which were supposed to have been intercepted between her and Bothwell, and which were certainly extravagant love-letters confessing a plot to murder her husband.

I do not profess at all to be an expert on these things—that is what makes my position in the matter so singularly impertinent—but I know what everybody knows by this time: that some considerable parts of the Casket Letters have already been actually proved to be forgeries. They were forged by Maitland, possibly the greatest scoundrel of that pack of scoundrels, though the selection is a very delicate matter. Therefore I take it that a theory founded on the Casket Letters is pretty well suspect. I am not at all sure that that theory is needed. I merely advance as a general suggestion or outline that idea, which as I say seems to me to have been curiously neglected: that possibly Mary may have accepted Bothwell for a totally different reason. Being a Renaissance princess, being a vigorous and healthy woman, she may have had other feelings in the matter into which I take it it is not our affair to inquire. She may or may not have liked Bothwell as a husband forced upon her by circumstances; for I think there were other considerations which have been left out of account.

The conception of the right of a king or queen to the territory that they governed was to the people of those times what private property was to the people of the nineteenth century, and what, for all I know, the absolute omnipotence of politicians may be to the people of the twenty-first century. I do not know what will be the next phase of the sacredness of power. But certainly those people had no doubt whatever that when they had been crowned and anointed and named King of Muscovy, or Norway, or Scotland, or Ireland, or anywhere else, they had a right to the thing as I have a right to my hat or my walking-stick; supposing indeed that I have any such right, which would be the subject of another lecture. What it seems to me has been left out of the discussion is this: that so far as I know—I repeat I am not a historical scholar on the point and it is possible facts may be advanced against me—there is not a jot or tittle or trace of evidence that James

Hepburn, Lord Bothwell, ever betrayed Queen Mary to the English. Now that cannot be said of a single one of the other nobles, religious leaders, and all the rest, that surrounded her. They were all, I take it, more or less, in one form or another, engaged in treasonable communication with Elizabeth. There was one strong, vigorous, militant, upstanding man, of military temper, a fighter, of whom there is no evidence that he was ever a traitor to his Queen. He was very probably a brute in all sorts of other ways, but that was not the point. It seems to me that Mary had a perfectly straightforward, political motive for putting herself under the protection of Bothwell, assuming that she was from her point of view defending the absolute, sacred rights of Scottish independence. You must always remember Scottish independence was one of the great romances of the Middle Ages. I should say that the Scots were one of the earliest people to feel Nationalism in the sense that we mean it to-day. They had by a kind of unexpected good luck achieved their independence at Bannockburn and they were immensely proud of it ever afterwards. They were proud of the fact that Scotland was a separate nation—and that feeling has not died out. I see my friend, Mr. Compton Mackenzie, is even standing as a Nationalist Scottish candidate for Glasgow. Anyhow, that feeling was intense and strong and it is an important point to realise that Mary and her friends were the Scottish patriots. There may be a lot to be said against Cardinal Beaton. There may, for all I know, be something to be said for John Knox. But Cardinal Beaton was the patriot and John Knox was, in the modern use of that word, the traitor. He was the man who was willing to allow England, the richer and more powerful country and the ancient and hereditary enemy, to prevail in policy in that perilous hour.

Supposing that Mary was filled with that national idea, or at least accepted it as part of the duties of her position, it does seem to me somewhat significant that the person with whom she associated herself was the one man, as far as I know, among the great nobility of Scotland who was "national". That is to say, he was not in any kind of way affected by the treasonable communications with Elizabeth. Again I speak under correction, it is possible that some of the extremely scholarly and modern people present may produce from their pockets at this very moment an autograph letter from James Hepburn appealing to Cecil to send a little more money. But I have never heard of any such document, and I do know that communications of that kind were extraordinarily common between Cecil and all the other Scottish leaders of the time, among whom Mary had to choose. I would therefore suggest (as a general idea) that it is just possible that, while we admit Mary was a most romantic figure, and all of us who are male are ready to fall in love with her at a moment's notice, it is just possible we have been a little too romantic about her; or rather, shall we say, we have supposed she was a little more romantic than she was. It seems to me very arguable that she possessed exactly that quality which has always been attributed to Elizabeth (and I think not unjustly on the whole), the quality that we call "public spirit"; that she did think she had a terribly difficult job in front of her, that she could perceive with a single glance that she had to choose among a pack of howling savages, one not much better than the other; and that upon the whole the best—and God knows that is saying a bad thing about the nobility of Scotland of that time—was this great, big, squinting brute called Bothwell. It is possible she was in love with him as well—God knows what kind of men women can be in love with. But I think that that argument has been pressed too far, as if it were the only possible argument in the case. It seems to me very arguable that Mary was really trying to be the Sovereign of Scotland, to keep up its ancient, traditional independence as Cardinal Beaton in his own way had tried to do; and that her main thoughts were directed towards finding such of her barony as would be loyal to the national cause; that she stood in that sense, erect and a little sublime in defence of what she regarded as her rights. In other words, if I may repeat again the words of Swinburne in a sense totally different to that which Swinburne meant—

> No maiden stepping all unwary
> Through snares unseen,
> But one to live and die for, Mary
> The Queen.

I think that is what Mary thought.

Now we come to Swinburne and what I may call the next stage after the stage of Thackeray. Thackeray (as I say) may be taken as representing the ordinary Victorian view; that is, Elizabeth was a lioness and everybody knew it. It was obvious by a similar style of logic that Mary was a snake. He took that for granted, he did not know that he was believing in a poem of his own creation; he thought he was believing in plain, historical facts, only he had never studied them. But then with Swinburne there came another change in what I may call the Victorian view of Mary, which is very interesting.

Swinburne practically said, "Of course Mary did not care a rap about Scotland or England or Europe or Christendom or God or man or anything else. Of course she was wildly, passionately in love with Bothwell, and that is why she is a heroine of romance, a proper subject for my poetical dramas." In other words, he carried the romantic theory to another stage or another phase, by saying that Mary was merely a child of the appetites of the Renaissance. Swinburne, revolting against the ideals of *Idylls of the King*, was less idealistic, but not less romantic. He really substituted Guinevere lecturing Arthur for Arthur lecturing Guinevere. In short, he saved the myth of the Round Table by turning it round. But the myth is still mythical, as concerns sixteenth-century history.

The conflict between the Christian tradition and the Renaissance excitement, in all the people of that period, was very deep and subtle; in none more deep and subtle than in Shakespeare. But I take it as absolutely certain that, however complex and violent was the struggle, their Christianity was perfectly sincere. Shakespeare wallowed in paganism, but there are passages in Shakespeare which I defy any independent person to read without realising that he was what we call a Christian; that he had that particular humility of mind which was the chemical change in mankind produced by Christianity.

In the same way Mary was, as I say, a thoroughly Renaissance person. I can imagine her "larking" to almost any extent; almost to the extent of a modern duchess; but she was a Christian all right. I cannot prove it; I can only refer you to certain passages of what she said and wrote that produce exactly that impression. The particular condition of a Christian under those circumstances is not that he does not do wicked things, for he does them perpetually; but that he knows that they are wicked. If Mary did murder her husband, she knew she was a murderess. Of that I am quite certain. If she did blaspheme and renounce her religion by being married to Bothwell by Protestant rites, she knew she was an apostate. That is the nuisance of being a Catholic—that you always know. She knew all right. I will not here dogmatize on whether she did commit some of those crimes or sins or not; but I am perfectly certain that Swinburne's conception of her as an absolutely abandoned or rather unconscious pagan is absolutely false. A Papist princess might be immoral; she could not possibly be unmoral. I daresay not many of you may have read so far off and distant an author as Swinburne; in plays like *Chastelard* and *Bothwell* he draws with extraordinary beauty and vividness the picture of what we now call a "vamp". The only difference is that whereas Thackeray thought she was a vamp and abused her for it, Swinburne thought she was a vamp and admired her for it. But a vampire is a fabulous animal; invented by such poets and romancers.

I think that Swinburne and Thackeray were both modern and therefore romantic and sentimental. They read into the actions of the great princess, ruling at a crisis of history, consulting with excellent information and a very clear intellect, the course she was to pursue, they read into that a sort of three-volume novel notion; that everything in her life was determined by sex. They were not vulgar enough to talk about sex appeal; but they could talk about nothing but sex.

Whatever may have been her actual conduct, most of the ordinary charges against her are founded upon the most trivial and childish coincidences. They might have happened to anybody and were only remarked because she had bitter enemies and they happened to her. The incident of the young lunatic Chastelard is an example of what I mean. He was a wild French Renaissance poet, very far gone in the drunkenness which men reached by drinking the great wine of the ancients. He came to her Court and she was polite to him and liked to see him, because he was a civilised man and civilised men were scarce in Scotland in those times. There is nothing whatever to show, as far as I know, that she was anything but friendly and pleasant to him. But he, I suppose, was a somewhat unbalanced person and it went to his head. He, as I daresay you all know, broke violently into her bedchamber one night; I should think very likely drunk, certainly irresponsible. She screamed and howled as was natural; and among the things that she is alleged to have screamed and howled was that somebody should come and kill him, which (from the sixteenth-century point of view) was simply the respectable and conventional way of behaving. Not the most virtuous of virgin queens, not even if she had about seven lovers like Elizabeth, could possibly have done a more correct and Victorian thing than to scream out that somebody should kill him. But the unnaturally poisonous enemies she happened to possess, with great ingenuity, interpreted that as meaning that she had some guilty secret and that unless he was killed at once, Chastelard would reveal it. I think you will see in that the characteristic spirit of blackmail, if I may so call it, that pervades so much of the more blackguard journalism and politics of our own time. Anyhow, that was the interpretation put upon it; but it seems to me a perfectly absurd interpretation. Chastelard was not killed on the spot, he was led away, and in due course tried and executed, because his act amounted to high treason according to the laws of that time. He made a very magnificent end, as did many of the great men of the Renaissance. He refused, I am glad to say, the ministrations of the Puritan ministers, and stood upon the scaffold reciting, aloud and alone, that great ode of Ronsard to Death:

> Je te salue, auguste et profitable mort.

If he had time to give the company that rather long recitation, he had time to tell tales if he chose. The theory that he had some deadly secret to reveal about Mary and that he must not be allowed to live for an instant because he would reveal it, is obviously falsified by the simple fact that he lived for days afterwards and never said anything. The simple fact was that Mary was frightened and screamed, and even queens do not always know what they say when they scream.

There are all sorts of other things of the same sort in her history. Heaven alone knows how even anybody so stupid as Darnley, let alone so stupid as many modern historians, ever got the idea that the poor hunchback, Rizzio, her secretary, was her lover. Mary was the kind of person who could have chosen from a fairly large selection of lovers and had certainly no necessity to fall back upon a low-born hunchback who took down her letters. Upon this point there was simply a malicious *parti pris*, a one-sided and persistent desire to show that she was a thoroughly bad woman. I have not pretended for a moment that she might not, for all I know, have become technically guilty in this or that respect, but those examples certainly prove nothing in that connexion.

But the admirers of Mary have been more cruel to her than her accusers. All those who have turned her into a sort of glorious dream of boyish romance have left out that much larger political and intellectual sphere in which she really ranged. There is nothing whatever against Mary Stuart that I know of, as a great woman of history, except one very simple fact—that she failed. That is to say she was defeated in the duel, somewhat brutally, by the simple expedient of cutting off her head; that is the only reason, as far as I know, why Mary Stuart does not stand in history exactly as Elizabeth stands now. She was very much more of a lioness than Elizabeth. She was a much more vigorous woman, she had on the whole a keener intellect, she was certainly a person of much greater bodily force and courage. In other words, she was not an invalid. She was a strong rider, she danced until even the modern girl would be left far behind, she was a thoroughly full-blooded, efficient, normal person and there was nothing the matter with her, except that she did not have a normal destiny.

Without going into that aspect of the question at length, I take it one may say very few women have ever had so extraordinary a history from the point of view of personal relations as hers: as that of losing a boy husband, losing another very exotic boy husband, being married a short time to a jolly great, hulking brute, and then spending the whole of the rest of her life, up to comparatively young middle-age, absolutely alone in a fortress. It was her destiny that was abnormal; it was her tragedy that she was not abnormal enough to suit it.

On the other hand, Elizabeth, though she was a person of many talents and probably of some virtues, was very abnormal. She came of an abnormal family. Her only sister, though a good woman according to her lights, was extremely morbid and her lights were comparatively dim. Her only brother was so diseased that he had died as a child. Her whole stock from that point of view was rotten; and in that sense, so was she. It is very much to her credit that she put up as magnificent a show as she did and managed to become a legend. But the legend that with her powerful leonine statesmanship she decreed the killing of Mary Stuart, and still more the legend that with her spiteful feminine jealousy she decreed the killing of Mary Stuart, are both quite equally fabulous. If I may put it roughly, the ordinary, popular Catholic theory was that Elizabeth was jealous of Mary Stuart for her fascinations and therefore killed her. The popular Protestant theory was that Elizabeth saw before her a magnificent, statesmanlike plan for the liberation of the world, and Mary Stuart stood in her way. I believe both these stories are quite false. I am not a scholar, but from all the facts that I know, I do not think Elizabeth wanted to execute Mary Stuart.

I think Elizabeth, like all the great princesses and princes of her time, was possessed of an intensely strong feeling of the greatness of royalty and the sacredness of the anointed head (the feeling that you find running through all Shakespeare's plays) and that she herself had a great horror of killing a queen. The people who really killed Mary Stuart were the "new millionaires" as we should say nowadays, the people who had received the Church lands at the Reformation: the Cecils, the Russells, and all the gang who were horribly afraid that if a Catholic sovereign came to the Throne it was just possible that they might have to disgorge some of the money. The simple key of the whole situation was, as I say, the fact that Queen Elizabeth was very ill. In our boyhood histories we used to read the phrases written in letters to the King of Scotland by Elizabeth's courtiers, saying that "her Grace was breaking up fast." Alas poor woman, she was "breaking up fast" the greater part of her life, and it was practically certain the end would come before long. Mary, who as I say was almost the athletic modern girl, showed not the slightest intention of breaking up even in prison.

Now if Elizabeth had died before Mary, by every recognized principle of the age, by every dogma of royal inheritance, it was absolutely inevitable that Mary Stuart should become Queen of England. That was what Cecil and the lords were afraid of. They were quite simply afraid of Elizabeth dying and Mary surviving. Therefore by a short and simple method they ensured that Mary should not survive. She is perhaps the one example in all human history of a person who was killed for being in good health. It is not so much that point that I would insist on, as on the correlative and incidental results of good health; one of which is that I think she did all her life have a much more clear, dignified, rational, political outlook than is generally allowed for. How much personal emotions did interfere with what she did or said, I suppose nobody can know.

I think she felt three things very strongly: first, that she was by law and title Queen of Scotland, and the fact that she was the immediate neighbour of a much wealthier and more powerful queen strung up that sense taut and sensitive and imperious. I think she also had the feeling that she stood, in no unreal sense, for civilisation. All those old, romantic stories about her remembering her childhood in France, about her writing poems and exchanging them with Ronsard, about her loving to dally with Italian and French foreigners like Chastelard and Rizzio, all those stories really refer to the deep oppressive sense that barbarism was submerging Europe, that blunt and brutal forces from the North and West were overwhelming all that she and her sort had loved. I think she did intensely and tragically value those things, as one values things that are lost or are likely to be lost.

Lastly, I think she was perfectly sincere in her religion. I am not going to argue on that particular topic to-night. I can only say that if she violated her religion by murder and apostasy and perjury and adultery and various other things, she did no more than many a man and woman has done who was absolutely sincere in religion. But I do not think she did. I think all that picture is exaggerated. I think she believed that the faith that she held was necessary for the culture that she valued, and that she saw the world upon the whole in a clearer pattern and with a plainer purpose than Elizabeth did. If ever there was a person in this world (and I have not intended these remarks to be an attack on Elizabeth) who was a character in many ways sympathetic and certainly very much an object of compassion—if ever there was a person in the world who was bewildered, it was Elizabeth. If ever there was a person who did not know whether she was on her head or her heels, did not know whether she agreed or not with all that was taking place, it was "The Lioness of Protestantism". She was the typical example of a person, cultivated, in many ways large-minded, accomplished, thoroughly a woman of the world, understanding a great deal of the world in which she lived, but without the faintest ghost of a notion—I will not say of where the world was going, but even of where she wanted it to go. To the day of her death she was never certain if she was a Catholic or a Protestant, or whether England was Catholic or Protestant; she did not know even whether she wanted it to be Catholic or Protestant. She was a typical and supreme example of the other type of civilisation: the spirit of doubt. In other words, our sympathies may go out to Elizabeth in some ways more even than to Mary, because in that way Elizabeth was very modern. She was extraordinarily like the modern girl. She did not dance as well as Mary or ride or hunt or run about as well as Mary; but she doubted; she did not know where she was, like the modern girl.

Mary, it seems to me, had a much clearer conception of where she was, or at least of where she wanted to be. She inherited much more clearly a civilisation and a philosophy, and she fought for it as far as she could, under all sorts of limitations of personal faults and weaknesses of course, until the day of her death. I do not believe Elizabeth on her deathbed knew what she had fought for. She had had in some ways more glory than any historical character, and certainly glory has accumulated since past any comparison; the Armada had been scattered before her, Virginia had been founded, the British Empire had begun, and the great glories of England were beginning to clamour around her. She did not understand it. She simply wondered what had happened. To the day of her death she hated married priests. A little while before her death she called out in mysterious and inexplicable anger to the Archbishop of York, "I know you are only hedge priests"; she died with prayers read over her, every now and then signing to the people to go on. Elizabeth carried to the grave with her a mystery that we perhaps cannot solve and which I think she did not solve. But I do not think that Mary in that sense was a mystery to herself. I think she was simply a very unfortunate woman, but remained to the last a woman pretty clearly knowing what she thought was right and wrong, even if she had done what was wrong; pretty clearly knowing what would make her happy even if she had never had it; vigorous, erect, normal. That is the curious tragedy of these two women and I think the story of Elizabeth is the more tragic.

I think you have got to read into Mary something that has been read in part only, the general sense of the sixteenth century of the glory and the responsibility of the princess—

Some faults the gods will give to fetter
Man's highest intent,
But surely you were something better
Than innocent.
No maiden stepping all unwary
Through snares unseen,
But one to live and die for, Mary
The Queen.

George MacDonald

(Introduction to *George MacDonald and His Wife* by Greville MacDonald)

GKC as MC, 1929

Certain magazines have symposiums (I will call them "symposia" if I am allowed to call the two separate South Kensington collections "musea") in which persons are asked to name "Books that have Influenced Me," on the lines of "Hymns that have Helped Me." It is not a very realistic process as a rule, for our minds are mostly a vast uncatalogued library; and for a man to be photographed with one of the books in his hand generally means at best that he has chosen at random, and at worst that he is posing for effect. But in a certain rather special sense I for one can really testify to a book that has made a difference to my whole existence, which helped me to see things in a certain way from the start; a vision of things which even so real a revolution as a change of religious allegiance has substantially only crowned and confirmed. Of all the stories I have read, including even all the novels of the same novelist, it remains the most real, the most realistic, in the exact sense of the phrase the most like life. It is called *The Princess and the Goblin*, and is by George MacDonald, the man who is the subject of this book.

When I say it is like life, what I mean is this. It describes a little princess living in a castle in the mountains which is perpetually undermined, so to speak, by subterranean demons who sometimes come up through the cellars. She climbs up the castle stairways to the nursery or the other rooms; but now and again the stairs do not lead to the usual landings, but to a new room she has never seen before, and cannot generally find again. Here a good great-grandmother, who is a sort of fairy godmother, is perpetually spinning and speaking words of understanding and encouragement. When I read it as a child, I felt that the whole thing was happening inside a real human house, not essentially unlike the house I was living in, which also had staircases and rooms and cellars. This is where the fairy-tale differed from many other fairy-tales; above all, this is where the philosophy differed from many other philosophies. I have always felt a certain insufficiency about the ideal of Progress, even of the best sort which is a Pilgrim's Progress. It hardly suggests how near both the best and the worst things are to us from the first; even perhaps especially at the first. And though like every other sane person I value and revere the ordinary fairy-tale of the miller's third son who set out to seek his fortune (a form which MacDonald himself followed in the sequel called *The Princess and Curdie*), the very suggestion of travelling to a far-off fairyland, which is the soul of it, prevents it from achieving this particular purpose of making all the ordinary staircases and doors and windows into magical things.

Dr. Greville MacDonald, in his intensely interesting memoir of his father which follows, has I think mentioned somewhere his sense of the strange symbolism of stairs. Another recurrent image in his romances was a great white horse; the father of the princess had one, and there was another in *The Back of the North Wind*. To this day I can never see a big white horse in the street without a sudden sense of indescribable things. But for the moment I am speaking of what may emphatically be called the presence of household gods—and household goblins. And the picture of life in this parable is not only truer than the image of a journey like that of the Pilgrim's Progress, it is even truer than the mere image of a siege like that of The Holy War. There is something not only imaginative but intimately true about the idea of the goblins being below the house and capable of besieging it from the cellars. When the evil things besieging us do appear, they do not appear outside but inside. Anyhow, that simple image of a house that is our home, that is rightly loved as our home, but of which we hardly know the best or the worst, and must always wait for the one and watch against the other, has always remained in my mind as something singularly solid and unanswerable; and was more corroborated than corrected when I came to give a more definite name to the lady watching over us from the turret, and perhaps to take a more practical view of the goblins under the floor. Since I first read that story some five alternative philosophies of the universe have come to our colleges out of Germany, blowing through the world like the east wind. But for me that castle is still standing in the mountains and the light in its tower is not put out.

All George MacDonald's other stories, interesting and suggestive in their several ways, seem to be illustrations and even disguises of that one. I say disguises, for this is the very important difference between his sort of mystery and mere allegory. The commonplace allegory takes what it regards as the commonplaces or conventions necessary to ordinary men and women, and tries to make them pleasant or picturesque by dressing them up as princesses or goblins or good fairies. But George MacDonald did really believe that people were princesses and goblins and good fairies, and he dressed them up as ordinary men and women. The fairy-tale was the inside of the ordinary story and not the outside. One result of this is that all the inanimate objects that are the stage properties of the story retain that nameless glamour which they have in a literal fairy-tale. The staircase in *Robert Falconer* is as much of a magic ladder as the staircase in the *Princess and the Goblin*; and when the boys are making the boat and the girl is reciting verses to them, in *Alec Forbes*, and some old gentleman says playfully that it will rise to song like a magic Scandinavian ship, it always seemed to me as if he were describing the reality, apart from the appearance, of the incident. The novels as novels are uneven, but as fairy-tales they are extraordinarily consistent. He never for a moment loses his own inner thread that runs through the patchwork, and it is the thread that the fairy great-grandmother put into the hands of Curdie to guide him out of the mazes of the goblins.

The originality of George MacDonald has also a historical significance, which perhaps can best be estimated by comparing him with his great countryman Carlyle. It is a measure of the very real power and even popularity of Puritanism in Scotland that Carlyle never lost the Puritan mood even when he lost the whole of the Puritan theology. If an escape from the bias of environment be the test of originality, Carlyle never completely escaped, and George MacDonald did. He evolved out of his own mystical meditations a complete alternative theology leading to a completely contrary mood. And in those mystical meditations he learned secrets far beyond the mere extension of Puritan indignation to ethics and politics. For in the real genius of Carlyle there was a touch of the bully, and wherever there is an element of bullying there is an element of platitude, of reiteration and repeated orders. Carlyle could never have said anything so subtle and simple as MacDonald's saying that God is easy to please and hard to satisfy. Carlyle was too obviously occupied with insisting that God was hard to satisfy; just as some optimists are doubtless too much occupied with insisting that He is easy to please. In other words, MacDonald had made for himself a sort of spiritual environment, a space and transparency of mystical light, which was quite exceptional in his national and denominational environment. He said things that were like the Cavalier mystics, like the Catholic saints, sometimes perhaps like the Platonists or the Swedenborgians, but not in the least like the Calvinists, even as Calvinism remained in a man like Carlyle. And when he comes to be more carefully studied as a mystic, as I think he will be when people discover the possibility of collecting jewels scattered in a rather irregular setting, it will be found, I fancy, that he stands for a rather important turning-point in the history of Christendom, as representing the particular Christian nation of the Scots. As Protestants speak of the morning stars of the Reformation, we may be allowed to note such names here and there as morning stars of the Reunion.

The spiritual colour of Scotland, like the local colour of so many Scottish moors, is a purple that in some lights can look like grey. The national character is in reality intensely romantic and passionate—indeed, excessively and dangerously romantic and passionate. Its emotional torrent has only too often been turned towards revenge, or lust, or cruelty, or witchcraft. There is no drunkenness like Scotch drunkenness; it has in it the ancient shriek and the wild shrillness of the Maenads on the mountains. And of course it is equally true on the good side, as in the great literature of the nation. Stopford Brooke and other critics have truly pointed out that a vivid sense of colour appears in the mediæval Scottish poets before it really appears in any English poets. And it is absurd to be talking of the hard and shrewd sobriety of a national type that has made itself best known throughout the modern world by the prosaic literalism of *Treasure Island* and the humdrum realism of *Peter Pan*. Nevertheless, by a queer historical accident this vivid and coloured people have been forced to "wear their blacks" in a sort of endless funeral on an eternal Sabbath. In most plays and pictures, however, in which they are represented as wearing their blacks, some instinct makes the actor or the artist see that they fit very badly. And so they do.

The passionate and poetical Scots ought obviously, like the passionate and poetical Italians, to have had a religion which competed with the beauty and vividness of the passions, which did not let the devil have all the bright colours, which fought glory with glory and flame with flame. It should have balanced Leonardo with St. Francis; no young and lively person really thinks he can be balanced with John Knox. The consequence was that this power in Scottish letters, especially in the day (or night) of complete Calvinistic orthodoxy, was weakened and wasted in a hundred ways. In Burns it was driven out of its due course like a madness; in Scott it was only tolerated as a memory. Scott could only be a mediævalist by becoming what he would call an antiquary, or what we should call an aesthete. He had to pretend his love was dead, that he might be allowed to love her. As Nicodemus came to Jesus by night, the aesthete only comes to church by moonlight.

Now, among the many men of genius Scotland produced in the nineteenth century, there was only one so original as to go back to this origin. There was only one who really represented what Scottish religion should have been, if it had continued the colour of the Scottish mediæval poetry. In his particular type of literary work he did indeed realise the apparent paradox of a St. Francis of Aberdeen, seeing the same sort of halo round every flower and bird. It is not the same thing as any poet's appreciation of the beauty of the flower or bird. A heathen can feel that and remain heathen, or in other words remain sad. It is a certain special sense of significance, which the tradition that most values it calls sacramental. To have got back to it, or forward to it, at one bound of boyhood, out of the black Sabbath of a Calvinist town, was a miracle of imagination.

In noting that he may well have this place in history in the sense of religious and of national history, I make no attempt here to fix his place in literature. He is in any case one of the kind that it is most difficult to fix. He wrote nothing empty; but he wrote much that is rather too full, and of which the appreciation depends rather on a sympathy with the substance than on the first sight of the form. As a matter of fact, the mystics have not often been men of letters in the finished and almost professional sense. A thoughtful man will now find more to think about in Vaughan or Crashaw than in Milton, but he will also find more to criticise; and nobody need deny that in the ordinary sense a casual reader may wish there was less of Blake and more of Keats. But even this allowance must not be exaggerated; and it is in exactly the same sense in which we pity a man who has missed the whole of Keats or Milton, that we can feel compassion for the critic who has not walked in the forest of Phantastes or made the acquaintance of Mr. Cupples in the adventures of Alec Forbes.

Tolerating Other Religions

Illustrated London News, May 31, 1913

When I was a boy, in the old indescribable days which I can only describe as the great days of Stead, a thing met that was called the Parliament of Religions. It had all the evils of a Parliament. It had the narrow novelty, the deaf dignity, the profound isolation and unpopularity that a Parliament so often commands. A Member of Parliament must be a man who comes to think more of the men he argues with than of the men he argues for. The club is mightier than the constituency. This can be seen in all political Parliaments; it is notorious that in all such assemblies "those behind cry 'forward' and those before cry 'back.' " The back benches fight, while the front benches make peace.

All this, which is true of political Parliaments, was a little true even of the poor old Parliament of Religions. Every man was a very cultured representative of a very distant constituency. If it is hard to make a man represent Surrey, or even Surbiton, it is harder still to make him represent the central plains of Asia or the ultimate islands of Japan. Thus, as I say, the Parliament of Religions seemed almost as useless as the Parliament at Westminster.

Men did not come there to explain their religion. They came to explain it away. At that gathering, everyone had to have a silky manner, just as (at some social gatherings) everyone has to have a silk hat. It would be improper in the Parliament at Westminster to knock off another man's hat. It would be improper in the Parliament of Religions to knock off another man's head. Yet the whole object of theology and philosophy and pure reason is to knock off another man's head. As the philosophical world goes, just now, it is rather a compliment. One can pass through crowds of earnest modern thinkers without finding a head to knock off.

Yet only the other day I came across a little book by a man who was really defending one of the great philosophies of the earth, and not merely excusing it. His book is really an apologia, and not an apology. It is concerned with the creed of Zoroaster, the great Persian mystic who has left behind him the sect of the Parsees. It is published by Mr. Dent, and the name of the author on the title-page is Ardaser Scrabjee N. Wadia. I intend no flippancy about this highly intelligent author if I say that I do not know which part of this is his name, or his address, or the priestly or political titles attached to his name. I only intend to indicate my own blank ignorance of the subject—of all such subjects as Persia or Parsees. "Wadia" at the end of his name may be something like "Esquire," for all I know. "N." may be his telephone number, for all I know. I know nothing about his nation; I know nothing about his civilisation; I know nothing about him. But I do know something about his religion. I did not know it five hours ago, and I owe what I know to him. His book is one of the very few books about the religions of the world of which this can be said.

Generally, the difficulty is not to tolerate other people's religion. The trouble is to tolerate our own religion. Or rather (to speak more strictly), to get our own religion to tolerate us. Comparatively few modern religious people are intolerant. But a great many modern religious people are intolerable. Nor are these specially those that are called bigots; it is rather, I think, the other way. The person we really find exasperating is he who does not understand our beliefs, and yet also does not agree with his own. Now, the author of this book does agree with his own. His philosophy is not in the least like mine; but it seems to me to be one of the two or three intelligent alternatives to mine. It is that philosophy which is roughly, perhaps too roughly, described as Dualism: the theory that good and evil are, in one sense at least, exactly balanced in the universe: that, in one sense at least, their balance creates the universe. The very pattern of the cosmos, so to speak, is a pattern of crossed swords. Life and death are fencing for ever; and (I say, again, in one sense at least) the issue is always doubtful. With a movement of iron self-control, I here refrain from making a pun about a Dualist and a duellist.

The author writes like a man who really has ideas; for ideas are always most original when they are grown from the old religious origins. It is not a paradox; but a very common fact of human nature. A man's ideas are much more his own if they come out of his father's creed than if he had got them out of a book: just as a man's cabbages are much more his own if they come out of his father's field than if he had got them out of a shop. And there is something convincing even in a sort of weird simplicity which the writer shows, and which is often shown by men writing in the language of another civilisation: as where he speaks of "our revered Master—RUSKIN, to whom I belong so entirely and so devotedly that I invariably use his words, expressions, and even paragraphs as if they were my own." I feel myself on delicate ground; and I do not know whether I shall be considered as clearing him of the charge of imitation, or insulting him with the charge of bad imitation, if I say that I do not think there are any solid chunks of Ruskin really embedded in his prose. But there really are solid chunks of what is much more fresh and interesting for English readers; the real ideas of a real and able believer in the creed of Zoroaster.

The great principle of the Zoroastrian philosophy seems to be that the thorn is essential to the rose. Or, to put it more correctly, that the life of man is a chess-board, because chess is a royal game—the great game for the human intellect. And in chess it is necessary, not only that there should be black and white, but that black and white should be equal. There must be a pattern of black and white, and the pattern must be exact.

To all this view of life I should only answer that the chess-board is only a pattern, and therefore cannot be a picture. A black-and-white artist always treats one or other colour as the background. The artist may be scrawling black on white, when he is an illustrator in pen-and-ink. He may be scrawling white on black, when he is a schoolboy chalking the schoolmaster's nose on the blackboard. But the pen-and-ink artist knows that the page is white previous to the arrival of the pen and ink. The wicked schoolboy knows that the blackboard is black. So we, as Christians, should always believe that this is a white world with black spots, not a black world with white spots. I should always believe the good in it was its primary plan. Also, I should always remember that chess came from Persia.

The Efficiency of the Police

Illustrated London News, April 1, 1922

The plague of atrocious and anonymous murders has naturally been discussed as a problem of the police. It is usually thought sufficient to make a vague demand for more "organisation," for the modern man is in favour of introducing order into everything except his own ideas. But I think the remedy insufficient—first, because the British police are already more centralised and powerful than they were ever meant to be, or than our national tradition of liberty allowed of their being; and, second, because all this talk of mere organisation rests on a fallacy. Organisation very often means merely turning men into machinery; and it is quite a mistake to suppose that machinery as such is efficient. Machinery can move slow as well as fast—indeed, machinery left to itself does not move at all. Nothing could be more elaborately organised than the etiquette of a Chinese Court, or a palace in the last and darkest days of Byzantium or Spain. All Byzantine bureaucracies, all systems of officialism in decadent and declining empires, are most systematically organised. What is wanting in them is the breath of life—or, in other words, people taking some sort of interest in their work. Such an organisation is the very opposite of an organism. It has no vitality, because it does not truly believe in its own aim in life. This is the tragic consequence of the false relations touching industrial injustice in the modern world. We hear a great deal about the policy of "ca' canny"; but people do not seem to have learned the one real lesson from it. [Ca' canny is a Scots phrase: ca' or caw = to drive; canny = gently. It means go easy; go slow; do not exert yourself.] It is that it is just as possible to organise slackness as to organise efficiency; perhaps a little more easy. It is a certain attitude towards work, and the real reasons for that attitude, that are worthy of the attention of a thoughtful person. If I thought the police were inefficient, I should not be content with shuffling papers and rearranging labels, with putting one department under another department, or giving one unsuccessful official more power over another. I should inquire first whether the police were discontented, and whether, perhaps, they had some reason to be discontented.

But I doubt whether we need to argue that the police are particularly inefficient, and I think there are other causes. To begin with, the modern notion of universal official organisation is a physical impossibility, and almost a contradiction in terms. It implies that everybody should be shadowed, and therefore that every man must be his own shadow. It demands a policeman for every person, which could not be attained even if every person were a policeman. There are only a certain number of officials to go round; and, if we insist on using some of their energies for small and senseless objects, there will obviously be less for large and serious objects. If one of the officials is engaged in preventing people from buying chocolates after half-past eight, he has the less attention to give to people who send poisoned chocolates to other people whom they have the misfortune to dislike. If a policeman is engaged in preventing a man from standing treat to an old friend in a public-house, he cannot at the same moment be preventing another man from stabbing an old enemy in another public-house. The common sense of this consideration was as obvious as broad daylight to our fathers, and was embodied in the old legal tag of "De minimis non curat lex" ["the law does not care about 'minimums' or trifles"]. But that maxim has certainly been entirely reversed and repudiated in modern social legislation. Our officials are so much occupied in controlling diet and details of medical theory, and disputed points of decorum in the arts, that such a trifle as a corpse on a doorstep or an assassination a few yards from a lamp-post appears almost in the nature of an irritating and unexpected addition to their daily toils. They cannot be expected to concentrate on anything so barbaric and elementary. "De maximis non curat lex." ["The law does not care about the biggest matters."]

It is therefore the very opposite of the truth to say that the police fail through lack of organisation. It is much nearer the truth to say that they fail because society is being far too much organised. A scheme of official control which is too ambitious for human life has broken down, and broken down exactly where we need it most. Instead of law being a strong cord to bind what it is really possible to bind, it has become a thin net to cover what it is quite impossible to cover. It is the nature of a net so stretched to break everywhere; and the practical result of our bureaucracy is something very near to anarchy. But I agree that there are yet other causes for that anarchy. Our lawlessness is not only produced by our passion for making laws.

For one thing, as many must have pointed out, every tool of modern science is necessarily a double-edged tool, a tool that cuts both ways. A criminal can use a motor-car as well as a policeman; he can even use a telephone with almost as much effect. This is quite as true, of course, on a large scale as on a small one, as was proved by the huge historical fact of Prussia at war. When Dean Inge reproved me for resisting the eugenic projects of coercion, he comforted himself by saying that science would march on and continue to produce its marvels whatever idealists might say. I ventured to reply by pointing out to what sort of triumph the science of Germany did actually march, and what sort of marvels it did actually display to the admiration of mankind. There is no doubt that a Zeppelin is a wonderful thing; but that did not prevent it from becoming a horrible thing. If human sin can produce such abomination out of the beautiful vision of aviation, out of the science that takes the wings of the morning to abide in the uttermost parts of the sea, it is absurd to say that nothing evil can come out of a eugenical science that studies atavism and apes. The truth is that any advance in science leaves morality in its ancient balance; and it depends still on the inscrutable soul of man whether any discovery is mainly a benefit or mainly a calamity. This is, perhaps, the strongest argument for a morality superior to materialism, and a religion that refuses to be bullied by science. Moral progress must still be made morally; and a modern scientist who has invented the most complex mechanism, or liberated the most subtle gas, has still exactly the same spiritual problem before him as that which confronted Cain, when he stood with a ragged stone in his hand.

Modern discoveries like the motor and the telephone, like modern discoveries in poison gas or the mechanics of aviation, are therefore as much on the side of the criminal as of the policeman. But to this there may also be added, I think, another truth not wholly unconnected with it. It is a more tentative suggestion than the other; but I incline to think it is true. It is not unlikely that in the recent chaos of creeds and codes, from which we are only gradually emerging, there may be a much larger percentage than in steadier periods of really educated men in a mood to be the enemies of society. Where there is a popular religion and a recognised law of life, the opposition to it will be merely lawless, and a great deal of it will be merely senseless. But we have passed through a time of transition when even a sensible man might well be a sceptic, and when a sceptic might well be an anarchist. For mind as much as machinery depends for its good or evil not on its force, but on its direction. But if really educated and enlightened men have more and more turned in a criminal direction, there will be a great augmentation of the criminal force; and it will not be altogether surprising if it is sometimes too much for the police force.

About Beliefs

As I Was Saying, 1936

Some time ago, when a stir was made by a rather striking book called *Who Moved the Stone?* which might almost be described, with all reverence, as a divine detective story and almost a theological thriller, a pugnacious little paper in Fleet Street made a remark which has always hovered in my memory as more mysterious than any mystery story in the world. The writer said that any man who believes in the Resurrection is bound to believe also in the story of Aladdin in the *Arabian Nights*. I have no idea what he meant. Nor, I imagine, had he. But this curious conjunction of ideas recurs to my mind in connexion with a rather interesting suggestion made by Mr. Christopher Dawson about what we may call the History of Science. On the face of it, the remark I have quoted from the pugnacious paper seems to have no quality whatever except pugnacity. There is no sort of logical connexion between believing in one marvellous event and believing in another, even if they were exactly alike and not utterly different. If I believe that Captain Peary reached the North Pole, I am not therefore bound to believe that Dr. Cook also reached the North Pole, even if they both arrived with sledges and dogs out of the same snows. It is a fallacy, therefore, even where the two things are close enough to be compared. But the comparison between the Gospel miracle and the Arabian fairy-tale is about the most unfortunate comparison in the world. For in the one case there is a plain and particular reason for thinking the thing true, or at least meant to be true. And in the other case there is a plain and particular reason for realising that the tale is not only untrue, but is not even meant to be true.

The historical case for the Resurrection is that everybody else, except the Apostles, had every possible motive to declare what they had done with the body, if anything had been done with it. The Apostles might have hidden it in order to announce a sham miracle, but it is very difficult to imagine men being tortured and killed for the truth of a miracle which they knew to be a sham. In the case of the Apostles' testimony, the general circumstances suggest that it is true. In the case of the Arabian tale, the general circumstances avow and proclaim that it is false. For we are told in the book itself that all the stories were told by a woman merely to amuse the king and distract his attention from the idea of cutting off her head. A romancer in this personal situation is not very likely to confine herself strictly to humdrum accuracy, and it would be impossible more plainly to warn the reader that all the tales are taradiddles. In the one case, then, we have witnesses who not only think the thing true, but do veritably think it is as true as death, or truer than death. They therefore prefer death to the denial of its truth. In the other case we have a story-teller who, in trying to avoid death, has every motive to tell lies. If St. John the Baptist had wished to avoid being beheaded, and had saved his life by inventing a long string of Messianic or Early Christian legends on the spur of the moment, in order to hold the attention of King Herod, I should not regard any "resurrection myth" he might tell as a strong historical argument for the Resurrection. But, as the Apostles were killed as St. John was killed, I think their evidence cannot be identified by sound scholarship as a portion of the Arabian Nights.

I merely pause for a moment upon this wild and preposterous parallel as a passing example of the queer way in which sceptics now refuse to follow an argument and only follow a sort of association or analogy. But the real reason for recalling this strange remark about the Arabian Nights is to be found in a much more genuine analogy between Western Science and Eastern Sorcery. Nobody but a lunatic would look either for his facts or his faith in the Arabian Nights. But, oddly enough, there really was a touch of the Arabian magicians in the Arabian mathematicians. There really was a faint flavour of the Oriental wizardry about the quite genuine Oriental wisdom; even when that wisdom was really doing work for which the world will always be grateful, in geometry or chemistry, in mathematics or medicine. Thus we find the paradox: that a man might, after all, look for some of the elements of science in the Arabian Nights, though he would hardly look there for anything very edifying or elevating in the way of the elements of religion. In short, the old dim, or even dark, connexion between Medicine and Magic has a sort of hidden meaning of great historical interest. It is developed by Mr. Dawson in an essay on the Eastern element in early mediæval science, and occurs in a book of essays called *Mediæval Religion*.

But this particular point is not concerned with religion, but is connected in a curious way with science. The point is this: that Magic (in the ancient sense) and Medicine (in the modern sense) are really in one way very like each other, because they are both very unlike the pure and abstract idea of Science as conceived by the Ancient Greeks. Science only means knowledge; and for those ancients it did only mean knowledge. They wanted nothing but the pleasure of knowing; they were particularly proud of knowing a great deal of utterly useless knowledge. Thus the favourite science of the Greeks was Astronomy, because it was as abstract as Algebra. And when the Philistine among them said: "What are the Pleiades to me?" the Philosopher really answered the Philistine by saying: "They are all the more to me because they are nothing to me." We may say that the great Greek ideal was to have no use for useful things. The Slave was he who learned useful things; the Freeman was he who learned useless things. This still remains the ideal of many noble men of science, in the sense that they do desire truth as the great Greeks desired it; and their attitude is an eternal protest against the vulgarity of utilitarianism. But there was and is another side of science, also to be respected, which was from the first represented by things like Medicine. And if there were some association of Medicine with Magic, it was because Magic was always extremely *practical*.

The modern Magician, often a most respectable gentleman, may have altered his opinion that sticking pins in the wax image of a politician would be a practical act of social utility. But so the modern Medicine-Man may have altered his opinion that the blood of badgers mixed with wine and salt is always an immediate cure for rheumatism. But there is nothing in this change of opinion on the mere fact or details that differs from any other modern change in medical method, as in curing consumption first by shutting all the windows and then by opening all the windows. The point is that both types of Medicine-Man were employed by people who wanted something prompt and practical, such as killing politicians or curing rheumatism. And the note of this sort of science, which Mr. Dawson traces to the East, is that it always boasts of possessing Power, as distinct from the other sort set upon enjoying Truth. We have most of us met the kind of theosophical mystic who is always whispering that he can show us the Path to Power; that if we will only say "I am Wisdom; I am Power" seventy-seven times before the looking-glass we shall control the cosmos. There was some such note even in mediæval medicine. Mediæval science was really more practical than Pagan science, but sometimes it did really sound a little too practical to be quite wholesome. So some modern hygienic idealists are rather more concerned about health than is quite healthy. It is hard to dwell perpetually on this element of power without poisoning it with some element of pride. So, queerly enough, Aladdin and his Wonderful Lamp really has some remote relation with the miracles of science, though hardly any with the miracles of religion.

The Common Man

The Common Man, 1950

The explanation, or excuse, for this essay is to be found in a certain notion, which seems to me very obvious, but which I have never, as it happens, seen stated by anybody else. It happens rather to cut across the common frontiers of current controversy. It can be used for or against Democracy, according to whether that swear-word is or is not printed with a big D. It can be connected, like most things, with religion; but only rather indirectly with my own religion. It is primarily the recognition of a fact, quite apart from the approval or disapproval of the fact. But it does involve the assertion that what has really happened, in the modern world, is practically the precise contrary of what is supposed to have happened there.

The thesis is this: that modern emancipation has really been a new persecution of the Common Man. If it has emancipated anybody, it has in rather special and narrow ways emancipated the Uncommon Man. It has given an eccentric sort of liberty to some of the hobbies of the wealthy, and occasionally to some of the more humane lunacies of the cultured. The only thing that it has forbidden is common sense, as it would have been understood by the common people. Thus, if we begin with the seventeenth and eighteenth centuries, we find that a man really has become more free to found a sect. But the Common Man does not in the least want to found a sect. He is much more likely, for instance, to want to found a family. And it is exactly *there* that the modern emancipators are quite likely to begin to frustrate him; in the name of Malthusianism or Eugenics or Sterilisation or at a more advanced stage of progress, probably, Infanticide. It would be a model of modern liberty to tell him that he might preach anything, however wild, about the Virgin Birth, so long as he avoided anything like a natural birth; and that he was welcome to build a tin chapel to preach a twopenny creed, entirely based on the text, "Enoch begat Methuselah," so long as he himself is forbidden to beget anybody. And, as a matter of historical fact, the sects which enjoyed this sectarian freedom, in the seventeenth or eighteenth centuries, were generally founded by merchants or manufacturers of the comfortable, and sometimes of the luxurious classes. On the other hand, it is strictly to the lower classes, to use the liberal modern title for the poor, that such schemes as Sterilisation are commonly directed and applied.

It is the same when we pass from the Protestant world of the seventeenth and eighteenth centuries to the Progressive world of the nineteenth and twentieth. Here the form of freedom mostly claimed, as a boast and a dogma, is the freedom of the Press. It is no longer merely a freedom of pamphlets but a freedom of papers; or rather, it is less and less a freedom at all, and more and more a monopoly. But the important point is that the process, the test, and the comparison are the same as in the first example. Modern emancipation means this: that anybody who can afford it can publish a newspaper. But the Common Man would not want to publish a newspaper, even if he could afford it. He might want, for instance, to go on talking politics in a pothouse or the parlour of an inn. And that is exactly the sort of really popular talk about politics which modern movements have often abolished: the old democracies by forbidding the pothouse, the new dictatorships by forbidding the politics.

Or again, it is the boast of recent emancipated ethics and politics not to put any great restraints upon anybody who wants to publish a book, especially a scientific book, full of psychology or sociology; and perhaps unavoidably full of perversions and polite pornography. As that modern tendency increased, it was less and less likely that the police would interfere very much with a man publishing the sort of book that only the wealthy could publish with sumptuous artistic plates or scientific diagrams. It is much more probable, in most modern societies, that the police would be found interfering with a man singing a song, of a coarse and candid description, bawling out a ballad of the grosser sort, or even using the more restrained medium of prose with a similar lack of restraint. Yet there is a great deal to be said for song, or even speech, of the old ribald sort, as compared with writing of the new sort, when it is at once analytic and anarchic. The old obscenity had a gusto and a great virility even in its violence, which is not easily rendered in a diagram or a table of statistics; and the old was always normal and never had any of the horrors of abnormality. The point is that, here again, the Common Man does not generally want to write a book, whereas he may occasionally want to sing a song. He certainly does not want to write a book on psychology or sociology—or to read, it. But he does want to talk, to sing, to shout, to yell and howl on due and suitable occasions; and, rightly or wrongly, it is when he is thus engaged that he is much more likely to fall foul of a policeman than when he is (as he never is) writing a scientific study of a new theory of sex. The upshot of uplift, in the modern sense, is the same in practise as in the previous examples. In the actual atmosphere of the age, men will still be arrested for using a certain kind of language, long after they cannot be arrested for writing a certain kind of literature.

It would be easy to give other examples; but these contemporary examples are already too continuous to be a coincidence. It is equally true, for instance, that the liberating movement of the eighteenth century, the life in the American and French Revolutions, while it did really vindicate many virtues of republican simplicity and civic liberty, also accepted as virtues several things that were obviously vices: that had been recognised as vices long before, and are now again beginning to be recognised as vices so long afterwards. Where even ambition had once been a pardonable vice, avarice became an utterly unpardonable virtue. Liberal economics too often meant merely giving to those already rich the liberty to grow richer, and magnificently granting to the poor the permission to remain rather poorer than before. It was much more certain that the usurer was released to practise usury than that the peasant was released from the practises of the usurer. It was much more certain that the Wheat Pit was as big as the Bottomless Pit, than that the man who grew wheat would ever be found anywhere except at the bottom.

There was a sense in which "liberal economics" were a proclamation of freedom, for the few who were rich enough to be free. Nobody thought there was anything queer about talking of prominent public men "gambling" in the Wheat Pit. But all this time, there were laws of all kinds against normal human gambling; that is, against games of chance. The poor man was prevented from gambling, precisely because he did not gamble so much as the rich man. The beadle or the policeman might stop children from playing chuckfarthing; but it was strictly because it was only a farthing that was chucked. Progress never interfered with the game of chuck-fortune, because much more than a farthing was being chucked. The enlightened and emancipated age especially encouraged those who chucked away other people's fortunes instead of their own. But anyhow, the comparison remains continuous and clear. Progress, in the sense of the progress that has progressed since the sixteenth century, has upon every matter persecuted the Common Man; punished the gambling he enjoys and permitted the gambling he cannot follow; restrained the obscenity that might amuse him and applauded the obscenity that would certainly bore him; silenced the political quarrels that can be conducted among men and applauded the political stunts and syndicates that can only be conducted by millionaires; encouraged anybody who had anything to say against God, if it was said with a priggish and supercilious accent; but discouraged anybody who had anything to say in favour of Man, in his common relations to manhood and motherhood and the normal appetites of nature. Progress has been merely the persecution of the Common Man.

Progress has a hagiology, a martyrology, a mass of miraculous legends of its own, like any other religion; and they are mostly false and belong to a false religion. The most famous is the fancy that the young and progressive person is always martyred by the old and ordinary person. But it is false. It is the old and ordinary person who is almost always the martyr. It is the old and ordinary person who has been more and more despoiled of all his old and ordinary rights. In so far as this progress progresses, it is far more likely that six million men will be forbidden to go to sleep, because six men say that certain breathing exercises are a substitute for slumber, than that any of the six million somnambulists will wake up sufficiently to clout the six men over their highbrowed but half-witted heads. There is no normal thing that cannot now be taken from the normal man. It is much more likely that a law will be passed to forbid the eating of grain (notoriously the parent of poisons like beer and whisky) than that it will be even faintly suggested, to men of that philosophy, that the economic evil is that men cannot grow grain, and that the ethical evil is that men are still despised for growing it. Given the purely progressive principle, and nothing else as a guide to our future, it is entirely possible that they may be hanged or buried alive for growing it. But of course, in a scientific age, they will be electrocuted—or perhaps only tortured by electricity.

Thus far my thesis is this: that it is not the Uncommon Man who is persecuted; but rather the Common Man. But this brings me into direct conflict with the contemporary reaction, which seems to say, in effect, that the Common Man had much better be persecuted. It is quite certain that many modern thinkers and writers honestly feel a contempt for the Common Man; it is also quite certain that I myself feel a contempt for those who feel this contempt. But the actual issue must be faced more fully; because what is called the reaction against democracy is at this moment the chief result of democracy. Now on this quarrel I am democratic, or at least defiant of the attacks of democracy. I do not believe that most modern people have seen the real point of the advantage or disadvantage of popular rule; and my doubt can be very largely suggested and summarised under this title of the Common Man.

To put it briefly; it is now the custom to say that most modern blunders have been due to the Common Man. And I should like to point out what appalling blunders have in fact been due to the Uncommon Man. It is easy enough to argue that the mob makes mistakes; but as a fact it never has a chance even to make mistakes until its superiors have used their superiority to make much worse mistakes. It is easy to weary of democracy and cry out for an intellectual aristocracy. But the trouble is that every intellectual aristocracy seems to have been utterly unintellectual. Anybody might guess beforehand that there would be blunders of the ignorant. What nobody could have guessed, what nobody could have dreamed of in a nightmare, what no morbid mortal imagination could ever have dared to imagine, was the mistakes of the well-informed. It is true, in a sense, to say that the mob has always been led by more educated men. It is much more true, in every sense, to say that it has always been misled by educated men. It is easy enough to say the cultured man should be the crowd's guide, philosopher and friend. Unfortunately, he has nearly always been a misguiding guide, a false friend, and a very shallow philosopher. And the actual catastrophes we have suffered, including those we are now suffering, have not in historical fact been due to the prosaic practical people who are supposed to know nothing, but almost invariably to the highly theoretical people who knew that they knew everything. The world may learn by its mistakes; but they are mostly the mistakes of the learned.

To go back no further than the seventeenth century, the quarrel between the Puritans and the populace was originally due to the pride of a few men in being able to read a printed book, and their scorn for people who had good memories, good traditions, good stories, good songs, and good pictures in glass or gold or graven stone, and therefore had less need of books. It was a tyranny of literates over illiterates. But it was the literates who were narrow, sullen, limited, and often oppressive; it was the illiterates who were, at least relatively, gay and free and fanciful and imaginative and interested in everything. The Uncommon Men, the elect of the Calvinist theory, did undoubtedly lead the people along the next stretch of the path of progress; but what it led to was a prison. The book-reading rulers and statesmen managed to establish the Scottish Sabbath. Meanwhile, a thousand traditions, of the sort they would have trampled out, yet managed to trickle down from the mediæval poor to the modern poor, and lingering as legends in countless cottages and farmhouses, were collected by Scott (often repeated orally by people who could not read or write) to combine in the construction of the great Scottish Romances, which profoundly moved and partly inspired the Romantic Movement throughout the world.

When we pass to the eighteenth century, we find the same part played by a new and quite contrary party; differing from the last in everything except in being the same sort of rather dried up aristocracy. The new Uncommon Men, now leading the people, are no longer Calvinists, but a dry sort of Deists drying up more and more like Atheists; and they are no longer pessimists but the reverse; only their optimism is often more depressing than pessimism. There were the Benthamites, the Utilitarians, the servants of the Economic Man; the first Free-Traders. They have the credit of having first made clear the economic theories of the modern state; and the calculations on which were mainly based the politics of the nineteenth century. It was they who taught these things scientifically and systematically to the public, and even to the populace. But what were the things, and what were the theories? Perhaps the best and broadest of them was a most monstrous and mythical superstition of Adam Smith; a theological theory that providence had so made the world that men might be happy through their selfishness; or, in other words, that God would overrule everything for good, if only men could succeed in being sufficiently bad. The intellectuals in this epoch taught definitely and dogmatically that if only men would buy and sell freely, lend or borrow freely, sweat or sack freely, and in practise, steal or swindle freely, humanity would be happy. The Common Man soon found out how happy; in the Slums where they left him and in the Slump to which they led him.

We need not continue, through the last two centuries, all the tale of the frenzy and folly inflicted by the fickleness of the educated class on the relative stability of the uneducated. The fickle intellectuals next rushed to the other extreme, and became Socialists, despising small property as they had despised popular tradition. It is quite true that these intellectuals had a lucid interval in which they proclaimed some primary truths along with many priggish falsehoods. Some of them did rightly exalt liberty and human dignity and equality, as expressed in the Declaration of Independence. But even that was so much mishandled that there is now a disposition to deny the truth along with the falsehood. There has been a reaction against Democracy; or, in plain words, the prigs are now too bored even to go on with their normal routine about the Common Man; the familiar routine of oppressing him in practise and adoring him in theory.

I do not adore him, but I do believe in him; at least I believe in him much more than I believe in them. I think the actual history of the relations between him and them, as I have narrated it, is enough to justify my preference. I repeat that they have had all the educational advantages over him; they have always led him; and they have always misled him. And even in becoming reactionaries, they remain as raw and crude as when they were revolutionaries. Their anti-democracy is as much stuffed with cant as their democracy. I need only allude to the detestable new fashion of referring to ordinary men as morons. First, it is pedantry, the dullest form of vanity; for a moron is only the Greek for a fool; and it is mostly sham pedantry, for most of those who mention morons hardly know they are talking Greek, still less why on earth they should. It also involves this moral evil: that a man who says that men are mostly fools knows at least that he has often made a fool of himself; whereas the morons are thought of like monkeys; as if they were a fixed tribe or caste. The Common Man may well be the victim of a new series of tyrannies, founded on this scientific fad of regarding him as a monkey. But it is doubtful whether he can be much more persecuted for having the instincts of a moron, than he has already been for having the instincts of a man.

Two Stubborn Pieces of Iron

The Common Man, 1950

In discussing such a proposal as that of the co-education of the sexes it is very desirable first of all to realise clearly what it is that we want the thing to do. The thing might be upheld for quite opposite reasons. It might be supposed to increase delicacy or to decrease it. It might be valued because it was a sphere for sentiment or because it was a damper for sentiment. My sympathies would move me in a discussion entirely according to what difference its upholders thought it would make. For myself, I doubt whether it would make much difference at all. Everyone must agree with co-education for very young children; and I cannot believe that even for elder children it would do any great harm. But that is because I think the school is not so important as people think it nowadays. The home is the really important thing, and always will be. People talk about the poor neglecting their children; but a little boy in the street has more traces of having been brought up by his mother than of having been taught ethics and geography by a pupil teacher. And if we take this true parallel of the home we can see, I think, exactly what co-education can do and what it cannot do. The school will never make boys and girls ordinary comrades. The home does not make them that. The sexes can work together in a schoolroom just as they can breakfast together in a breakfast-room; but neither makes any difference to the fact that the boys go off to a boyish companionship which the girls would think disgusting, while the girls go off to a girl companionship which the boys would think literally insane. Co-educate as much as you like, there will always be a wall between the sexes until love or lust breaks it down. Your co-educative playground for pupils in their teens will not be a place of sexless camaraderie. It will be a place where boys go about in fives sulkily growling at the girls, and where the girls go about in twos turning up their noses at the boys.

Now if you accept this state of things and are content with it as the result of your co-education, I am with you; I accept it as one of the mystical first facts of Nature. I accept it somewhat in the spirit of Carlyle when somebody told him that Harriet Martineau had "accepted the Universe," and he said, "By God, she'd better." But if you have any idea that co-education would do more than parade the sexes in front of each other twice a day, if you think it would destroy their deep ignorance of each other or start them on a basis of rational understanding, then I say first that this will never happen, and second that I (for one) should be horribly annoyed if it did.

I can reach my meaning best by another route. Very few people ever state properly the strong argument in favour of marrying for love or against marrying for money. The argument is not that all lovers are heroes and heroines, nor is it that all dukes are profligates or all millionaires cads. The argument is this, that the differences between a man and a woman are at the best so obstinate and exasperating that they practically cannot be got over unless there is an atmosphere of exaggerated tenderness and mutual interest. To put the matter in one metaphor, the sexes are two stubborn pieces of iron; if they are to be welded together, it must be while they are red-hot. Every woman has to find out that her husband is a selfish beast, because every man is a selfish beast by the standard of a woman. But let her find out the beast while they are both still in the story of "Beauty and the Beast." Every man has to find out that his wife is cross—that is to say, sensitive to the point of madness: for every woman is mad by the masculine standard. But let him find out that she is mad while her madness is more worth considering than anyone else's sanity.

This is not a digression. The whole value of the normal relations of man and woman lies in the fact that they first begin really to criticise each other when they first begin really to admire each other. And a good thing, too. I say, with a full sense of the responsibility of the statement, that it is better that the sexes should misunderstand each other until they marry. It is better that they should not have the knowledge until they have the reverence and the charity. We want no premature and puppyish "knowing all about girls." We do not want the highest mysteries of a Divine distinction to be understood before they are desired, and handled before they are understood. That which Mr. Shaw calls the Life Force, but for which Christianity has more philosophical terms, has created this early division of tastes and habits for that romantic purpose, which is also the most practical of all purposes. Those whom God has sundered, shall no man join.

It is, therefore, a question of what are really the co-educators' aims. If they have small aims, some convenience in organisation, some slight improvement in manners, they know more about such things than I. But if they have large aims, I am against them.

The Revival of Philosophy—Why?

The Common Man, 1950

The best reason for a revival of philosophy is that unless a man has a philosophy certain horrible things will happen to him. He will be practical; he will be progressive; he will cultivate efficiency; he will trust in evolution; he will do the work that lies nearest; he will devote himself to deeds, not words. Thus struck down by blow after blow of blind stupidity and random fate, he will stagger on to a miserable death with no comfort but a series of catchwords; such as those which I have catalogued above. Those things are simply substitutes for thoughts. In some cases they are the tags and tail-ends of somebody else's thinking. That means that a man who refuses to have his own philosophy will not even have the advantages of a brute beast, and be left to his own instincts. He will only have the used-up scraps of somebody else's philosophy; which the beasts do not have to inherit; hence their happiness. Men have always one of two things: either a complete and conscious philosophy or the unconscious acceptance of the broken bits of some incomplete and shattered and often discredited philosophy. Such broken bits are the phrases I have quoted: efficiency and evolution and the rest. The idea of being "practical," standing all by itself, is all that remains of a Pragmatism that cannot stand at all. It is impossible to be practical without a Pragma. And what would happen if you went up to the next practical man you met and said to the poor dear old duffer, "Where is your Pragma?" Doing the work that is nearest is obvious nonsense; yet it has been repeated in many albums. In nine cases out of ten it would mean doing the work that we are least fitted to do, such as cleaning the windows or clouting the policeman over the head. "Deeds, not words" is itself an excellent example of "Words, not thoughts." It is a deed to throw a pebble into a pond and a word that sends a prisoner to the gallows. But there are certainly very futile words; and this sort of journalistic philosophy and popular science almost entirely consists of them.

Some people fear that philosophy will bore or bewilder them; because they think it is not only a string of long words, but a tangle of complicated notions. These people miss the whole point of the modern situation. These are exactly the evils that exist already; mostly for want of a philosophy. The politicians and the papers are always using long words. It is not a complete consolation that they use them wrong. The political and social relations are already hopelessly complicated. They are far more complicated than any page of mediæval metaphysics; the only difference is that the mediævalist could trace out the tangle and follow the complications; and the moderns cannot. The chief practical things of to-day, like finance and political corruption, are frightfully complicated. We are content to tolerate them because we are content to misunderstand them, not to understand them. The business world needs metaphysics—to simplify it.

I know these words will be received with scorn, and with gruff reassertion that this is no time for nonsense and paradox; and that what is really wanted is a practical man to go in and clear up the mess. And a practical man will doubtless appear, one of the unending succession of practical men; and he will doubtless go in, and perhaps clear up a few millions for himself and leave the mess more bewildering than before; as each of the other practical men has done. The reason is perfectly simple. This sort of rather crude and unconscious person always adds to the confusion; because he himself has two or three different motives at the same moment, and does not distinguish between them. A man has, already entangled hopelessly in his own mind, (1) a hearty and human desire for money, (2) a somewhat priggish and superficial desire to be progressing, or going the way the world is going, (3) a dislike to being thought too old to keep up with the young people, (4) a certain amount of vague but genuine patriotism or public spirit, (5) a misunderstanding of a mistake made by Mr. H. G. Wells, in the form of a book on Evolution. When a man has all these things in his head, and does not even attempt to sort them out, he is called by common consent and acclamation a practical man. But the practical man cannot be expected to improve the impracticable muddle; for he cannot clear up the muddle in his own mind, let alone in his own highly complex community and civilisation. For some strange reason, it is the custom to say of this sort of practical man that "he knows his own mind." Of course this is exactly what he does not know. He may in a few fortunate cases know what he wants, as does a dog or a baby of two years old; but even then he does not know why he wants it. And it is the why and the how that have to be considered when we are tracing out the way in which some culture or tradition has got into a tangle. What we need, as the ancients understood, is not a politician who is a business man, but a king who is a philosopher.

I apologise for the word "king," which is not strictly necessary to the sense; but I suggest that it would be one of the functions of the philosopher to pause upon such words, and determine their importance and unimportance. The Roman Republic and all its citizens had to the last a horror of the word "king." It was in consequence of this that they invented and imposed on us the word "Emperor." The great Republicans who founded America also had a horror of the word "king"; which has therefore reappeared with the special qualification of a Steel King, an Oil King, a Pork King, or other similar monarchs made of similar materials. The business of the philosopher is not necessarily to condemn the innovation or to deny the distinction. But it is his duty to ask himself exactly what it is that he or others dislike in the word "king." If what he dislikes is a man wearing the spotted fur of a small animal called the ermine, or a man having once had a metal ring placed on the top of his head by a clergyman, he will decide one way. If what he dislikes is a man having vast or irresponsible powers over other men, he may decide another. If what he dislikes is such fur or such power being handed on from father to son, he will enquire whether this ever occurs under commercial conditions to-day. But, anyhow, he will have the habit of testing the thing by the thought; by the idea which he likes or dislikes; and not merely by the sound of a syllable or the look of four letters beginning with a "R."

Philosophy is merely thought that has been thought out. It is often a great bore. But man has no alternative, except between being influenced by thought that has been thought out and being influenced by thought that has not been thought out. The latter is what we commonly call culture and enlightenment to-day. But man is always influenced by thought of some kind, his own or somebody else's; that of somebody he trusts or that of somebody he never heard of, thought at first, second or third hand; thought from exploded legends or unverified rumours; but always something with the shadow of a system of values and a reason for preference. A man does test everything by something. The question here is whether he has ever tested the test.

I will take one example out of a thousand that might be taken. What is the attitude of an ordinary man on being told of an extraordinary event: a miracle? I mean the sort of thing that is loosely called supernatural, but should more properly be called preternatural. For the word "supernatural" applies only to what is higher than man; and a good many modern miracles look as if they came from what is considerably lower. Anyhow, what do modern men say when apparently confronted with something that cannot, in the cant phrase, be naturally explained? Well, most modern men immediately talk nonsense. When such a thing is currently mentioned, in novels or newspapers or magazine stories, the first comment is always something like, "But my dear fellow, this is the twentieth century!" It is worth having a little training in philosophy if only to avoid looking so ghastly a fool as that. It has on the whole rather less sense or meaning than saying, "But my dear fellow, this is Tuesday afternoon." If miracles cannot happen, they cannot happen in the twentieth century or in the twelfth. If they can happen, nobody can prove that there is a time when they cannot happen. The best that can be said for the sceptic is that he cannot say what he means, and therefore, whatever else he means, he cannot mean what he says. But if he only means that miracles can be *believed* in the twelfth century, but cannot be believed in the twentieth, then he is wrong again, both in theory and in fact. He is wrong in theory, because an intelligent recognition of possibilities does not depend on a date but on a philosophy. An atheist could disbelieve in the first century and a mystic could continue to believe in the twenty-first century. And he is wrong, in fact, because there is every sign of there being a great deal of mysticism and miracle in the twenty-first century; and there is quite certainly an increasing mass of it in the twentieth.

But I have only taken that first superficial repartee because there is a significance in the mere fact that it comes first; and its very superficiality reveals something of the subconsciousness. It is almost an automatic repartee; and automatic words are of some importance in psychology. Let us not be too severe on the worthy gentleman who informs his dear fellow that it is the twentieth century. In the mysterious depths of his being even that enormous ass does actually mean something. The point is that he cannot really explain what he means; and *that* is the argument for a better education in philosophy. What he really means is something like this, "There is a theory of this mysterious universe to which more and more people were in fact inclined during the second half of the eighteenth and the first half of the nineteenth centuries; and up to that point at least, this theory did grow with the growing inventions and discoveries of science to which we owe our present social organisation—or disorganisation. That theory maintains that cause and effect have from the first operated in an uninterrupted sequence like a fixed fate; and that there is no will behind or within that fate; so that it must work itself out in the absence of such a will, as a machine must run down in the absence of a man. There were more people in the nineteenth century than in the ninth who happened to hold this particular theory of the universe. I myself happened to hold it; and therefore I obviously cannot believe in miracles." That is perfectly good sense; but so is the counter-statement; "I do not happen to hold it; and therefore I obviously can believe in miracles."

The advantage of an elementary philosophic habit is that it permits a man, for instance, to understand a statement like this, "Whether there can or can not be exceptions to a process depends on the nature of that process." The disadvantage of not having it is that a man will turn impatiently even from so simple a truism; and call it metaphysical gibberish. He will then go off and say: "One can't have such things in the twentieth century"; which really is gibberish. Yet the former statement could surely be explained to him in sufficiently simple terms. If a man sees a river run downhill day after day and year after year, he is justified in reckoning, we might say in betting, that it will do so till he dies. But he is not justified in saying that it cannot run uphill, until he really knows why it runs downhill. To say it does so by gravitation answers the physical but not the philosophical question. It only repeats that there is a repetition; it does not touch the deeper question of whether that repetition could be altered by anything outside it. And that depends on whether there *is* anything outside it. For instance, suppose that a man had only seen the river in a dream. He might have seen it in a hundred dreams, always repeating itself and always running downhill. But that would not prevent the hundredth dream being different and the river climbing the mountain; because the dream is a dream, and there *is* something outside it. Mere repetition does not prove reality or inevitability. We must know the nature of the thing and the cause of the repetition. If the nature of the thing is a Creation, and the cause of the thing a Creator, in other words if the repetition itself is only the repetition of something willed by a person, then it is *not* impossible for the same person to will a different thing. If a man is a fool for believing in a Creator, then he is a fool for believing in a miracle; but not otherwise. Otherwise, he is simply a philosopher who is consistent in his philosophy.

A modern man is quite free to choose either philosophy. But what is actually the matter with the modern man is that he does not know even his own philosophy; but only his own phraseology. He can only answer the next spiritual message produced by a spiritualist, or the next cure attested by doctors at Lourdes, by repeating what are generally nothing but phrases; or are, at their best, prejudices.

Thus, when so brilliant a man as Mr. H. G. Wells says that such supernatural ideas have become impossible "for intelligent people," he is (for that instant) not talking like an intelligent person. In other words, he is not talking like a philosopher; because he is not even saying what he means. What he means is, not "impossible for intelligent men," but, "impossible for intelligent monists," or, "impossible for intelligent determinists." But it is not a negation of *intelligence* to hold any coherent and logical conception of so mysterious a world. It is not a negation of intelligence to think that all experience is a dream. It is not unintelligent to think it a delusion, as some Buddhists do; let alone to think it a product of creative will, as Christians do. We are always being told that men must no longer be so sharply divided into their different religions. As an immediate step in progress, it is much more urgent that they should be more clearly and more sharply divided into their different philosophies.

If I Only Had One Sermon to Preach

The Common Man, 1950

If I had only one sermon to preach, it would be a sermon against Pride. The more I see of existence, and especially of modern practical and experimental existence, the more I am convinced of the reality of the old religious thesis; that all evil began with some attempt at superiority; some moment when, as we might say, the very skies were cracked across like a mirror, because there was a sneer in Heaven.

Now the first fact to note about this notion is a rather curious one. Of all such notions, it is the one most generally dismissed in theory and most universally accepted in practise. Modern men imagine that such a theological idea is quite remote from them; and, stated as a theological idea, it probably is remote from them. But, as a matter of fact, it is too close to them to be recognised. It is so completely a part of their minds and morals and instincts, I might almost say of their bodies, that they take it for granted and act on it even before they think of it. It is actually the most popular of all moral ideas; and yet it is almost entirely unknown as a moral idea. No truth is now so unfamiliar as a truth, or so familiar as a fact.

Let us put the fact to a trifling but not unpleasing test. Let us suppose that the reader, or (preferably) the writer, is going into a public-house or some public place of social intercourse; a public tube or tram might do as well, except that it seldom allows of such long and philosophical intercourse as did the old public-house. Anyhow, let us suppose any place where men of motley but ordinary types assemble; mostly poor because the majority is poor, some moderately comfortable but rather what is snobbishly called common; an average handful of human beings. Let us suppose that the enquirer, politely approaching this group, opens the conversation in a chatty way by saying, "Theologians are of opinion that it was one of the superior angelic intelligences seeking to become the supreme object of worship, instead of finding his natural joy in worshipping, which dislocated the providential design and frustrated the full joy and completion of the cosmos." After making these remarks the enquirer will gaze round brightly and expectantly at the company for corroboration, at the same time ordering such refreshments as may be ritually fitted to the place or time, or perhaps merely offering cigarettes or cigars to the whole company, to fortify them against the strain. In any case, we may well admit that such a company will find it something of a strain to accept the formula in the above form. Their comments will probably be disjointed and detached; whether they take the form of "Lorlumme" (a beautiful thought slurred somewhat in pronunciation), or even "Gorblimme" (an image more sombre but fortunately more obscure), or merely the unaffected form of "Garn"; a statement quite free from doctrinal and denominational teaching, like our State compulsory education. In short, he who shall attempt to state this theory as a theory to the average crowd of the populace will doubtless find that he is talking in an unfamiliar language. Even if he states the matter in the simplified form, that Pride is the worst of the Seven Deadly Sins, he will only produce a vague and rather unfavourable impression that he is preaching. But he is only preaching what everybody else is practising; or at least is wanting everybody else to practise.

Let the scientific enquirer continue to cultivate the patience of science. Let him linger—at any rate let *me* linger—in the place of popular entertainment whatever it may be, and take very careful note (if necessary in a note-book) of the way in which ordinary human beings do really talk about each other. As he is a scientific enquirer with a note-book, it is very likely that he never saw any ordinary human beings before. But if he will listen carefully, he will observe a certain tone taken towards friends, foes, and acquaintances; a tone which is, on the whole, creditably genial and considerate, though not without strong likes and dislikes. He will hear abundant if sometimes bewildering allusion to the well-known weaknesses of Old George; but many excuses also, and a certain generous pride in conceding that Old George is quite the gentleman when drunk, or that he told the policeman off proper. Some celebrated idiot, who is always spotting winners that never win, will be treated with almost tender derision; and, especially among the poorest, there will be a true Christian pathos in the reference to those who have been "in trouble" for habits like burglary and petty larceny. And as all these queer types are called up like ghosts by the incantation of gossip, the enquirer will gradually form the impression that there is one kind of man, probably only one kind of man, perhaps, only one man, who is really disliked. The voices take on quite a different tone in speaking of him; there is a hardening and solidification of disapproval and a new coldness in the air. And this will be all the more curious because, by the current modern theories of social or anti-social action, it will not be at all easy to say why he should be such a monster; or what exactly is the matter with him. It will be hinted at only in singular figures of speech, about a gentleman who is mistakenly convinced that he owns the street; or sometimes that he owns the earth. Then one of the social critics will say, "'E comes in 'ere and 'e thinks 'e's Gawd Almighty." Then the scientific enquirer will shut his note-book with a snap and retire from the scene, possibly after paying for any drinks he may have consumed in the cause of social science. He has got what he wanted. He has been intellectually justified. The man in the pub has precisely repeated, word for word, the theological formula about Satan.

Pride is a poison so very poisonous that it not only poisons the virtues; it even poisons the other vices. This is what is felt by the poor men in the public tavern, when they tolerate the tippler or the tipster or even the thief, but feel something fiendishly wrong with the man who bears so close a resemblance to God Almighty. And we all do in fact know that the primary sin of pride has this curiously freezing and hardening effect upon the other sins. A man may be very susceptible and in sex matters rather loose; he may waste himself on passing and unworthy passions, to the hurt of his soul; and yet always retain something which makes friendship with his own sex at least possible, and even faithful and satisfying. But once let that sort of man regard his own weakness as a strength, and you have somebody entirely different. You have the Lady-Killer; the most beastly of all possible bounders; the man whom his own sex almost always has the healthy instinct to hate and despise. A man may be naturally slothful and rather irresponsible; he may neglect many duties through carelessness, and his friends may still understand him, so long as it is really a careless carelessness. But it is the devil and all when it becomes a careful carelessness. It is the devil and all when he becomes a deliberate and self-conscious Bohemian, sponging on principle, preying on society in the name of his own genius (or rather of his own belief in his own genius), taxing the world like a king on the plea that he is a poet, and despising better men than himself who work that he may waste. It is no metaphor to say that it is the devil and all. By the same fine old original religious formula, it is all of the devil. We could go through any number of social types illustrating the same spiritual truth. It would be easy to point out that even the miser, who is half-ashamed of his madness, is a more human and sympathetic type than the millionaire who brags and boasts of his avarice and calls it sanity and simplicity and the strenuous life. It would be easy to point out that even cowardice, as a mere collapse of the nerves, is better than cowardice as an ideal and theory of the intellect; and that a really imaginative person will have more sympathy with men who, like cattle, yield to what they know is panic, than with a certain particular type of prig who preaches something that he calls peace. Men hate priggishness because it is the driest form of pride.

Thus there is a paradox in the whole position. The spiritual idea of the evil of pride, especially spiritual pride, was dismissed as a piece of mysticism not needed by modern morality, which is to be purely social and practical. And, as a fact, it is very specially needed because the morality is social and practical. On the assumption that we need care for nothing except making other human beings happy, this is quite certainly the thing that will make them unhappy. The practical case against pride, as a mere source of social discomfort and discord, is if possible even more self-evident than the more mystical case against it, as a setting up of the self against the soul of the world. And yet though we see this thing on every side in modern life, we really hear very little about it in modern literature and ethical theory. Indeed, a great deal of modern literature and ethics might be meant specially for the encouragement of spiritual pride. Scores of scribes and sages are busy writing about the importance of self-culture and self-realisation; about how every child is to be taught to develop his personality (whatever that may be); about how every man must devote himself to success, and every successful man must devote himself to developing a magnetic and compelling personality; about how every man may become a superman (by taking Our Correspondence Course) or, in the more sophisticated and artistic type of fiction, how one specially superior superman can learn to look down on the mere mob of ordinary supermen, who form the population of that peculiar world. Modern theory, as a whole, is rather encouraging egoism. But we need not be alarmed about that. Modern practise, being exactly like ancient practise, is still heartily discouraging it. The man with the strong magnetic personality is still the man whom those who know him best desire most warmly to kick out of the club. The man in a really acute stage of self-realisation is a no more pleasing object in the club than in the pub. Even the most enlightened and scientific sort of club can see through the superman; and see that he has become a bore. It is in practise that the philosophy of pride breaks down; by the test of the moral instincts of man wherever two or three are gathered together; and it is the mere experience of modern humanity that answers the modern heresy.

There is indeed another practical experience, known to us all, even more pungent and vivid than the actual unpopularity of the bully or the bumptious fool. We all know that there is a thing called egoism that is much deeper than egotism. Of all spiritual diseases it is the most intangible and the most intolerable. It is said to be allied to hysteria; it sometimes looks as if it were allied to diabolic possession. It is that condition in which the victim does a thousand varying things from one unvarying motive of a devouring vanity; and sulks or smiles, slanders or praises, conspires and intrigues or sits still and does nothing, all in one unsleeping vigilance over the social effect of one single person. It is amazing to me that in the modern world, that chatters perpetually about psychology and sociology, about the tyranny with which we are threatened by a few feeble-minded infants, about alcoholic poisoning and the treatment of neurotics, about half a hundred things that are near the subject and never on the spot—it is amazing that these moderns really have so very little to say about the cause and cure of a moral condition that poisons nearly every family and every circle of friends. There is hardly a practical psychologist who has anything to say about it that is half so illuminating as the literal exactitude of the old maxim of the priest; that pride is from hell. For there is something awfully vivid and appallingly fixed about this madness at its worst, that makes that short and antiquated word seem much more apt than any other. And then, as I say, the learned go wandering away into discourses about drink or tobacco, about the wickedness of wine glasses or the incredible character of public-houses. The wickedest work in this world is symbolised not by a wine glass but by a looking-glass; and it is not done in public-houses, but in the most private of all private houses; which is a house of mirrors.

The phrase would probably be misunderstood; but I should begin my sermon by telling people not to enjoy themselves. I should tell them to enjoy dances and theatres and joy-rides and champagne and oysters; to enjoy jazz and cocktails and night-clubs if they can enjoy nothing better; to enjoy bigamy and burglary and any crime in the calendar, in preference to this other alternative; but never to learn to enjoy themselves. Human beings are happy so long as they retain the receptive power and the power of reaction in surprise and gratitude to something outside. So long as they have this they have as the greatest minds have always declared, a something that is present in childhood and which can still preserve and invigorate manhood. The moment the self within is consciously felt as something superior to any of the gifts that can be brought to it, or any of the adventures that it may enjoy, there has appeared a sort of self-devouring fastidiousness and a disenchantment in advance, which fulfils all the Tartarean emblems of thirst and of despair.

Difficulties can easily be raised, of course, in any such debate by the accident of words being used in different senses; and sometimes in quite contrary senses. For instance, when we speak of somebody being "proud of" something, as of a man being proud of his wife or a people proud of its heroes, we really mean something that is the very opposite of pride. For it implies that the man thinks that something outside himself is needed to give him great glory; and such a glory is really acknowledged as a gift. In the same way, the word will certainly be found misleading, if I say that the worst and most depressing element in the mixed elements of the present and the immediate future, seems to me to be an element of impudence. For there is a kind of impudence that we all find either amusing or bracing; as in the impudence of the guttersnipe. But there again the circumstances disarm the thing of its real evil. The quality commonly called "cheek" is not an assertion of superiority; but rather a bold attempt to balance inferiority. When you walk up to a very wealthy and powerful nobleman and playfully tip his hat over his eyes (as is your custom) you are not suggesting that you yourself are above all human follies, but rather that you are capable of them, and that he also ought to have a wider and richer experience of them. When you dig a Royal Duke in the waistcoat, in your playful manner, you are not taking yourself too seriously, but only, perhaps, not taking him so seriously as is usually thought correct. This sort of impudence may be open to criticism, as it is certainly subject to dangers. But there is a sort of hard intellectual impudence, which really treats itself as intangible to retort or judgment; and there are a certain number among the new generations and social movements, who fall into this fundamental weakness. It is a weakness; for it is simply settling down permanently to believe what even the vain and foolish can only believe by fits and starts, but what all men wish to believe and are often found weak enough to believe; that they themselves constitute the supreme standard of things. Pride consists in a man making his personality the only test, instead of making the truth the test. It is not pride to wish to do well, or even to look well, according to a real test. It is pride to think that a thing looks ill, because it does not look like something characteristic of oneself. Now in the general clouding of clear and abstract standards, there is a real tendency to-day for a young man (and even possibly a young woman) to fall back on that personal test, simply for lack of any trustworthy impersonal test. No standard being sufficiently secure for the self to be moulded to suit it, all standards may be moulded to suit the self. But the self as a self is a very small thing and something very like an accident. Hence arises a new kind of narrowness; which exists especially in those who boast of breadth. The sceptic feels himself too large to measure life by the largest things; and ends by measuring it by the smallest thing of all. There is produced also a sort of subconscious ossification; which hardens the mind not only against the traditions of the past, but even against the surprises of the future. *Nil admirari* becomes the motto of all nihilists; and it ends, in the most complete and exact sense, in nothing.

If I had only one sermon to preach, I certainly could not end it in honour, without testifying to what is in my knowledge the salt and preservative of all these things. This is but one of a thousand things in which I have found the Catholic Church to be right, when the whole world is perpetually tending to be wrong; and without its witness, I believe that this secret, at once a sanity and a subtlety, would be almost entirely forgotten among men. I know that I for one had hardly heard of positive humility until I came within the range of Catholic influence; and even the things that I love most, such as liberty and the island poetry of England, had in this matter lost the way, and were in a fog of self-deception. Indeed there is no better example of the definition of pride than the definition of patriotism. It is the noblest of all natural affections, exactly so long as it consists of saying, "May I be worthy of England." It is the beginning of one of the blindest forms of Pharisaism when the patriot is content to say, "I am an Englishman."

And I cannot count it an accident that the patriot has generally seen the flag as a flame of vision, beyond and better than himself, in countries of the Catholic tradition, like France and Poland and Ireland; and has hardened into this heresy of admiring merely his own breed and bone and inherited type, and himself as a part of it, in the places most remote from that religion, whether in Berlin or Belfast. In short, if I had only one sermon to preach, it would be one that would profoundly annoy the congregation, by bringing to their attention the permanent challenge of the Church. If I had only one sermon to preach, I should feel specially confident that I should not be asked to preach another.

Scipio and the Children

The Spice of Life, 1964

I have lately found myself in the town of Tarragona; famous for its vinegar, which it wisely sends abroad, rather than the wine, which it still more wisely drinks at home. I have myself ordered a fair amount of the wine; I omitted to order any of the vinegar. These things are an allegory; for there is something of the same contrast between the acid taste of party politics, especially anti-clerical politics, which is all that is exported to the English papers from Spain, and the rich and joyful vintage of popular life and humour, of which nobody can get the gusto except by going to Spain. I have always noted that there is never anything new in the news; and the things which the traveller recognizes are never the things that the journalist reports. For instance, the thing that struck me first and last in Spain was the Spanish children; especially the Spanish little boys, and their relation to the Spanish fathers of the Spanish little boys. The love of fathers and sons in this country is one of the great poems of Christendom; it has, like a bewildering jewel, a hundred beautiful aspects, and especially that supremely beautiful aspect; that it is a knock in the eye for that nasty-minded old pedant Freud.

I was sitting at a café table with another English traveller, and I was looking at a little boy with a bow and arrows, who discharged very random shafts in all directions, and periodically turned in triumph and flung himself into the arms of his father, who was a waiter. That part of the scene was repeated all over the place, with fathers of every social type and trade. And it is no good to tell me that such humanities must be peculiar to the progressive and enlightened Catalans, in that this incident happened in a Catalan town, for I happen to remember that I first noticed the fact in Toledo and afterwards even more obviously in Madrid. And it is no good to tell me that Spaniards are all gloomy and harsh and cruel, for I have seen the children; I have also seen the parents. I might be inclined to call them spoilt children; except that it seems as if they could not be spoilt. I may also remark that one element which specially haunts me, in the Spanish Peninsula, is the very elusive element called Liberty. Nobody seems to have the itch of interference; nobody is moved by that great motto of so much social legislation; "Go and see what Tommy is doing, and tell him he mustn't." Considering what this Tommy was doing, I am fairly sure that in most progressive countries, somebody would tell him he mustn't. He shot an arrow that hit his father; probably because he was aiming at something else. He shot an arrow that hit me; but I am a BROAD target. His bow and his archery were quite inadequate; and would not have been tolerated in the scientific Archery School into which he would no doubt have been instantly drafted in any state in which sport is taken as seriously as it should be. While I was staring at him, and at some other little boys who had assembled, also to stare at him, the English traveller interrupted my dream by saying suddenly:

"What is there to *see* in Tarragona?"

I was instantly prompted to answer, and almost did answer, "Why, of course, the boy with the bow and arrows! There is also the waiter."

But I stopped myself in time, remembering the strange philosophy of sightseeing; and then I found my mind rather a blank. I knew next to nothing about the town, and said so. I said the Cathedral was very fine; and then added with increasing vagueness; "I'm afraid I don't know anything at all about

Tarragona. I have a hazy idea that Scipio got buried here or born here. I can't even remember which."

"Who was it who was buried or born?" he inquired patiently.

"Scipio," I said, with an increasing sense of weakness; then I added as in feeble self-defence, "Africanus."

He inquired whether I meant that the man was an African. I feared, in any case, that the word "African" would not instantly summon up before his imagination the figure of St. Augustine; or even of Hannibal. It would more probably suggest to him a coal-black negro. So I said that I was sure he was not an African; I believed he was a Roman; certainly he was a Roman General; and I thought it was too early in history for a Roman General to have really belonged to what were afterwards the Roman Provinces. I had always understood that Carthage, or the Carthaginian influence, practically prevailed over all these parts at that time. And even as I said the words a thought came to me, like a blinding and even a blasting light.

The traveller was very legitimately bored. After the mysterious manner of his kind, he was not bored with sightseeing, but he was bored with history; especially ancient history. I do not blame him for that; I only puzzle upon why a man bored with history should take endless trouble to visit historic sites. He was patently one of those who think that all those things happened such a long time ago that they cannot make much difference now. But it had suddenly occurred to me that this rather remote example really might, perhaps, make a great deal of difference now. I tried to tell him so; and he must have formed the impression that I was raving mad.

"Would it be all the same," I asked, "if that little boy were thrown into a furnace as a religious ceremony, when his family went to church on Sunday? That is what Carthage did; it worshipped Moloch; and sacrificed batches of babies as a regular religious ritual. That is what Scipio Africanus did; he defeated Carthage, when it had nearly defeated the world. Somehow, I seem to feel a fine shade of difference."

My companion did not reply; and I continued to watch the archer; and though Apollo was a Pagan god, I am glad that such a sun-god slew the Punic Python; and that even before the Faith, those ancient arrows cast down Moloch for us all.

The Philosophy of Islands

The Spice of Life, 1964

Suppose that in some convulsion of the planets there fell upon this earth from Mars, a creature of a shape totally unfamiliar, a creature about whose actual structure we were of necessity so dark that we could not tell which was creature and which was clothes. We could see that it had, say, six red tufts on its head, but we should not know whether they were a highly respectable head-covering or simply a head. We should see that the tail ended in three yellow stars, but it would be difficult for us to know whether this was part of a ritual or simply a tail. Well, man has been from the beginning of time this unknown monster. People have always differed about what part of him belonged to himself, and what part was merely an accident. People have said successively that it was natural to him to do everything and anything that was diverse and mutually contradictory; that it was natural to him to worship God, and natural to him to be an atheist; natural to him to drink water, and natural to him to drink wine; natural to him to be equal, natural to be unequal; natural to obey kings, natural to kill them. The divergence is quite sufficient to justify us in asking if there are not many things that are really natural, which really appear early and strong in every normal human being, which are not embodied in any of his after affairs. Whether there are not morbidities which are as fresh and recurrent as the flowers of spring. Whether there are not superstitions whose darkness is as wholesome as the darkness that falls nightly on all living things. Whether we have not treated things essential as portents; whether we have not seen the sun as a meteor, a star of ill-luck.

It would at least appear that we tend to become separated from what is really natural, by the fact that we always talk about those people who are really natural as if they were goblins. There are three classes of people, for instance, who are in a greater or less degree elemental: children, poor people, and to some extent, and in a darker and more terrible manner, women. The reason why men have from the beginning of literature talked about women as if they were more or less mad, is simply because women are natural, and men, with their formalities and social theories, are very artificial. It is the same with children; children are simply human beings who are allowed to do what everyone else really desires to do, as for instance, to fly kites, or when seriously wronged to emit prolonged screams for several minutes. So again, the poor man is simply a person who expends upon treating himself and his friends in public-houses about the same proportion of his income as richer people spend on dinners or cabs; that is, a great deal more than he ought. But nothing can be done until people give up talking about these people as if they were too eccentric for us to understand, when, as a matter of fact, if there is any eccentricity involved, we are too eccentric to understand them. A poor man, as it is weirdly ordained, is definable as a man who has not got much money; to hear philanthropists talk about him one would think he was a kangaroo. A child is a human being who has not grown up; to hear educationists talk one would think he was some variety of a deep-sea fish. The case of the sexes is at once more obvious and more difficult. The stoic philosophy and the early church discussed woman as if she were an institution, and in many cases decided to abolish her. The modern feminine output of literature discusses man as if he were an institution, and decides to abolish him. It can only timidly be suggested that neither man nor woman is an institution, but things that are really quite natural and all over the place.

If we take children, for instance, as examples of the uncorrupted human animal, we see that the very things which appear in them in a manner primary and prominent, are the very things that philosophers have taught us to regard as sophisticated and over-civilised. The things which really come first are the things which we are accustomed to think come last. The instinct for a pompous intricate and recurring ceremonial, for instance, comes to a child like an organic hunger; he asks for a formality as he might ask for a drink of water.

Those who think, for instance, that the thing called superstition is something heavily artificial, are very numerous; that is those who think that it has only been the power of priests or of some very deliberate system that has built up boundaries, that has called one course of action lawful and another unlawful, that has called one piece of ground sacred and another profane. Nothing it would seem, except a large and powerful conspiracy, could account for men so strangely distinguishing between one field and another, between one city and another, between one nation and another. To all those who think in this way there is only one answer to be given. It is to approach each of them and whisper in his ear: "Did you or did you not as a child try to step on every alternate paving-stone? Was that artificial and a superstition? Did priests come in the dead of night and mark out by secret signs the stones on which you are allowed to tread? Were children threatened with the oubliette or the fire of Smithfield if they failed to step on the right stone? Has the Church issued a bill '*Quisquam non pavemente*'?" ["Whatsoever is not pavement," but also, "Whatsoever does not nourish the mind." An apparent Latin pun from Chesterton.] No! On this point on which we were really free, we invented our servitude. We chose to say that between the first and the third paving-stone there was an abyss of the eternal darkness into which we must not fall. We were walking along a steady and safe and modern road, and it was more pleasant to us to say that we were leaping desperately from peak to peak. Under mean and oppressive systems it was no doubt our instinct to free ourselves. But this truth written on the paving-stones is of even greater emphasis, that under liberal systems it was our instinct to limit ourselves. We limited ourselves so gladly that we limited ourselves at random, as if limitation were one of the adventures of boyhood.

People sometimes talk as if everything in the religious history of man had been done by officials. In all probability things like the Dionysian cult or the worship of the Virgin were almost entirely forced by the people on the priesthood. And if children had been sufficiently powerful in the State, there is no reason why this paving-stone religion should not have been accepted also. There is no reason why the streets up which we walk should not be emblazoned so as to commemorate the memory of a superstition as healthy as health itself.

For what is the idea in human nature which lies at the back of this almost automatic ceremonialism? Why is it that a child who would be furious if told by his nurse not to walk off the kerbstone, invents a whole desperate system of footholds and chasms in a plane in which his nurse can see little but a commodious level? It is because man has always had the instinct that to isolate a thing was to identify it. The flag only becomes a flag when it is unique; the nation only becomes a nation when it is surrounded; the hero only becomes a hero when he has before him and behind him men who are not heroes; the paving-stone only becomes a paving-stone when it has before it and behind it things that are not paving-stones.

There are two other obvious instances, of course, of the same instinct; the perennial poetry of islands, and the perennial poetry of ships. A ship like the Argo or the Fram is valued by the mind because it is an island, because, that is, it carries with it, floating loose on the desolate elements, the resources, and rules and trades, and treasuries of a nation, because it has ranks, and shops and streets, and the whole clinging like a few limpets to a lost spar. An island like Ithaca or England is valued by the mind because it is a ship, because it can find itself alone and self-dependent in a waste of water, because its orchards and forests can be numbered like bales of merchandise, because its corn can be counted like gold, because the starriest and dreariest snows upon its most forsaken peaks are silver flags flown from familiar masts, because its dimmest and most inhuman mines of coal or lead below the roots of things are definite chattels stored awkwardly in the lowest locker of the hold.

In truth, nothing has so much spoilt the right artistic attitude as the continual use of such words as "infinite" and "immeasurable." They were used rightly enough in religion, because religion, by its very nature, consists of paradoxes. Religion speaks of an identity which is infinite, just as it spoke of an identity that was at once one and three, just as it might possibly and rightly speak of an identity that was at once black and white.

The old mystics spoke of an existence without end or a happiness without end, with a deliberate defiance, as they might have spoken of a bird without wings or a sea without water. And in this they were right philosophically, far more right than the world would now admit because all things grow more paradoxical as we approach the central truth. But for all human imaginative or artistic purposes nothing worse could be said of a work of beauty than that it is infinite; for to be infinite is to be shapeless, and to be shapeless is to be something more than mis-shapen. No man really wishes a thing which he believes to be divine to be in this earthly sense infinite. No one would really like a song to last for ever, or a religious service to last for ever, or even a glass of good ale to last for ever. And this is surely the reason that men have pursued towards the idea of holiness, the course that they have pursued; that they have marked it out in particular spaces, limited it to particular days, worshipped an ivory statue, worshipped a lump of stone. They have desired to give to it the chivalry and dignity of definition, they have desired to save it from the degradation of infinity. This is the real weakness of all imperial or conquering ideals in nationality. No one can love his country with the particular affection which is appropriate to the relation, if he thinks it is a thing in its nature indeterminate, something which is growing in the night, something which lacks the tense excitement of a boundary. No Roman citizen could feel the same when once it became possible for a rich Parthian or a rich Carthaginian to become a Roman citizen by waving his hand. No man wishes the thing he loves to grow, for he does not wish it to alter. No man would be pleased if he came home in the evening from work and found his wife eight feet high.

The dangers upon the side of this transcendental insularity are no doubt considerable. There lies in it primarily the great danger of the thing called idolatry, the worship of the object apart from or against the idea it represents. But he must surely have had a singular experience who thinks that this insular or idolatrous fault is the particular fault of one age. We are likely to suffer primary painful resemblance to the men of Thermopylae, the Zealots, who raged round the fall of Jerusalem. If we are rushing upon any destruction it is not, at least, upon this.

The Artistic Side

The Coloured Lands, 1938

In the days of my early youth, in the days of the Yellow Book and the Green Carnation, there were many idle fancies that were quite harmless because they were fanciful, as well as one or two which hardened into evil imaginations. A curious legend has arisen that the Yellow Book, with its grave contributions by Henry James or its innocent contributions by Kenneth Graham, was a book of black, or at least of yellow magic. As a matter of fact, the Yellow Book might almost have been a Blue Book, so far as the harmless and humdrum sobriety of much of its printed matter went; and even the Green Carnation was not so green as it was painted. These things were seen afterwards in the lurid light that shone backwards from the shameful illumination of one individual career; but at the time most of us saw very little harm in them; or at least very little harm of this particular kind. The peacock's feather of the aesthete had not yet proved itself a true type of ill-luck; and a man might be irritated with Whistler for posing so persistently as a Butterfly, without associating him with the real moth that corrupts; or any of the subsequent corruption.

Among the pleasing fancies that occurred to us in those early days was a sense of the poetry of London; and, in the days when I wrote a fortunately forgotten work called "The Napoleon of Notting Hill," I quite honestly felt that I was adorning a neglected thing, when I felt impelled to write about lamp-posts as one-eyed giants or hansom cabs as yawning dragons with two flaming optics, or painted omnibuses as coloured ships or castles, or all the rest of it. And, now, after many years of controversy and complications, and collisions with all sorts of other questions, I come back to the same feeling in a new way, but with something of an undiminished freshness. I still hold, every bit as firmly as when I wrote "The Napoleon of Notting Hill," that the suburbs ought to be either glorified by romance and religion or else destroyed by fire from heaven, or even by firebrands from the earth. I still hold that it is the main earthly business of a human being to make his home, and the immediate surroundings of his home, as symbolic and significant to his own imagination as he can; whether the home be in Notting Hill or Nicaragua, in Palestine or in Pittsburgh. But an experience of the mingled strands of modern life has led me to consider the problem in a slightly different way; though I will claim to have added to my views rather than abandoned them.

I know no better exercise in that art of wonder, which is the life of man and the beginning of the praise of God, than to travel in a train through a long, dark, almost uninterrupted tunnel: until the traveller has grown almost accustomed to dusk and a dead blank background of brick. At last, after long stretches and at long intervals, the wall will suddenly break in two, and give a glowing glimpse of the land of the living. It may be a chasm of daylight showing a bright and busy street. It may be a similar flash of light on a long, lonely road of poplars, with a solitary human figure plodding across the vast countryside. I know not which of the two gives a more startling stab of human vitality. Sometimes the grey façade is broken by the lighted windows of a house, almost overhanging the railway-line; and for an instant we look deep into a domestic interior; chamber within chamber of a glowing and coloured human home. That is the way in which objects ought to be seen; separate; illuminated; and above all, contrasted against blank night or bare walls; as indeed these living creations do stand eternally contrasted with the colourless chaos out of which they came. Travelling in this fashion, the other day, I was continually haunted, and almost tormented, with an impression that I could not disentangle; nor am I at all confident that I can disentangle it here.

It seemed to me that I saw very strange sights; which ought to have been significant sights. I looked suddenly through an open window into a little room that was filled with blue light; something much bluer than we see in moonlight, even once in a blue moon. It came apparently from the blue shade that completely hooded a lamp standing on the table; there was nothing else on the table but an open book, which gleamed almost pale blue in that bleak luminosity. There was nobody there; there was nothing else. And I had an indescribable subconscious sense that it ought to mean something; and there massed vaguely at the back of my mind, like blue clouds, the colours that cling about the Blessed Virgin in the old pictures and the visions seen in narrow rooms and cells. Then again I saw a square patch of burning red, which was but the red curtain covering a lighted room. But there was a shadow that moved sharply across it, lifting long arms, arms of an unnatural exaggerated length, and making the black pattern of a cross upon the burning scarlet. It was impossible not to feel that somebody had made a signal to the train. And yet somebody had only stretched his arms, probably with a yawn, before going indifferently to bed. All along that night journey there were these signals signifying nothing. And I grew conscious, in a way quite beyond expression, that there is indeed a poetry of modern life, and of the modern cities; but it is in some strange way a poetry of misfits; a tangle of misunderstood messages; an alphabet all higgledy-piggledy in a heap. Beautiful things ought to mean beautiful things. And the case for simpler conditions is that, on the whole, they do. That indestructibility of religion, and even of ritualism, which puzzles the poor old rationalist so much, is not a little due to the fact that in ritual, for the first time, modern men see forms and colours placed where they mean something. Anybody can see why the priest's vestment on common days is green like the common fields, and on martyrs' days red as blood. But that blood-red curtain I saw from the train either commemorated no martyrdom; or the man crucified within did not know that his martyrdom was commemorated.

What Is Right with the World

The Apostle and the Wild Ducks, 1975

The above excellent title is not of my own invention. It was suggested to me by the Editor of *T. P.'s Weekly* and I consented to fill up the bill, partly because of the pleasure I have always had from the paper itself, and partly because it gives me an opportunity of telling an egotistical story, a story which may enlighten the public about the general origin of such titles.

I have always heard of the brutality of publishers and how they crush and obscure the author; but my complaint has always been that they push him forward far too much. I will not say that, so far from making too little of the author, they make too much of him; that this phrase is capable of a dark financial interpretation which I do not intend. But I do say that the prominent personalities of the literary world are very largely the creations of their publishers, in so far as they are not solely the creations of their wives. Here is a small incident out of my own existence. I designed to write a sort of essay, divided into sections, on one particular point of political error. This fallacy, though small and scholastic at first sight, seemed to me to be the real mistake in most modern sociological works. It was, briefly, the idea that things that have been tried have been found wanting. It was my purpose to point out that in the entanglements of practise this is untrue; that an old expedient may easily be the best thing for a new situation; that its principle may be useful though its practise failed; that its practise may have failed because its principle was abandoned; and so on. Therefore, I claimed, we should look for the best method, the ideal, whether it is in the future or the past. I imagined this book as a drab-coloured, decorous little philosophical treatise, with no chapters, but the page occasionally broken by section-headings at the side. I proposed to call my analysis of a radical error "What is wrong," meaning where the mistake is in our logical calculation. But I had highly capable and sympathetic publishers, whose only weakness was that they thought my unhappy monologue much more important than I did. By some confusion of ecstasy (which entirely through my own fault I failed to check) the title was changed into the apocalyptic trumpet-blast "What's Wrong With the World." It was divided up into three short, fierce chapters, like proclamations in a French riot. Outside there was an enormous portrait of myself looking like a depressed hairdresser, and the whole publication had somehow got the violence and instancy of a bombshell. Let it be understood that I do not blame the publishers in the least for this. I could have stopped it if I had minded my own affairs, and it came out of their beautiful and ardent souls. I merely mention it as an instance of the error about publishers. They are always represented as cold and scornful merchants, seeking to keep your writers in the background. Alas (as Wordsworth so finely says), alas! the enthusiasm of publishers has oftener left me mourning.

Upon the whole, I am rather inclined to approve of this method of the publisher or editor making up the title, while the author makes up the remarks about it. Any man with a large mind ought to be able to write about anything. Any really free man ought to be able to write to order. Some of the greatest books in the world—*Pickwick*, for instance—were written to fulfil a scheme partly sketched out by a publisher. But I only brought together these two cases of titles that came to me from outside because they do illustrate the necessity of some restatement in such a case. For these two titles are, when it comes to the fulfilment, at once too complex and too simple. I would never have dreamed of announcing, like some discovery of my own, what is wrong with the world. What is wrong with the world is the devil, and what is right with it is God; the human race will travel for a few more million years in all sorts of muddle and reform, and when it perishes of the last cold or heat it will still be within the limits of that very simple definition. But in an age that has confused itself with such phrases as "optimist" and "pessimist", it is necessary to distinguish along more delicate lines. One of the strangest things about the use of the word "optimist" is that it is now so constantly used about the future. The house of man is criticised not as a house, but as a kind of caravan; not by what it is, but by where it is going to. None are more vitally and recklessly otherworldly than those modern progressives who do not believe in another world.

Now, for the matter of that, I do think the world is getting very much better in very many vital respects. In some of them, I think, the fact could hardly be disputed. The one perfectly satisfactory element at the present crisis is that all the prophecies have failed. At least the people who have been clearly proved to be wrong are the people who were quite sure they were right. That is always a gratifying circumstance. Now why is it that all these prophecies of the wise have been confounded and why has the destiny of men taken so decisive and so different a course? It is because of the very simple fact that the human race consists of many millions of two-legged and tolerably cheerful, reasonably unhappy beings who never read any books at all and certainly never hear of any scientific predictions. If they act in opposition to the scheme which science has foreseen for them, they must be excused. They sin in ignorance. They have no notion that they are avoiding what was really unavoidable. But, indeed, the phrases loosely used of that obscure mass of mankind are a little misleading. To say of the bulk of human beings that they are uneducated is like saying of a Red Indian hunter that he has not yet taken his degree. He has taken many other things. And so, sincerely speaking, there are no uneducated men. They may escape the trivial examinations, but not the tremendous examinations of existence. The dependence of infancy, the enjoyment of animals, the love of woman, and the fear of death—these are more frightful and more fixed than all conceivable forms of the cultivation of the mind. It is idle to complain of schools and colleges being trivial. Schools and colleges must always be trivial. In no case will a college ever teach the important things. For before a man is twenty he has always learnt the important things. He has learnt them right or wrong, and he has learnt them all alone.

We therefore come back to the primary truth, that what is right with the world has nothing to do with future changes, but is rooted in original realities. If groups or peoples show an unexpected independence or creative power; if they do things no one had dreamed of their doing; if they prove more ferocious or more self-sacrificing than the wisdom of the world had ever given them credit for, then such inexplicable outbursts can always be referred back to some elementary and absolute doctrine about the nature of men. No traditions in this world are so ancient as the traditions that lead to modern upheaval and innovation. Nothing nowadays is so conservative as a revolution. The men who call themselves Republicans are men walking the streets of deserted and tiny city-states, and digging up the great bones of pagans. And when we ask on what republicanism really rests, we come back to that great undemonstrable dogma of the native dignity of man. And when we come back to the lord of creation, we come back of necessity to creation; and we ask ourselves that ultimate question which St. Thomas Aquinas (an extreme optimist) answered in the affirmative: Are these things ultimately of value at all?

What is right with the world is the world. In fact, nearly everything else is wrong with it. This is that great truth in the tremendous tale of Creation, a truth that our people must remember or perish. It is at the *beginning* that things are good, and not (as the more pallid progressives say) only at the end. The primordial things—existence, energy, fruition—are good so far as they go. You cannot have evil life, though you can have notorious evil livers. Manhood and womanhood are good things, though men and woman are often perfectly pestilent. You can use poppies to drug people, or birch trees to beat them, or stones to make an idol, or corn to make a corner; but it remains true that, in the abstract, before you have done anything, each of these four things is in strict truth a glory, a beneficent speciality and variety. We do praise the Lord that there are birch trees growing amongst the rocks and poppies amongst the corn; we do praise the Lord, even if we do not believe in Him. We do admire and applaud the *project* of a world, just as if we had been called to council in the primal darkness and seen the first starry plan of the skies. We are, as a matter of fact, far more certain that this life of ours is a magnificent and amazing enterprise than we are that it will succeed. These evolutionary optimists who call themselves Meliorists (a patient and poor-spirited lot they are) always talk as if we were certain of the end, though not of the beginning. In other words, they don't know what life is aiming at, but they are quite sure it will get there. Why anybody who has avowedly forgotten where he came from should be quite so certain of where he is going to I have never been able to make out; but Meliorists are like that. They are ready to talk of existence itself as the product of purely evil forces. They never mention animals except as perpetually tearing each other in pieces; but a month in the country would cure that. They have a real giddy horror of stars and seas, as a man has on the edge of a hopelessly high precipice. They sometimes instinctively shrink from clay, fungoids, and the fresh young of animals with a quivering gesture that reveals the fundamental pessimist. Life itself, crude, uncultivated life, is horrible to them. They belong very largely to the same social class and creed as the lady who objected that the milk came to her from a dirty cow, and not from a nice clean shop. But they are sure how everything will end.

I am in precisely the opposite position. I am much more sure that everything is good at the beginning than I am that everything will be good at the end. That all this frame of things, this flesh, these stones, are good things, of that I am more brutally certain than I can say. But as for what will happen to them, that is to take a step into dogma and prophecy. I speak here, of course, solely of my personal feelings, not even of my reasoned creed. But on my instincts alone I should have no notion what would ultimately happen to this material world I think so magnificent. For all I know it may be literally and not figuratively true that the tares are tied into bundles for burning, and that as the tree falleth so shall it lie. I am an agnostic, like most people with a positive theology. But I do affirm, with the full weight of sincerity, that trees and flowers are good at the beginning, whatever happens to them at the end; that human lives were good at the beginning, whatever happens to them in the end. The ordinary modern progressive position is that this is a bad universe, but will certainly get better. I say it is certainly a good universe, even if it gets worse. I say that these trees and flowers, stars and sexes, are primarily, not merely ultimately, good. In the Beginning the power beyond words created heaven and earth. In the Beginning He looked on them and saw that they were good.

All this unavoidable theory (for theory is always unavoidable) may be popularly pulled together thus. We are to regard existence as a raid or great adventure; it is to be judged, therefore, not by what calamities it encounters, but by what flag it follows and what high town it assaults. The most dangerous thing in the world is to be alive; one is always in danger of one's life. But anyone who shrinks from this is a traitor to the great scheme and experiment of being. The pessimist of the ordinary type, the pessimist who thinks he would be better dead, is blasted with the crime of Iscariot. Spiritually speaking, we should be justified in punishing him with death. Only, out of polite deference to his own philosophy, we punish him with life.

But this faith (that existence was fundamentally and purposely good) is not attacked only by the black, consistent pessimist. The man who says that he would sooner die is best answered by a sudden blow with the poker, for the reply is rightly logical, as well as physically very effective. But there has crept through the culture of modern Europe another notion that is equally in its own way an attack on the essential rightness of the world. It is not avowedly pessimistic, though the source from which it comes (which is Buddhism) is pessimistic for those who really understand it. It can offer itself—as it does among some of the high-minded and distinguished Theosophists—with an air of something highly optimistic. But this disguised pessimism is what is really wrong with the world—at least, especially with the modern world. It is essential to arrest and to examine it.

There has crept into our thoughts, through a thousand small openings, a curious and unnatural idea. I mean the idea that unity is itself a good thing; that there is something high and spiritual about things being blended and absorbed into each other. That all rivers should run into one river, that all vegetables should go into one pot—that is spoken of as the last and best fulfilment of being. Boys are to be "at one" with girls; all sects are to be "at one" in the New Theology; beasts fade into men and men fade into God; union in itself is a noble thing. Now union in itself is not a noble thing. Love is a noble thing; but love is not union. Nay, it is rather a vivid sense of separation and identity. Maudlin, inferior love poetry does, indeed, talk of lovers being "one soul", just as maudlin, inferior religious poetry talks of being lost in God; but the best poetry does not. When Dante meets Beatrice, he feels his distance from her, not his proximity; and all the greatest saints have felt their lowness, not their highness, in the moment of ecstasy. And what is true of these grave and heroic matters (I do not say, of course, that saints and lovers have never used the language of union too, true enough in its own place and proper limitation of meaning)—what is true of these is equally true of all the lighter and less essential forms of appreciation of surprise. Division and variety are essential to praise; division and variety *are* what is right with the world. There is nothing specially right about mere contact and coalescence.

In short, this vast, vague idea of unity is the one "reactionary" thing in the world. It is perhaps the only connection in which that foolish word "reactionary" can be used with significance and truth. For this blending of men and women, nations and nations, is truly a return to the chaos and unconsciousness that were before the world was made. There is, of course, another kind of unity of which I do not speak here; unity in the possession of truth and the perception of the need for these varieties. But the varieties themselves; the reflection of man and woman in each other, as in two distinct mirrors; the wonder of man at nature as a strange thing at once above and below him; the quaint and solitary kingdom of childhood; the local affections and the colour of certain landscapes—these actually are the things that are the grace and honour of the earth; these are the things that make life worth living and the whole framework of things well worthy to be sustained. And the best thing remains; that this view, whether conscious or not, always has been and still is the view of the living and labouring millions. While a few prigs on platforms are talking about "oneness" and absorption in "The All," the folk that dwell in all the valleys of this ancient earth are renewing the varieties for ever. With them a woman is loved for being unmanly, and a man loved for being unwomanly. With them the church and the home are both beautiful, because they are both different; with them fields are personal and flags are sacred; they are the virtue of existence, for they are not mankind but men.

The rooted hope of the modern world is that all these dim democracies do still believe in that romance of life, that variation of man, woman, and child upon which all poetry has hitherto been built. The danger of the modern world is that these dim democracies are so very dim, and that they are especially dim where they are right. The danger is that the world may fall under a new oligarchy—the oligarchy of prigs. And if anyone should promptly ask (in the manner of the debating clubs) for the definition of a prig, I can only reply that a prig is an oligarch who does not even know he is an oligarch. A circle of small pedants sit on an upper platform, and pass unanimously (in a meeting of none) that there is no difference between the social duties of men and of women, the social instruction of men or of children. Below them boils that multitudinous sea of millions that think differently, that have always thought differently, that will always think differently. In spite of the overwhelming majority that maintains the old theory of life, I am in some real doubt about which will win. Owing to the decay of theology and all the other clear systems of thought, men have been thrown back very much upon their instincts, as with animals. As with animals, their instincts are right; but, as with animals, they can be cowed. Between the agile scholars and the stagnant mob, I am really doubtful about which will be triumphant. I have no doubt at all about which ought to be.

Europe at present exhibits a concentration upon politics which is partly the unfortunate result of our loss of religion, partly the just and needful result of our loss of our social inequality and iniquity. These causes, however, will not remain in operation for ever. Religion is returning from her exile; it is more likely that the future will be crazily and corruptly superstitious than that it will be merely rationalist.

On the other hand, our attempts to right the extreme ill-balance of wealth must soon have some issue; something will be done to lessen the perpetual torture of incompetent compassion; some scheme will be substituted for our malevolent anarchy, if it be only one of benevolent servitude. And as these two special unrests about the universe and the State settle down into more silent and enduring system, there will emerge more and more those primary and archaic truths which the dust of these two conflicts has veiled. The secondary questions relatively solved, we shall find ourselves all the more in the presence of the primary questions of Man.

For at present we all tend to one mistake; we tend to make politics too important. We tend to forget how huge a part of a man's life is the same under a Sultan and a Senate, under Nero or St. Louis. Daybreak is a never-ending glory, getting out of bed is a never-ending nuisance; food and friends will be welcomed; work and strangers must be accepted and endured; birds will go bedwards and children won't, to the end of the last evening. And the worst peril is that in our just modern revolt against intolerable accidents we may have unsettled those things that alone make daily life tolerable. It will be an ironic tragedy if, when we have toiled to find rest, we find we are incurably restless. It will be sad if, when we have worked for our holiday, we find we have unlearnt everything but work. The typical modern man is the insane millionaire who has drudged to get money, and then finds he cannot enjoy even money. There is danger that the social reformer may silently and occultly develop some of the madness of the millionaire whom he denounces. He may find that he has learnt how to build playgrounds but forgotten how to play. He may agitate for peace and quiet, but only propagate his own mental agitation. In his long fight to have a half-holiday he may angrily deny those ancient and natural things, the zest of being, the divinity of man, the sacredness of simple things, the health and humour of the earth, which alone make a half-holiday even half a holiday or a slave even half a man.

There is danger in that modern phrase "divine discontent." There is truth in it also, of course; but it is only truth of a special and secondary kind. Much of the quarrel between Christianity and the world has been due to this fact; that there are generally two truths, as it were, at any given moment of revolt or reaction, and the ancient underlying truism which is nevertheless true all the time. It is sometimes worth while to point out that black is not so black as it is painted; but black is still black, and not white. So with the merits of content and discontent. It is true that in certain acute and painful crises of oppression or disgrace, discontent is a duty and shame could call us like a trumpet. But it is not true that man should look at life with an eye of discontent, however high-minded. It is not true that in his primary, naked relation to the world, in his relation to sex, to pain, to comradeship, to the grave, or to the weather, man ought to make discontent his ideal; it is black lunacy. Half his poor little hopes of happiness hang on his thinking a small house pretty, a plain wife charming, a lame foot not unbearable, and bad cards not so bad. The voice of the special rebels and prophets, recommending discontent, should, as I have said, sound now and then suddenly, like a trumpet. But the voices of the saints and sages, recommending contentment, should sound unceasingly, like the sea.

The Spice of Life

The Spice of Life, 1964

Forgive me if I begin by enacting the part which I have played at so many dinner-parties, I mean the part of the skeleton at the feast. Pardon me if the first few words that reach you resemble a hollow voice from the tomb. For the truth is that the very title of this series makes me feel a little funereal. When I was asked to speak on the Spice of Life, I am sorry to say that the first thought that crossed my perverse and morbid mind was that spices, as spices, are quite as much associated with death as with life. Corpses embalmed and preserved were always swathed amid spices; mummies also, I suppose. I am no Egyptologist to decide the point. But even if they were, you would hardly go sniffing round a mummy in the British Museum, drawing deep breaths and saying, "This is indeed the spice of life." Egypt was almost a civilisation organised as a funeral procession; it is hardly an exaggeration to say that the living lived to serve the dead. And yet I suppose that an actual Egyptian walking about alive, was in no hurry to be spiced. Or take a homelier scene nearer home. Suppose you are chased by a mad bull; we will not debate which animal enjoys more of the spice of life; but both at the moment will give unmistakable signs of life. But the quadruped must wait until he is killed and cut up into cold beef, before he can have the pride and privilege of being spiced beef. In short, I want you to remember first of all that there has been in history, not only the spice of life, but something else that may fairly be called the spice of death. And I mention it first because it is a sort of parable; and there are a good many things in the modern world that seem to me to be dead, not to say damned, and yet are considered very spicy.

I will not dwell on this morbid parallel. Heaven forbid that I should suggest that some ladies are rather like mummies walking about, with very beautiful faces painted on the mummy-cases: or that some young gentlemen going the pace exhibit all the culture and selective subtlety of mad bulls. I am concerned with a much more important question at the back of this one. It seems to me that a great many people, whom I am far from calling mummies or mad bulls, are at this moment paying rather too much attention to the spice of life, and rather too little attention to life. Do not misunderstand me. I am very fond of spiced beef and all the spices; I always dread that the Puritan reformers will suddenly forbid mustard and pepper as they did malt and hops; on the absurd ground that salt and mustard are as unnecessary as music. But while I resist the suggestion that we must eat beef without mustard, I do recognize that there is now a much deeper and more subtle danger that men may want to eat mustard without beef. I mean that they may lose their appetite; their appetite for beef and bread and cheese and the broad daylight of life; and depend entirely on spices and condiments. I have even been blamed for defending the spices of life against what was called the Simple Life. I have been blamed for making myself a champion of beer and skittles. Fortunately, if I was a champion of skittles, there was never any danger of my being a champion at skittles. But I have played ordinary games like skittles, always badly; but all healthy people will agree that you never enjoy a game till you enjoy being beaten at the game. I have even played golf in Scotland before Arthur Balfour brought it to England and it became a fashion and then a religion. I have been since inhibited by a difficulty in regarding a game as a religion, and the horrid secret of my failure is that I never could quite see the difference between cricket and golf, as I played them when I was a boy, and puss-in-the-corner and honey-pots as I played them when I was a child. Perhaps those nursery games are now forgotten; anyhow, I will not reveal what good games they were, lest they should become fashionable. If once they were taken seriously in that most serious world, the world of Sport, enormous results will follow. The shops will sell a special Slipper for Hunt-the-Slipper, or a caddy will follow the player with a bag full of fifteen different slippers. Honey-pots will mean money-pots; and there will be a "corner" in puss-in-the-corner.

Anyhow, I have enjoyed like everybody else those sports and spices of life. But I am more and more convinced that neither in your special spices nor in mine, neither in honey-pots nor quart-pots, neither in mustard nor in music, nor in any other distraction from life, is the secret we are all seeking, the secret of enjoying life. I am perfectly certain that all our world will end in despair, unless there is some way of making the mind itself, the ordinary thought we have at ordinary times, more healthy and more happy than they seem to be just now, to judge by most modern novels and poems. You have to be happy in those quiet moments when you remember that you are alive; not in those noisy moments when you forget. Unless we can learn again to enjoy life, we shall not long enjoy the spices of life. I once read a French fairytale that expressed exactly what I mean. Never believe that French wit is shallow; it is the shining surface of French irony, which is unfathomable. It was about a pessimist poet who decided to drown himself; and as he went down to the river, he gave away his eyes to a blind man, his ears to a deaf man, his legs to a lame man, and so on, up to the moment when the reader was waiting for the splash of his suicide; but the author wrote that this senseless trunk settled itself on the shore and began to experience the joy of living: *la joie de vivre*. The joy of being alive. You have to go deep, and perhaps to grow old, to know how true that story is.

If I were to ask myself where and when I have been happiest, I could of course give the obvious answers, as true of me as of everybody else; at some dance or feast of the romantic time of life; at some juvenile triumph of debate; at some sight of beautiful things in strange lands. But it is much more important to remember that I have been intensely and imaginatively happy in the queerest because the quietest places. I have been filled with life from within in a cold waiting-room in a deserted railway-junction. I have been completely alive sitting on an iron seat under an ugly lamp-post at a third-rate watering place. In short, I have experienced the mere excitement of existence in places that would commonly be called as dull as ditch-water. And by the way, is ditch-water dull? Naturalists with microscopes have told me that it teems with quiet fun. Even that proverbial phrase will prove that we cannot always trust what is proverbial, when it professes to describe what is prosaic. I doubt whether the fifteen gushing fountains to be found in your ornamental garden contain creatures so amusing as those the microscope reveals; like the profiles of politicians in caricature. And that is only one example out of a thousand, of the things in daily life we call dull that are not really so dull after all. And I am confident that there is no future for the modern world, unless it can understand that it has not merely to seek what is more and more exciting, but rather the yet more exciting business of discovering the excitement in things that are called dull.

What we have to teach the young man of the future, is how to enjoy himself. Until he can enjoy himself, he will grow more and more tired of enjoying everything else. What we have to teach him is to amuse himself. At this moment he is more and more dependent upon anything which he thinks will amuse him. And, to judge by the expression of his face, it does not amuse him very much. When we consider what he receives, it is indeed a most magnificent wonder and wealth and concentration of amusement. He can travel in a racing-car almost as quick as a cannon-ball; and still have his car fitted up with wireless from all the ends of the earth. He can get Vienna and Moscow; he can hear Cairo and Warsaw; and if he cannot see England, through which he happens to be travelling, that is after all a small matter. In a century, no doubt, his car will travel like a comet, and his wireless will hear the noises in the moon. But all this does not help him when the car stops; and he has to stand stamping about in a line, with nothing to think about. All this does not help him even when the wireless stops and he has to sit still in a silent car with nothing to talk about. If you consider what are the things poured into him, what are the things he receives, then indeed they are colossal cataracts of things, cosmic Niagaras that have never before poured into any human being are pouring into him. But if you consider what comes out of him, as a result of all this absorption, the result we have to record is rather serious. In the vast majority of cases, nothing. Not even conversation, as it used to be. He does not conduct long arguments, as young men did when I was young. The first and startling effect of all this noise is silence. Second, when he does have the itch to write or say something, it is always an itch in the sense of an irritation.

Everything has its better and baser form; and there is irritation and irritation. There is a great deal of difference between the irritation of Aldous Huxley and the irritation of some nasty little degenerate in a novel by Aldous Huxley. But honestly I do not think I am unfair to the whole trend of the time, if I say that it is intellectually irritated; and therefore without that sort of rich repose in the mind which I mean, when I say that a man when he is alone can be happy because he is alive. For instance, a man of genius of the same generation, for whom I have a very special admiration, is Mr. T. S. Eliot. But nobody will deny that there was a sense in which, originally, even his inspiration was irritation. He began with pure pessimism; he has since found much finer and more subtle things; but I hardly think he has found repose. And it is just here that I will have the effrontery to distinguish between his generation and mine. It used to be thought impudent for a boy to criticise an old gentleman, it now requires far more sublime impudence for an older man to criticise a younger. Yet I will defend my own idea of the spiritual spice of life against even the spirituality that finds this ordinary life entirely without spice. I know very well that Mr. Eliot described the desolation he found more than the desolation he felt. But I think that "The Waste Land" was at least a world in which he had wandered. And as I am describing the recent world, I may as well describe it as he has described it, in "The Hollow Men"—though nobody would describe him as a hollow man. This is the impression of many impressions.

> This is the way the world ends
> This is the way the world ends
> This is the way the world ends
> Not with a bang but a whimper.

Now forgive me if I say, in my old-world fashion, that I'm damned if I ever felt like that. I recognize the great realities Mr. Eliot has revealed; but I do not admit that this is the deepest reality. I am ready to admit that our generation made too much of romance and comfort, but even when I was uncomfortable I was more comfortable than that. I was more comfortable on the iron seat. I was more happy in the cold waiting-room. I knew the world was perishable and would end, but I did not think it would end with a whimper, but if anything with a trump of doom. It is doubtless a grotesque spectacle that the great-grandfathers should still be dancing with indecent gaiety, when the young are so grave and sad; but in this matter of the spice of life, I will defend the spiritual appetite of my own age. I will even be so indecently frivolous as to break into song, and say to the young pessimists:—

Some sneer; some snigger; some simper;
In the youth where we laughed and sang,
And *they* may end with a whimper
But *we* will end with a bang.

INDEX